ASSAULT PISTOLS, RIFLES AND SUBMACHINE GUNS

DUNCAN LONG

ASSAULT PISTOLS, RIFLES AND SUBMACHINE GUNS

PALADIN PRESS
BOULDER, COLORADO

Assault Pistols, Rifles and Submachine Guns
by Duncan Long
Copyright © 1986 by Duncan Long

ISBN 0-87364-353-4
Printed in the United States of America

Published by Paladin Press, a division of
Paladin Enterprises, Inc., P.O. Box 1307,
Boulder, Colorado 80306, USA.
(303) 443-7250

Direct inquiries and/or orders to the above address.

ACKNOWLEDGMENTS

I must extend my thanks to the many companies that so graciously loaned or gave me equipment and firearms for testing during the writing of this book, as well as for the help of Paladin Press.

Thanks to my dad for his work in processing photos. And my usual special thanks to Maggie, Kristen, and Nicholas.

CONTENTS

INTRODUCTION

To the purist, assault rifles are lightweight selective-fire weapons that chamber an intermediate round between the size of pistol and rifle cartridges. I stood by that definition before I started getting down to the nitty-gritty of this book. I often pointed to the German *Sturmgewehr* ("storming rifle" or "assault rifle") as an example of what an assault rifle should be. It seems cut and dried until you check into the original German terms.

The German *Sturmgewehr* was called the MP44. The MP stood for *maschinen pistole*. The way most of us purists got around that one was with a story of how this designation was used to fool Hitler or to keep the weapon secret from the Allies. I don't think that theory holds up too well; chances are the Germans just didn't know what to call this new type of rifle. Certainly an argument could be made that it was more like a submachine gun (which the Germans called a maschinen pistole) than the large-caliber rifles of the period. East Germany still classifies their AK-style rifles as maschinen pistoles; I doubt that they're still trying to pull the wool over Hitler's eyes! At any rate, Hitler liked the weapon well enough to give it its Sturmgewehr moniker, and that term has stuck to this type of rifle to this day.

Another example of terms often ignored by those who use English almost exclusively is the StuG57. The German-speaking Swiss designed the StuG57. They didn't refrain from calling the rifle a Sturmgewehr even though it was chambered for the 7.5×55mm Schmidt-Rubin. The Schmidt-Rubin round fires a 174-grain, .308 caliber bullet and has a total length slightly greater than the .308 Winchester rifle cartridge. A purist would have to maintain that the poor Swiss either didn't realize that they were using the wrong type of cartridge in their rifle or didn't know the meaning of *sturmgewehr*. Since the Swiss were using the term before anyone else had given

much thought to the term "assault rifle," maybe we should give them credit with knowing what they were doing.

The next problem arises if you make a semiauto-only model of one of these selective-fire rifles. According to the purists, an assault rifle has to be selective fire. Yet, if you think about it, it's a little hard to accept the idea that firearms with extended magazines, pistol grip stock, etc., cease to be assault rifles by changing a bit of metal.

Much the same thing happens with the term "battle rifle." The purist defines a battle rifle as a combat weapon chambered for a full-powered rifle round. Simple. But what happens if a manufacturer takes a "battle rifle" and chambers it for a smaller cartridge? A good example of this is the AR-10 in .308 Winchester which was scaled down to become the AR-15 in .223 Remington. The same thing happened with the .308 HK-91 which was scaled down to .223 as the HK-93. Thus, a minor change creates a major reclassification if we go by the purist's definition. The reverse can also happen: the Mini-14 in .223 would be an assault rifle, while with a few modifications and a new chambering, it becomes a battle rifle in its XGI/.308 form.

It's a little hard to see how a different chambering can change a weapon that much. I think the manufacturers are on the right track when they call all these rifles "assault rifles" rather than distinguishing between assault rifles, battle rifles, and semiauto, former assault rifles, or however a purist would classify a semiauto assault rifle.

The indiscriminate usage of the term "assault rifle" in the United States has caused it to mean any weapon that looks like an assault rifle and fires something bigger than a pistol round. "Assault rifle" has come to mean a rifle that has an extended magazine, straight-lined

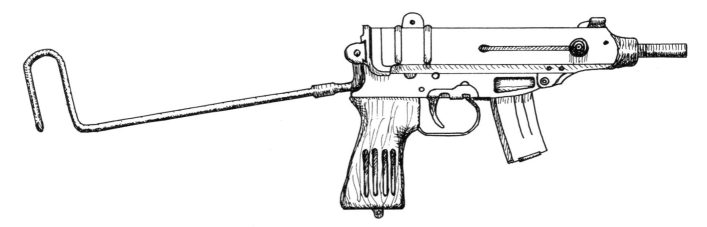

The Czechoslovakian Model 61 submachine gun, developed as a tanker's weapon, can be used both as a pistol and as a light submachine gun. Due to its lightweight wire stock, which folds over the upper receiver, the weapon can easily be carried on a sling or even in a pistol holder.

stock, and usually the "required" pistol grip, though even that is a little iffy when you start looking at a conventionally designed rifle like the Mini-14.

Another term that some may shudder at is my use of "carbine." Carbine originally meant any short-barreled lightweight rifle designed for troops on horseback. There aren't many soldiers on horseback these days. The U.S. Army has already crossed that bridge by applying the term to the M1 Carbine developed for use in World War II. With a 16-inch barrel and light weight, it met all but the horseback qualifications. So carbine has come to mean any short-barreled, lightweight rifle.

If one takes a good long look at the M1 Carbine, however, it's really an assault rifle: extended magazine, selective fire, lightweight, even an intermediate cartridge. Assault rifle or carbine?

We're also back to changing the designation by removing a bit of metal if we're not careful. How about a rifle like the AR-15 Commando ("Shorty")? Does chopping off four inches of barrel make it a carbine? To add to the confusion, the British until recently called their submachine guns "machine carbines."

Again, I'm going to fall back on the modern trend and classify semiauto rifles which fire pistol-caliber rounds as carbines and all the battle rifles as well as the M1 Carbine as assault rifles. This is shaky territory, but that's the nature of things.

What about semiauto-only versions of submachine guns? In this book, they'll be lumped in with the carbines, along with selective-fire, short-barreled submachine guns that have the overall size and weight of a modern carbine. This may be far from satisfactory but if it isn't done, we again end up with a few inches of metal changing the major classification of weapons.

Which brings us to the final group of weapons:

"machine pistols" and "assault pistols."

As tactics and weapons change, some firearms become obsolete. As the firepower of the rifle increases and its weight decreases, the submachine gun is being slowly edged out of its traditional role, but it isn't vanishing from combat. Rather, it is often used in place of the pistol or shotgun. With the U.S. military referring to their new 9mm pistol as a "personal defense weapon," surely the pistol's days are numbered; shotguns are about as common as slingshots in today's hot spots. The pistol and shotgun may soon disappear from the battlefield.

Or will they? Current work in the CAWS (Close Assault Weapon Systems) program is producing a selective-fire shotgun for the infantry. And let's not forget police, home owners, bodyguards, and others. Certainly the handgun still rules the roost in civilian combat.

Even as the pistol is apparently being eased out of the military, two major trends are tending to keep both the submachine gun and pistol on the scene: the use of larger-capacity magazines coupled with burst-fire modes with pistols and the reduction of submachine guns to pistol size. The line between the pistols and submachine guns is gradually eroding, just as the overlap between carbines, assault rifles, and battle rifles has occurred. Thus, it is probable that even as the submachine gun and pistol are supposedly on the verge of leaving the field of combat, both will remain viable products in the world marketplace as they are altered and used in unexpected ways.

It will probably be only a matter of time before the light "carbine," machine gun, machine pistol, or whatever we'll be calling it, replaces the semiauto pistol worn by officers, drivers, or other special personnel. In fact, it's already happening; the Sterling Para Pistol—a chopped version of the Sterling submachine gun—is being issued to British tank crews. This stockless "pistol" has a 4-inch barrel and a 10-round magazine; it has less firepower than many modern 9mm pistols and weighs nearly twice as much! It will be interesting to see how this game of substitution and weapons chopping ends.

Marketplace considerations come into play as well. While a full-automatic weapon has only a limited market, one manufactured in both auto and semi-auto only will often enjoy handsome profits, thanks to a free society's inexhaustible compulsion to purchase firearms. Adding to the confusion in the United States are BATF (Bureau of Alcohol, Tobacco and Firearms) regulations which allow the semiauto version of a submachine gun to be one of two forms: a handgun (?) with a short barrel and no shoulder stock or a carbine, a long-barreled monstrosity with the standard stock, which becomes a long-snouted, semiauto "carbine." Surely "assault pistol" is a more meaningful—if overly colorful—term for the first variety, while "carbine" is what I've chosen for the latter.

But you can see that we've beaten around the bush again, for now we can make a chopped-down submachine gun into a totally different weapon by giving it a nose and tail job! Is a submachine gun without a stock a totally different weapon? Surely not. So I've reserved the term "assault pistol" for those weapons which are pistol sized, though generally they are a few pounds heavier than actual semiauto pistols. I try to avoid the term "machine pistol" except for a select few weapons. While firearms like the Czech Model 61 "Skorpion," MAC-10/11, Uzi Pistol, Holmes MP-83, or TEC-9, with their small size and automatic fire, certainly make the idea of the machine pistol come to life, it must be remembered that the term was first used by the Germans in World War I. Their maschinen pistoles were stocked weapons like the Mauser and, later, the MP-40 submachine gun. So, if we remain purists, it looks like we're destined to chase about in circles.

I guess the bottom line for each of us is that "my words mean what I say they mean." Artistic license, if you will, but with small-arms development in its present state of flux, I think the time when purists and historians can start classifying weapons into well-defined groups will be around A.D. 2200, after all the dust has settled and current trends have come to fruition. In the meantime, I hope you'll find the same enjoyment and interest I have as you study the strange combat weapons to which our savage modern age has given birth.

1. A BRIEF HISTORY

One thing stands out in the recent history of firearms development: When a firearm is first tested, or worse yet, fielded with a minimum of testing, it generally functions poorly. In other words, the longer a weapon is used and modified, the more reliable it tends to become. Two U.S. rifles, the M1 Garand and the M16, are good examples.

When the Garand was introduced, it was the first time a semiauto rifle replaced a bolt-action. Many individuals opposed the Garand as a matter of principle, but the main problem was that it didn't function reliably. Though adopted by the U.S. military in 1936, it wasn't until around 1942 that the Marines actually started equipping their men with Garands rather than bolt-action Springfields.

As improvements continued to be made, the Garand become more and more reliable until, in 1945, General George Patton was to write, "In my opinion, the M1 [Garand] is the greatest battle implement ever devised." Even so, the rifle still often refused to chamber the last round in a clip if the clip wasn't charged from the correct side!

Much the same thing happened, as we'll see, with the AR-15 rifle. When the M16 (AR-15) was first fielded, the old M14 rifle (which was itself plagued by too tight a gas piston when first issued) suddenly became "the best rifle available" when compared to the lightweight—and new—M16. Like the Garand, the M16 had real problems when U.S. troops received it. Yet, during NATO tests conducted in the late 1980s to choose a standard .223 cartridge, guess which rifle performed nearly flawlessly? The M16, the oldest design, outshone the newer bullpups and even the tough, heavy, and "super-reliable" Galil. It was the same M16 rifle; only the bugs had been removed.

All this boils down to several important points: 1) a number of good designs fall by the wayside because they don't have time to be developed; 2) a lot of good soldiers have fallen by the wayside as well because a weapon has been fielded before being perfected; 3) almost any "bug-ridden" firearm with a good basic design can be made into a dependable rifle with a little work.

There's a fourth point that comes up when you delve further into the facts: An awful lot of weapons problems are caused by poor magazines and/or bad ammunition. So if you ever have to pick up a firearm and stake your life on it, give it some thought and make a worthwhile firearm choice beforehand.

PISTOL-CALIBER CARBINES, SUBMACHINE GUNS, AND ASSAULT PISTOLS

As mentioned earlier, every few years the experts mourn the passing of the submachine gun. And yet the weapons continue to be built, new submachine guns are constantly being marketed, and even the old models like the Thompson continue to sell like hotcakes. What's going on?

Certainly the pistol cartridge has lost ground on the battlefield. The FMJ (full metal jacket) bullets required by the conventions of war make pistols far from effective in battle. Too, modern assault rifles are often as light and compact as many submachine guns and have a very mild recoil while still delivering the punch of a rifle round. Today's assault rifle outperforms most submachine guns.

But in the area of antiterrorism, bodyguarding, police work, or home defense, the modern pistol-caliber weapon offers a lot of advantages over the assault rifle. For one thing, those not limited by the conventions of

Early Garands were full of bugs. Yet, as improvements continued to be made, the Garand became increasingly reliable. In 1945, General George Patton wrote, "In my opinion, the M1 [Garand] is the greatest battle implement ever devised." Photo courtesy of Springfield Armory.

Springfield Armory's modern "Tankers" version of the Garand shows how fine the line is between a modern assault rifle and the semiauto military rifle. Photo courtesy of Springfield Armory.

In the areas of antiterrorism, bodyguarding, police work, or home defense, the modern pistol-caliber weapon offers many advantages over an assault rifle. For those not limited by the conventions of war, modern expanding bullets are capable of inflicting great damage while not penetrating through walls to endanger innocent bystanders. Shown above are the HK-94 carbine and the HK-P9S, both chambered for 9mm Luger.

Compared to new cartridges like the 5.56mm NATO, the pistol cartridge has lost ground on the battlefield. New assault rifles can be as light and small as many submachine guns with a very mild recoil while still having the punch of a rifle. Today's assault rifle outperforms most submachine guns. Top: the "old-style" 9mm carbine (HK-94); bottom: the Colt "Commando" chambered for 5.56mm.

war have found that modern expanding bullets can inflict great damage while not penetrating through walls to endanger innocent bystanders. Thus, the weapon that is anemic on the battlefield with FMJ bullets becomes a tiger with suitable ammunition.

This carries over even into the semiautomatic versions of submachine guns offered on the civilian market. It cannot be over-stressed that in the semiauto mode, the ammunition used in a pistol-caliber weapon can make the difference between an impotent weapon and a deadly, accurate firearm. (For more information on ammunition suitable for combat, see my book *Combat Ammunition: Everything You Need to Know* available from Paladin Press.)

Another point in favor of the pistol-caliber firearm is that modern weapons that make use of plastics and alloys are often quite compact and lightweight. While some submachine guns like the Thompson and Uzi weigh in nearly as heavy as a rifle, the TEC-9, H&K MP5K, and Uzi Pistol all handle nearly as easily as a pistol and have the firepower of large-capacity magazines.

In a society where citizens are free to own guns, we also have the "Walter Mitty effect." A lot of carbines and "pistols" are simply submachine guns modified to fire semiauto only—adult toys, which appeal to the Walter Mitty types. While these can serve as self-defense weapons, one often has to wonder if a revolver or pistol might not work just as well. The mystique of the submachine gun sells. How did this all begin?

With the trend toward greater firepower and smaller calibers, the submachine gun was the logical outgrowth of the larger machine guns developed in the late 1800s. While early automatic weapons were crew-served firearms similar to mortars or cannons, a number of designers recognized the need for a mobile gun capable of overwhelming firepower. The problem came to a head when both sides became bogged down in Europe during World War I. The opposing armies were all but trapped in their trenches by nearly immobile machine guns. An easily carried weapon capable of great firepower was needed. While one off-the-shelf solution was the shotgun, such a weapon was long and awkward to use and its ammunition was bulky and water-sensitive. Added to this was the problem of supplying another type of ammunition and the limited range of the shotgun should the user need to defend himself beyond 50 yards. A better solution was needed, and three different firearms were developed nearly simultaneously, independently, and apparently with each inventor unaware of the others' work.

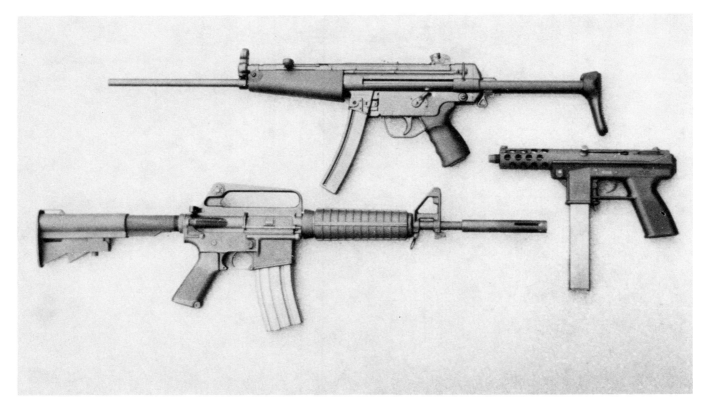

While some submachine guns can be as large as a rifle, and weigh just as much, new weapons are quite small and nearly as easy to handle as a pistol; such weapons have the firepower offered by extended magazines. Shown are the larger HK-94 (top) and the SGW 9mm Carbine (bottom). The TEC-9 (center, right) has as much firepower with a fraction of the size and weight.

In Germany, Hugo Schmeisser was working on his submachine gun; in the United States, John T. Thompson was doing nearly the same work. While Thompson and Schmeisser were working on their weapons, Tullio Marengoini, working for Beretta of Italy, developed the Moschetto Automatico M1918, which was actually fielded before the German weapon. The weapon had a 25-round magazine, fired the 9mm Glisenti round, and weighed a then-light 7¼ pounds. It should be noted that Italy already had the 9mm Beretta Villar Perosa, which might be viewed as a submachine gun if the Italian military hadn't deployed it as an anti-aircraft weapon in 1915! Too, the two-barrel/double magazine arrangement of the weapon made it far from lightweight—a good idea gone awry if ever there was one. This weapon was modified to use a stock the same year that the M1918 was introduced; one way or another, the Italians would have had a submachine gun.

While the Germans and Italians were using their weapons on the battlefield, the United States managed to tie down the deployment of the submachine gun to their forces. At the end of the war, the American submachine guns were sitting on the docks in the States.

Following the war, development of the submachine gun nearly stood still. Thompson saw the weapon he'd hoped would help end war and crime misused by criminals and ignored by the military both in Britain and the United States.

While the United States and British militaries rested on their laurels, the German army readied itself for World War II with the development of the 9mm MP38 and MP40. These were manufactured largely from sheet-metal stampings and were devoid of wooden furniture. They were simple to make, and while they didn't look pretty, they could be quickly stamped out in large quantities and placed into the hands of German troops. (The MP40 is so well designed and reliable that many continue to be used in Third World countries.)

When Britain entered World War II, its military was in a shambles since it had been all but dismantled at the end of World War I. Though the British used U.S.-made Thompsons for some time, they soon developed a pattern which could be easily and cheaply produced through the use of welding and sheet-metal stamping. This design was known as the STEN, and a number of variations were created during the war. Nearly four million of the weapons were stamped out by Britain and Canada.

Unfortunately for the United States, the Thompson was hard to make since it required a machined receiver and wood stocks; the heavy (eleven pounds empty) weapon required a lot of materials in its manufacture which could become scarce during wartime. So, shortly after the outbreak of World War II, the United States designed the M3 grease gun, which could be stamped out at less than $20 per unit (keeping in mind that a dollar bought a lot more back then). The M3 went into production and, along with the M1 .30 Carbine, gradually replaced the heavy Thompson.

The Soviets created the PPSh41 for use in World War II. Though it had a wooden stock and the look of a conventional rifle, it relied on sheet-metal stampings and could also be quickly produced in large numbers. Over five million PPSh41s were produced by the USSR; China produced large numbers as well, its model being designated as Type 50.

Following World War II, a trend started toward the development of smaller lightweight submachine guns. While far from new (stocked pistols like the Mauser capable of firing full-automatic were common before World War I), this trend came about through the logical change in the submachine gun rather than as an outgrowth of the pistol.

Major changes in submachine-gun design have led many weapons historians to divide submachine guns into "generations" or groupings as follows: Submachine guns with wooden stocks and milled or forged receivers are first-generation firearms; steel stampings and welds

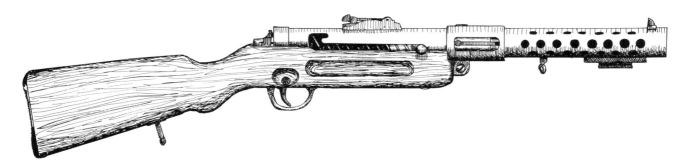

Among the first successful submachine guns developed in World War I was the German MP18, created by Hugo Schmeisser.

mark the second generation; and the use of plastics, telescoping bolts, and/or smaller size marks the third generation, which developed after World War II. While other changes are sometimes suggested as marking a fourth generation, no such trend is currently apparent, though the use of different magazine designs, trigger pulls that allow the selection of semi- or full-auto fire without the use of a selector switch, barrel design, rate-slowing mechanisms, etc., all will no doubt be considered and debated by future historians.

It should also be noted that the swing to third-generation weapons has not been made by the military by and large. While some armies do use third-generation submachine guns, especially for special troops, such weapons are most common among civilian users, secret police, bodyguards, or clandestine groups where the weapon's small size and massive firepower are needed. Larger weapons like the grease gun, H&K MP5, or British Sterling have more in common with second-generation weapons than those of the third and are generally the ones selected by military users, with a few exceptions like the Uzi and Steyr M69 which just squeak into the third-generation category despite their large size.

Examples of second-generation submachine guns developed during or after World War II are the British Sterling, the Smith & Wesson M76, the French MAT 49, and the Beretta M12. Interestingly, all modern Western submachine guns have pretty well been limited to the 9mm Parabellum. As far as sales of weapons go, the Sterling is in first place, the Uzi gets second, the out-of-production M49 is third, the Beretta M12 is in fourth place, and the in-and-out-of-production Ingram MAC-10 ranks fifth. Not far behind in the military sales race are the H&K MP5 series, the Walther MP-L and MP-K, the Argentine MEMS, the Brazilian/Danish Madsen, and a number of other lesser-known models.

If the Uzi is viewed as a transitional firearm marking the beginning of the third generation, then the Ingram MAC-10 would certainly be a full-fledged member of the third generation. Though heavy, it is very compact, and like other third-generation weapons, it has never been widely accepted by the military. The company making it finally went bankrupt in 1976, though several companies purchased the rights and continue to manufacture it.

Eastern Europe has also been busy creating submachine guns since World War II. Probably the most notable example is the Czech M61 (Skorpion), chambered for the .32 ACP with a 10- or 20-round magazine. Weighing in at 2.9 pounds with a telescoping bolt, it is probably one of the best examples of a third-generation weapon.

As world militaries rely more and more on assault rifles to fill the submachine-gun role, it is probable that the West will take the lead in submachine gun development as commercial manufacturers create new weapons. To this end, a number of companies have tried to capture two different markets: the police market, which—except for SWAT units in the United States—is mainly in Europe, where the submachine gun doesn't seem to alarm citizens the way it does here; and the civilian market—with semiauto versions designed to get around many of the U.S. firearms laws.

While there are few limitations on submachine guns for police use, two measures have to be taken to meet the civilian market. One is to lengthen the barrel to 16 inches to meet BATF requirements and the other is to do away with the stock so that the weapon becomes a pistol—in the eyes of the law at least. These measures create a semiauto weapon that can be purchased as easily by a U.S. citizen as any other firearm and place the manufacturer in the running toward capturing a chunk of a seemingly inexhaustible market.

Some of today's submachine guns may very well be the beginning of the fourth generation. The lightweight Intratec TEC-9 is a very good example of current innovations among stockless versions of the "semiauto submachine gun." Its lower receiver is made entirely of plastic (except for the serial plate, which is by law made of metal), and the upper receiver is created from an extruded steel tube with the barrel welded into one end. The weapon locks together with a forward pin for easy takedown, and the barrel is threaded to accept standard MAC-10 silencers. The "heavy" version of the stockless "pistol" weighs only 3.2 pounds, while the shorter TEC-9M weighs only 2.7 pounds. Coupled with its reliable double-feed ramp and 36-round magazines, the weapon can be used like a pistol but has the firepower of a carbine. All this at a price lower than most semiauto pistols! Similar weapons like the Uzi Pistol, the JATI, and the Sterling Para Pistol may well be the beginning of a trend toward small submachine guns as selective-fire versions work their way into use by secret police, bodyguards, SWAT teams, and so on.

Current tactics and aiming/sighting technology lag behind the development of these abbreviated weapons. New aiming systems such as lasers or all-tracer loads may enable these weapons to be used to their full potential. The death notice of the submachine gun and pistol-caliber carbine is probably premature.

ASSAULT RIFLES

The U.S. BAR (Browning Automatic Rifle) of 1918

came close to being the first assault rifle. With its 20-round detachable magazine, selective fire, and one-man carrying capability, it was ahead of its time. But for the fact that it was saddled with the overly powerful .30-06 round, it might have been the lightweight rifle that was to be developed decades later. Despite the BAR's forward-looking design and combat effectiveness, military planners relegated the heavy "rifle" to a light-

machine gun role rather than developing it into an infantry rifle. Likewise, the M1 .30 Carbine just missed the assault rifle boat when it was given what amounted to a pistol round rather than a rifle cartridge. So the first official "assault rifle" was created toward the close of World War II. German innovations set the stage for what was to follow.

Work on the German weapon dated back to a

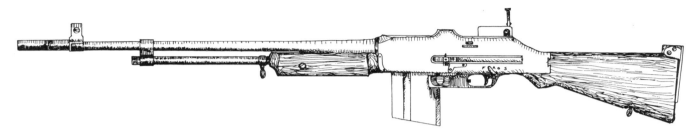

The U.S. BAR (Browning Automatic Rifle) of 1918 came close to being the first "assault rifle." With its 20-round magazine and selective fire, it was ahead of its time. But for the fact that it was saddled with an overly powerful round (the .30-06), it might have been the lightweight rifle that was to be developed decades later.

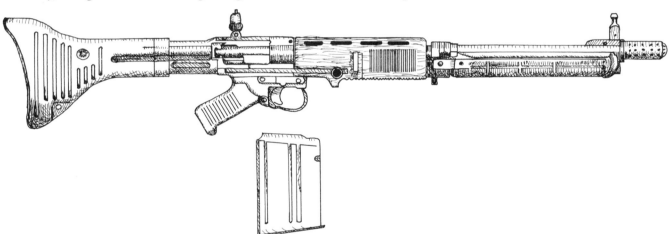

The German FG 42, with its overly powerful cartridge, proved to be too much of a good thing. It probably paved the way, however, for later development of smaller cartridges.

The German effort to develop a cartridge smaller than the standard 7.92 Kurz led to the development of the MP43. The final product from the German development was the Sturmgewehr, which can be directly traced to modern rifles like those of CETME and Heckler & Koch.

development contract offered in 1934 to the Polte Werke for a cartridge smaller than the standard 7.92 Kurz. This cartridge led to the development of *Machinenkarabiner*, or Machine Carbines, by Haenel, the MKb 42(H), and Walther, MKb 42(W). In 1943, the designation *Machinenkarabiner* was changed to *Machinen Pistole*, the designation used for German submachine guns. A number of features still found on modern combat rifles include laminated wooden stocks, sheet-metal stampings for the receiver, a selector located above the pistol grip on the left side of the receiver, a 30-round magazine, and a simple field-stripping design. Only the 11.5-pound weight of the firearm separates it from modern assault rifles.

The final product was the *Sturmgewehr* which was developed as the MP43, later redesignated the MP44 and later still the StG44. Following the war, the rifle can be directly traced through a series of changes which led to modern rifles like the CETME and Heckler & Koch series of rifles and submachine guns.

Unfortunately, while the USSR was creating a very efficient rifle and round that took advantage of the forward-looking German idea, U.S. military decision-makers refused to give up the powerful, long-range rifle round, even after numerous studies showed that the World War I/World War II vintage round was too powerful for normal combat needs. Because the United States insisted on a powerful round, it was impossible to develop a small, lightweight weapon without excessive recoil, especially in the automatic mode. Designers were virtually locked into creating a heavy rifle to go with the round.

Another course of thinking also bogged down U.S. military planners. Besides helping to hamstring the American infantry with less-than-ideal rifles for several decades, it may well have led to the Korean stalemate and later to great problems in Vietnam. The thinking was that past military concepts were made obsolete by nuclear weapons. While this may seem overly simplistic now, this thinking had a profound effect on strategy, tactics, and weapon design. To such a line of thought, the foot soldier existed only to guard nuclear weapons installations. Whether a soldier's weapon was ideal for the conventional battlefield made little difference. As this view gained popularity, studies which showed that a lighter weapon would be more desirable in combat came to mean little to military planners. The Korean "incident" was viewed as an aberration rather than the rule of the game.

In the meantime, one commercial company in the United States was trying to look toward what the future gun market would be. This company, Armalite, became

a part of the Fairchild Engine and Airplane Corporation in the early 1950s. After joining the company, Armalite started to develop firearms incorporating the advantages in speed and economy that could be realized by producing weapons using modern plastics and alloys and newer manufacturing techniques rather than the labor-intensive methods then employed. Weapons created by Armalite have influenced weapons design over the last half of the twentieth century and will probably continue to do so. The same can be said of the designers who worked for the company: Eugene Stoner, L. James Sullivan, and Robert Fremont.

One of the first limited successes the Armalite company enjoyed was the development of the AR-10. This rifle, originally chambered for the .30-06 cartridge, was modified for the new 7.62mm NATO standard cartridge. The AR-10 (along with the FN LAR) was submitted in 1956 for testing as a possible replacement for the M1 Garand but the U.S. Army chose the M14, which had been designed in-house by Army personnel.

While Armalite was doing its work during the early Fifties, the SPIW (Special Purpose Individual Weapon) project was being carried out by the U.S. military. It was principally aimed at producing a multiple-projectile weapon through the use of flechettes packaged in one round similar to that of a shotgun. The project had only limited success due to the problems of range and the large dispersion of the projectiles created by the researchers. The rounds precluded accurate single shots and the weapon could not fire out to the 300-yard maximum combat range. Though the flechette round did not gain acceptance at the time, it did lead to production of a flechette round for 40mm grenade launchers which later appeared mounted under the barrel of the AR-15.

Although efforts were even made to mount single flechettes into saboted rifle rounds, the SPIW program was generally seen as a failure. Its final outcome was to make military planners decide to stick with conventional ammunition. While the SPIW research has not led to any actual weapon, the work continues at the time of this writing and may yet create a breakthrough that will perhaps greatly change the current trend in U.S. weapons.

After floundering about with the SPIW research and discovering the drawbacks of the .308-caliber rifles, the military decided—with browbeating from civilian leaders—to try a smaller caliber weapon. The U.S. Continental Army Command (CONARC) asked Winchester and Armalite to submit rifles for testing. Armalite scaled down their AR-10 to a new experimental round and on March 31, 1985, ten AR-15s were delivered to the Infantry Board for trial. Winchester's offering

Although the FN LAR was rejected by the U.S. military during 1956 tests, it was adopted by a large number of other countries. Shown is the SAR-48 version. Photo courtesy of Springfield Armory.

Springfield Armory's SAR-48, a semiauto version of the FN LAR, is shown here.

looked like a sort of scaled-down M14. The AR-15 looked like a sci-fi weapon and outshone the Winchester rifle in tests as well.

Though the AR-15 did well, the military seemed to be dragging its heels, and Armalite sought to divest itself of the AR-15, while Winchester withdrew its entry from the running. In the meantime, Colt Firearms Corporation bought the manufacturing license for the AR-15 and AR-10 from Armalite in 1959.

Armalite went on to perfect the AR-18 to compete against the AR-15 design they had sold to Colt. At about the same time, Eugene Stoner joined the competition

with the Stoner 63 weapons system. The AR-15 won the military contract and has been refined over the years to become the star weapon of the Western world.

In the USSR and its satellites, as well as a number of nonaligned countries, the AK-47 design has been adopted with great success. The AK-47 was created around a cartridge that dates back to World War II. The rifle and its variants have a very rugged design that has proven to be as nearly foolproof as a rifle can be. The trade-off is a lot of weight. Nevertheless, the design is very trouble-free, and huge numbers of AKs have been manufactured.

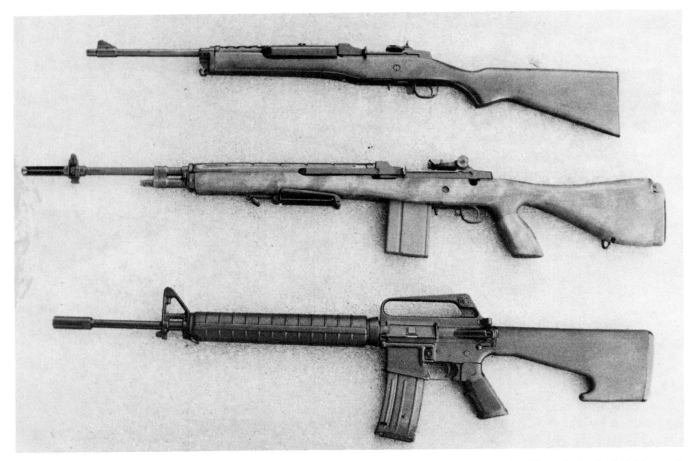

Three solutions to the problems of the U.S. M14 rifle: the Mini-14 (top), a scaled-down M14; the E2 stock for the M14 (center); and the AR-15 rifle (bottom).

Two trends in military rifles are showing up at the present time. One is the creation of "chopped" rifles to serve as submachine guns. This is generally done by cutting the barrel down to ten to twelve inches and adding a folding or telescoping stock. While muzzle flash (and sometimes weight) is greater than that of a submachine gun, the weapon also has more power than its pistol-cartridge-firing counterpart and supplying parts and ammunition is much easier since the rifle differs little from the standard infantry weapon. In a time when a country may be fighting a battle halfway around the world, such logistical considerations are by no means minor.

The second trend may bring an end to the chopped rifle even as it does away with the need for the traditional submachine gun. This is the movement toward the "bullpup" weapon design. The bullpup design is hardly new; General Patton had a bullpup modification of his own before World War II. It creates a light, short rifle without shortening the barrel to the point where it cuts down on bullet velocity or creates excessive muzzle noise and flash. The bullpup design places the pistol grip ahead of the magazine and most of the receiver mechanism. The rear of the receiver becomes the stock, and the rifle is shortened by the length of a regular stock.

Whether the bullpup is the wave of the future remains to be seen. It's possible that the infantry doesn't need such a short weapon, though anyone who has ridden in a troop carrier would argue otherwise. Certainly the United States seems perfectly happy with its full-length rifle, even though several inches could be trimmed from the 20-inch barrel with negligible loss of velocity.

Weapons of the future could be quite radical even if no major technological breakthroughs occur. New plastics reinforced by glass and carbon fibers could be used for receivers (especially in rifle designs where the bolt locks into the barrel), and aluminum or other light metals could be used to create barrels lined with steel sleeves (which Armalite was experimenting with in the 1950s). Coupled with smaller caliber cartridges, such rifles could easily weigh in at around four to five pounds, thereby making even current lightweight weapons seem heavy by comparison.

Rifle configuration and materials are not the only areas in which major changes may occur in the not too distant future; there are currently two U.S. military projects which may lead to the development of new weapons. One program is the ACR (Advanced Combat Rifle) and the other the CAWS (Close Assault Weapon Systems) program. In late 1983, the U.S. Army issued two contracts, one to the AAI Corporation and the other to Heckler & Koch, Inc., for the development of caseless ammunition and prototype rifles for testing and demonstration.

Caseless ammunition is hardly a new concept. The German military actually produced some experimental caseless ammunition during World War II. In the 1950s, the U.S. Frankford Arsenal started experimenting with caseless ammunition and in the 1960s developed a caseless 7.62mm round with ballistics similar to the 7.62mm NATO. What's new is that new caseless ammunition is tough and works well, and weapons are being developed to deal with the problem of heat buildup (the standard brass cartridge acts as a heat sink to carry off a great deal of the heat generated by the burning powder).

Caseless ammunition would offer a number of advantages to rifle design. The rifle could be lighter and simpler since there would be no need for a mechanism to extract or eject fired cases. Too, the weapon would be more resistant to dirt and mud since an ejection port would not have to be part of the receiver. Without a metal case, the ammunition would be lighter, which would allow the soldier to carry a greater quantity of it.

With the simplified mechanism, such a weapon could cycle very quickly (up to 2,000 rounds per minute) so that when fired in an automatic or burst mode the recoil would be a steady push rather than successive jumps, and barrel climb would be nonexistent. This means that a very small caliber bullet might be used to create multiple hits.

Currently. Heckler & Koch is working on a caseless ammunition bullpup, the G11, while the AAI Corporation is working on another which looks more like a standard rifle and fires from either the closed or open bolt, a definite plus when heat buildup may be a problem. Both weapons use a burst capability coupled with a small caliber bullet to create greater wounding/hit capabilities.

Approaching the multiple-projectile weapon from a different angle, the CAWS program seems to be aimed at producing an updated selective-fire shotgun which would fire ammunition with almost double the range of conventional shotgun ammunition. Like the ACR program, the CAWS program is dependent on the creation of ammunition that allows the weapon to fulfill the military's needs.

While the CAWS program (with contracts given to the AAI Corporation and Heckler & Koch—Smith & Wesson developed its own series of M16-style assault shotguns) has produced some interesting weapons, ammunition success to date seems limited. The long-range capability of the rounds remains to be seen. Too, many critics of the CAWS program point out that the ammunition (unlike that of the ACR program) will be heavy and will not offer precise, single-projectile shooting if and when it is needed. Troops carrying CAWS weapons would need the support of riflemen.

Since one of the major problems with small rifles is soaking up heat and recoil, new systems may be developed to handle these problems. Liquid recoil systems (perhaps even coupled with refrigeration systems) which augment the work done by springs may be seen on weapons of the future as could cooling systems using an electrostatic wind to blow air around the barrel. Such a system has been proposed by Stuart A. Hoenig of the University of Arizona and seems to pave the way for light-barreled weapons which could fire a large volume of small bullets from a closed bolt. Either system could use recoil energy to power the cooling system.

Optical systems may also go through some major changes in the future. The current trend is toward systems which allow the fighter to find his target more quickly. Through the use of fiber optics and laser-aiming systems, it is also possible that modern rifles may not need to be shouldered to obtain pinpoint accuracy. Fiber optics could couple an optical sight on the rifle to a pair of glasses worn by the soldier so that he could fire over or around obstacles without exposing his body to return fire. Such a system would give an overwhelming advantage to a defender and might lead to major changes in infantry tactics. Interestingly, this development may cause aimed fire to become more important than firing a number of projectiles in the general direction of an enemy. Optical systems might actually undo burst fire or CAWS-style research! Inexpensive laser or night-vision equipment would also vastly change the modern battlefield as well as combat in urban areas. Again, the precision shooting offered by a laser system could have a profound effect on infantry tactics.

One thing is certain: the weapons carried by the soldier will go through a lot of changes in the near future, if the past is any indication.

2. SUBMACHINE GUNS, CARBINES AND ASSAULT PISTOLS

An overview of submachine guns, carbines, and assault pistols currently available in the marketplace follows. Listed alphabetically by manufacturer, each weapon has a list of specifications for your reference.

BERETTA MODELLO 12 SUBMACHINE GUN

The Modello 12, a fine firearm created by the Pietro Beretta Company of Italy, was developed in the late 1950s and early 1960s. It is, as its name suggests, the twelfth in a line of experimental prototype models. Like many other modern submachine guns, it uses steel stampings and a telescoping bolt extending almost three-fourths of its length over the barrel; these features make it inexpensive and compact.

Two models of the weapon are available, one with a metal stock which folds to the right and one with a removable wooden stock. There has also been talk of a semiauto version for the police and civilian markets.

The receiver tube has grooves extending its full length. These can hold a lot of muck and grime so that the weapon can function in very dirty conditions. This design also does away with the need for machining expensive cleaning grooves on the bolt.

The Modello 12 has a grip safety on the front of its pistol grip, the selector on the left over the pistol grip, and the magazine release behind the magazine well. The charging handle is on the left side of the receiver tube. The weapon has a pistol grip handguard ahead of the magazine well.

Field-stripping the weapon is quite simple:

1. Remove the magazine and cycle the weapon to be sure it's empty; pull the trigger while holding the charging handle and ease it to its forward position.

2. Pull the barrel nut release catch (located at the rear of the barrel jacket) downward and unscrew the barrel nut.

3. Remove the barrel, nut, and bolt from the receiver by pulling them through the front of the receiver.

4. Remove the barrel nut over the muzzle end of the barrel. Pull the barrel toward the back of the bolt and out of it.

5. Lift the latch at the end of the receiver (behind the rear sight) and unscrew the end cap. Be careful, as the recoil spring is under pressure. Remove the recoil spring from the rear of the receiver.

Further disassembly is not recommended except for parts repair/replacement. Reassembly is basically the reverse of the above procedure.

The Modello 12 is a well-designed submachine gun, which has been adopted for use by the Italian armed forces.

Beretta Modello 12 Specifications

Barrel length	8 in.
Barrel twist	6 grooves, right-hand twist
Caliber	9mm Luger
Length (stock folded or removed)	16.4 in.
Length (stock extended)	25.4 in.
Magazine	20-, 30-, 40-round
Muzzle velocity	1250 fps
Cyclic rate	550 rpm
Weight unloaded (approx.)	6.5 lbs.

CZECH SKORPION MODELS

The Czechoslovakian Model 61 submachine gun was developed as a tanker's weapon and can be used both as a pistol and as a light submachine gun. The weapon has a wire stock which folds over the upper receiver so that the firearm can easily be carried on a sling, with some Skorpions having a sling loop welded to their tops, or even in a pistol holster.

The Model 61 is chambered for the diminutive .32 ACP (7.65mm Browning Short). While this is a marginal combat round in a pistol, the Skorpion's automatic capabilities make it effective in close combat.

The larger Model 68 is chambered for the 9mm Luger and designed mainly for export. The Model 61 is also manufactured for export by Yugoslavia as the M61. The Yugoslavian firm of Zastava is currently planning on exporting semiauto models chambered for .32 ACP as well as .380 ACP; these will be targeted for police use as well as the lucrative U.S. civilian market.

Other lesser-seen Czech models include the Model 64 chambered for .380 ACP (9mm Short) and the Model 65 which is chambered for 9mm Soviet (9mm × 18). Both are similar in size to the Model 61.

The various models of the Skorpion have been good sellers among African countries and often turn up among communist-backed terrorists thanks to the weapon's easily concealed size.

Because of the light weight of the bolt and the weapon's blow-back operation, a rate reducer is used to keep the cyclic rate of the Skorpion within useful limits. It consists of a hook on the inside of the receiver which hangs up the bolt for a fraction of a second during recoil. Another useful feature is the telescoping bolt which allows the weapon to have a long enough barrel to give good muzzle velocity without excessive protrusion from the receiver.

The pistol has two-position flip sights calibrated for 75 and (in the usual optimistic European manner) 150 meters. Glow-in-the-dark sights are also available, as is a silencer.

The magazine release is located on the left side of the receiver above the front of the trigger guard. The weapon has dual charging handles on each side of the upper receiver. The selector is located on the left of the receiver just above the pistol grip. The center position of the selector is "Safe," while the forward setting ("20") gives auto fire, and backward to "1" sets the weapon in the semiauto mode.

Field-stripping, which is quite simple, is as follows:

1. Remove the magazine and cycle the weapon to be sure it is empty. Place the stock in the extended position and ease the bolt into its fired position.

2. Push out the assembly pin at the front of the lower receiver from right to left.

3. Lift up the barrel end of the receiver and pull it out and away from the lower receiver. Be careful, as the recoil spring will be under tension.

4. Pull the charging handles backward as far as they will go, and pull them out of the bolt through the wide area at the rear of their receiver cuts.

5. Remove the bolt, recoil springs, and spring guides from the rear of the upper receiver.

This procedure will give the user access to the action springs, trigger, etc. Further disassembly is not recommended except for parts repair/replacement or to clean/lubricate the rate reducer assembly. This is accessible by removing the pistol grip cap and actuator spring. Reassembly is basically the reverse of the above procedure.

The Skorpion is a well-designed "assault pistol" with a lot of firepower in a small package. It will undoubtedly remain popular in communist and Third-World countries for some time.

Czech Model 61 Specifications

Barrel length . . . . 4.5 in.
Barrel twist . . . . 6 grooves, right-hand twist
Caliber . . . . .32 ACP
Length (stock folded) . . . . 10.7 in.
Length (stock extended) . . . . 20.6 in.
Magazine 10-, 20-round
Muzzle velocity . . . . 1040 fps
Cyclic rate . . . . 750 rpm
Weight unloaded (approx.) . . . . 2.9 lbs.

Czech Model 68 Specifications

Barrel length . . . . 5 in.
Caliber . . . . 9mm Luger
Length (stock folded) . . . . 12 in.
Length (stock extended) . . . . 23.4 in.
Magazine 10-, 20-, 30-round
Muzzle velocity . . . . 1300 fps
Cyclic rate . . . . 750 rpm
Weight unloaded (approx.) . . . . 4.4 lbs.

DEMRO TAC-1 AND XF-7 WASP

Though it looks somewhat like a Thompson submachine gun, the Demro TAC-1 is a semiauto carbine that is actually quite different from the older weapon. The TAC-1, available in either 9mm or .45 ACP, has a removable stock and a rear sight adjustable for windage and elevation. Operating with a blow-back action, the semiauto is one of the few that can fire from an open bolt without being removed from the U.S. market by the BATF. The 9mm version is nearly identical to the

.45 version but has a 32-round magazine. The TAC-1 has a walnut stock, pistol grip, and foregrip.

Early models of the TAC-1 had a combination lock on the left side of the receiver above the trigger; the manufacturer has mercifully removed this feature on newer weapons. Weapons without the combination lock are designated as the "TAC-1M." A grip safety and safety lever/selector (on the left of the receiver over the pistol grip) have been retained. A sister weapon which is nearly identical to the TAC-1M is the XF-7. The XF-7 has a folding stock and plastic furniture rather than wood.

Both carbines have the magazine release behind the magazine well, and the charging knob is located on the left side of the upper receiver. Selective-fire versions of the weapons are also occasionally encountered.

Field-stripping the TAC-1 is fairly straightforward (the XF-7 Wasp is nearly identical except for its folding stock):

1. Remove the magazine and cycle the weapon to be sure it is empty. Leave the bolt forward.

2. Release and remove the stock by depressing the release button located at the left rear of the receiver.

3. Push the latch release at the rear of the receiver and rotate the upper receiver and barrel assembly downward.

4. Lift the bolt carrier and bolt up and out of the lower receiver, rotating it out either side while restraining the recoil spring, which is under pressure.

5. Remove the recoil spring and its guide from the back of the bolt carrier.

6. Remove the charging handle from the bolt carrier to release the bolt, and remove it from the bolt carrier (take care that the extractor and its spring aren't dropped, as they are free in the bolt).

7. The upper receiver/barrel assembly can be removed by pushing out its pivot pin with the longer of the two stock-mounting rods.

Further disassembly is generally not required, and reassembly is a reversal of the above steps. When the bolt is placed back into its carrier, be sure to align the groove in the bolt with the ejector/spring guide. Depress the extractor as the bolt is pushed into place.

The Demro rifles are basically good designs and are probably among the best of the "plinker carbines," which may also be employed for combat.

Demro TAC-1 Specifications

Barrel length	16.8 in.
Caliber	.45 ACP
Length	35.7 in.
Magazine	30-round
Muzzle velocity	960 fps
Weight unloaded (approx.)	7.7 lbs.

ENFIELD MP-45

The Enfield MP-45 is a semiauto "assault pistol" that operates in the standard blow-back manner and fires from a closed bolt.

The MP-45 appears to be very similar to the KG-99/TEC-9 but is made of steel and chambered for the .45 ACP (a 9mm Luger version is under development). The pistol has several interesting points, including a modular trigger group, and the manufacturer offers a wide variety of accessories including carrying handles and scope mounts which can be quickly fastened to the front and rear sight "dog ears."

The magazine release is located to the rear of the magazine well, and the cross-bolt safety is just above the trigger. The charging handle is on the upper left of the receiver tube.

A carbine kit allows the user to quickly convert the weapon to an 18-inch barrel with a retractable wire stock. The stock is fastened to the barrel shroud rather than to the pistol to avoid problems with the U.S. law which restricts stocked handguns to barrel lengths of 16 inches or more.

A left-handed model of the weapon is also available, though the unit's upward charging handle, cross-bolt safety, and magazine release at the rear of the well are quite easy for left-handers to use.

A wide range of accessories is available for the MP-45. The barrel screws into the front of the receiver so that different length barrels are quickly interchangeable. The muzzle end of the barrel is threaded to accept silencers, barrel extensions, etc. Scope mounts, electric night sights, and an AR-15-style carrying handle are also available.

Magazines (as well as a loading tool) are offered with 10- and 30-round capacities as well as unwieldy 40- and 50-round sizes. Stainless steel 30- and 40-round magazines are also available.

Field-stripping the weapon is quite simple:

1. Remove the magazine and cycle the weapon to be sure it is empty.

2. Unscrew the barrel and shroud.

3. Pull out the charging handle. Be careful, as the recoil spring will be under tension and the bolt will be released to pop out the front of the receiver tube.

4. Remove the bolt, recoil spring, and spring guide from the front of the receiver tube.

5. To free the trigger group, remove the roll pin holding it in place. This will give access to the action springs, trigger, etc.

Further disassembly is not recommended except for

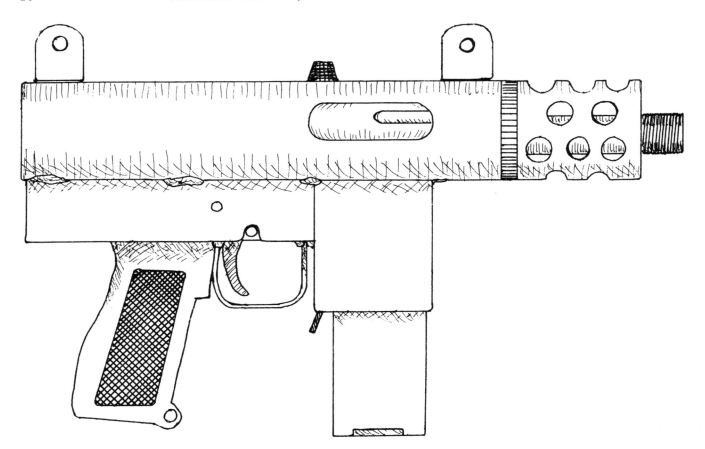

The heavy Enfield MP-45 has a modular trigger group and a wide variety of accessories, including carrying handles and scope mounts. Accessories can quickly be fastened to the front and rear sight "dog ears," which have machined holes for this purpose.

parts repair/replacement. Reassembly is basically the reverse of the above procedure.

Like most other blow-back weapons, the Enfield MP-45 may have trouble using ammunition with thin brass since the cartridge head is unsupported during the first part of recoil.

The Enfield MP-45 is a well-designed "assault pistol." Unfortunately, it is chambered for a round which seems to be slowly becoming obsolete and is extremely heavy for a gun of this type due to the use of heavy-gauge steel rather than plastics. Nevertheless, the MP-45 is a weapon worth considering for combat use.

Enfield MP-45 Specifications

Barrel length . . . . 4.5 in.
Barrel twist . 6 grooves, right-hand, 1-in-18 in. twist
Caliber . . . . .45 ACP
Length . . . . 11.8 in.
Magazine 10-, 30-, 40-, 50-round
Muzzle velocity . . . . 850 fps
Weight unloaded (approx.) . . . . 6 lbs.

GONCZ HIGH-TECH CARBINE AND PISTOL

The Goncz pistols and carbine are quite similar to the KG-99/TEC-9 in concept but use an alloy rather than plastic pistol grip and have the magazine well in the pistol grip, similar to the Uzi but with an improved angle. The forward end of the receiver extends around the barrel a short distance and is ventilated to create a shroud/foregrip.

Designed by Lajos J. Goncz, the carbine and pistols are nearly identical except for the carbine stock and barrel lengths plus slight modifications to keep the stock from being mounted on the shorter-barreled model's receiver. All are simple blow-back semiautos which fire from a closed bolt. The weapon's safety locks the firing pin. The barrel is threaded for accessories, and the firearms have a black oxide/anodized finish.

Both pistols and carbine are available in 9mm Luger, .30 Mauser, .38 Super, or .45 ACP. Magazine capacity is 18 and 32 rounds for all except the .45 ACP, which has 10- and 20-round magazines. The front sight is adjustable for elevation and the rear for windage. The charging handle is located on the upper left side of the receiver; the safety, on the left above the pistol grip; and the magazine release, on the grip behind the trigger in a manner similar to a semiauto pistol. The pistol grip is an integral part of the lower metallic receiver and has finger grooves and checkering molded into it. The carbine's original standard stock was made of plastic, but is presently offered in walnut. The pistol is available in the GS model with a threaded, 5-inch barrel or the GA model with a 9½-inch barrel, while the carbine has a 16-inch barrel. The GC is the standard carbine, while the GCH model has a halogen light source with its power supply in the stock. The halogen light allows the shooter to light up target areas at night (or become a flood-lit target if careless). The GCL carbine has a laser-aiming system.

At the time of this writing, the Goncz weapons had just been released and were not available for testing. It will be interesting to see how they perform and whether the market has room for yet another pistol/carbine combination.

Goncz Pistol Specifications
Barrel length . . . . 5 (or 9.5) in.
Caliber . . . . 9mm Luger, .30 Mauser,
.38 Super, .45 ACP
Length . . . . 11.5 (or 16) in.
Magazine 18-, 38-round
(10-, 20-round for .45)
Weight unloaded (approx.) . . . . 3.6 lbs.

Goncz Carbine Specifications
Barrel length . . . . 16.1 in.
Caliber . . . . 9mm Luger, .30 Mauser,
.38 Super, .45 ACP
Length . . . . 31 in.
Magazine 18-, 32-round
(10-, 20-round for .45)
Weight unloaded without laser or
halogen light system (approx.) . . . . .4.1 lbs.

INGRAM MAC-10/11 SUBMACHINE GUNS

Gordon Ingram marketed the Ingram Model 6 submachine gun in the early 1950s, but the Thompson-like weapon enjoyed only limited sales, and his company, Police Ordnance of Los Angeles, California, soon discontinued the gun. In 1969, Ingram went to work for the Military Armament Corporation of Powder Springs, Georgia, which was producing silencers, and a year later produced the Model 10, a weapon which was nearly as compact as a pistol with the firepower of

a submachine gun. This weapon has become known both as the "Ingram" and by its factory designation, the "MAC-10" (Military Armaments Corporation, Model 10).

The MAC-10 fires from an open bolt and uses a telescoping bolt which partially wraps around the barrel at the time of firing. The magazine well doubles as the pistol grip. This makes a short, well-balanced weapon which can be carried and fired with one hand. The MAC-10s were made in both 9mm Luger and .45 ACP. Later, a smaller version of the MAC-10, the MAC-11, was created in .380 ACP (9mm Browning Short). The MAC-10 enjoyed very limited use by the U.S. military in Vietnam and some sales were made to Chile and Yugoslavia.

In an effort to reach the civilian market, a semiauto version was marketed, designated the SM10 or SAP M10 and chambered for .45 and 9mm. The SM10s were stockless and thus legally classified as pistols. Later, carbine versions were developed and designated the SM10-A1 and SM11-A1. These weapons all fired from an open bolt and could be converted to full auto; when other companies started marketing full-auto conversion kits, the BATF ordered the company to discontinue production.

Sales of the Ingram weapons were never overwhelming. The company finally went bankrupt in 1978, and manufacturing rights for the MAC-11 were purchased by RPB Industries, Inc., of Atlanta, Georgia, and its sister company, SWD.

Knowing that sales of a weapon chambered for the .380 ACP would be small, RPB/SWD created a new 9mm Luger model of the MAC-11. This modification is designated the M11-9mm and is available in both semiauto and selective-fire versions. The M11-9mm has altered dimensions which lower its cyclic rate to 900 rpm and fires from a closed bolt; these two features have made the weapon considerably more accurate and easier to fire than the original MAC-10. The safety on the M11-9mm is located in the standard position on the auto versions of the weapon; on the semiauto versions, the AR-15-style safety is located on the right side of the receiver, just over the trigger.

Following the bankruptcy of Military Armaments Corporation, a new company was set up in Stephenville, Texas, which purchased the rights to the MAC-10. This new company adopted the original "Military Armaments Corporation" name even though it was a different corporate entity. The new company also modified the Ingram design somewhat and designated the modified version the M10A1. Both .45 and 9mm Luger versions are made, as well as semiauto closed-bolt

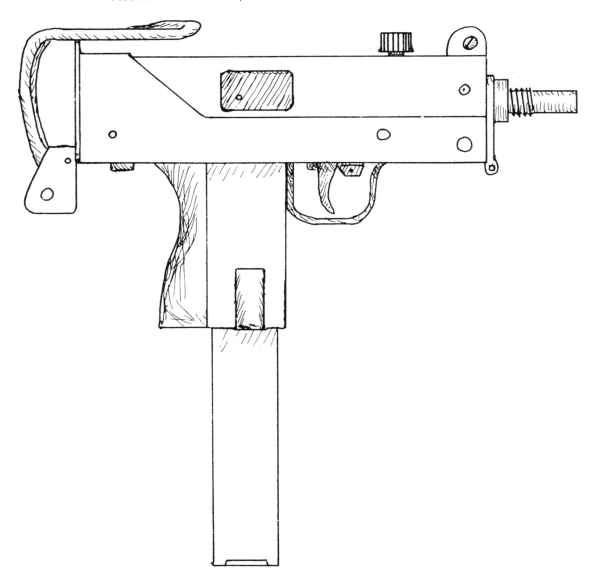

The U.S. MAC-10 fires from an open bolt and uses a telescoping bolt which partially wraps around the barrel at the time of firing. The magazine well doubles as the pistol grip. This makes a very short, well-balanced weapon which can be fired with one hand. The MAC-10s were made in both 9mm Luger and .45 ACP. Later, a smaller version, the MAC-11, was created for the .380 ACP (9mm Browning Short).

firearms. Conversion kits are available to change a weapon from one caliber to the other.

All versions of the Ingram weapons are made of stamped and welded steel with the magazine well welded to the lower receiver to make a strong, stationary pistol grip. The magazine release catch is located at the rear of the pistol grip.

Placing the magazine well in the grip also creates problems. It forces the pistol grip to be less steeply angled than is necessary for good pointing and makes the weapon so short that it is possible to shoot off the fingers of the off hand in the heat of battle. The latter hazard is not much improved by the strap, which is often mounted in the sling swivel under the barrel. Therefore,

many shooters use a silencer or barrel extension to create a handguard.

The silencer is readily mounted on the Ingram weapons since all barrels are threaded to accept it. The silencer is most useful with subsonic ammunition; supersonic bullets create a cracking sound as they break the sound barrier. Because of this, the suppressor is more successful on the .45 caliber model. The silencer created by the Military Armament Corporation was designed by Col. Mitch Werbell; it is one of the best sound suppressors available and has done much to promote the sales of the MAC-10/11.

The stock on the auto versions is short and not too stable. Most shooters end up using it to steady the weapon against their side or under their arm. Such shooting is quick but hardly accurate. (Due to the high cyclic rate, Ingram weapons are generally used only at extremely close ranges.)

A much sturdier stock is marketed by Choate Machine and Tool. This stock folds to the side of the Ingram and acts as a forward grip when folded; extended, it locks up tightly and allows the shooter to make quick, accurate shots. This stock greatly enhances the Ingram weapons' long-range capabilities with only a slight increase in weight.

All models have a charging knob on the top of the receiver which doubles as the safety and obstructs the sight picture when rotated a quarter turn to the safe position. Thus, the shooter can tell at a glance whether or not the safety is on.

A second "safety" is located in and to the side of the trigger guard where it is worked by the trigger finger (the only exception to this is with the semiauto M11-9mm which has an AR-15-style selector/safety on the receiver's right side). The M10-A1 has a slightly different safety that extends down into the trigger guard. The selector—missing on the semiauto versions—is located on the left side of the receiver ahead of the trigger guard.

The rear sight is an extension of the rear receiver plate; it consists of an aperture hole drilled into the metal. The front sight is a post protected by two ears. No adjustments can be made to the sights except by filng. The relatively crude sights often limit the capabilities of the weapon with some types of ammunition.

The magazines are modified magazines originally created for other weapons. While this makes for inexpensive magazines and cheap tooling up for the manufacturer, it also saddles the .45 Ingram with the M-3 grease gun magazine, never noted for its reliability. The 9mm Luger version fares better with the Swedish K and Walther MPL/K magazines. The MAC-11 fared as poorly as the MAC-10; its magazines are terrible, small versions of the single-column .45 magazine with a very limited ammunition capacity.

Currently, RPB/SWD offers a plastic Zytel magazine for the M11-9mm version. With slight modifications, it will work in the old MAC-11 as well as the 9mm MAC-10. RPD/SWD also offered a conversion kit for a time which allowed the user to convert the M11-9mm from 9mm Luger to .380 ACP and also reduced the cycling rate.

The Ingram weapons often have trouble feeding hollow-point or flat-nosed ammunition. Simple throating and polishing of the chamber and feed ramp will usually take care of this difficulty. Older guns also have

a tendency for the front receiver pin to "walk" out. This can be cured by substituting a threaded bolt or a bar with pins for the factory pin. The new M11-9mm uses a double pin that seems to have solved this problem.

To field-strip the Ingram weapons:
1. Remove the magazine and cycle the weapon. While restraining the bolt, pull the trigger and ease the bolt into its forward position (on auto versions). Unscrew and remove the suppressor or barrel extension.
2. Push the front receiver pin free and pull it out of the gun.
3. Rotate the barrel end of the upper receiver up and out of the lower receiver.
4. Pull the charging knob back and remove it through the larger opening in its channel.
5. Remove the bolt and recoil spring assembly which are now free.
6. The recoil spring and guide are held in place by a cross pin at the front of the guide. When possible, leave them installed. If it is necessary to remove the guide and spring from the bolt, compress the spring so that the guide extends out the front of the bolt, and drift out the pin to free the guide and spring. Use care since the spring is under tension.
7. The stock can be removed by depressing its release button and pulling it out.

The above steps give access to the various parts of the weapon which need to be cleaned. Further disassembly is not recommended. If it is necessary to remove the barrel, be sure to remove its roll pin before unscrewing it. The extractor can be removed for replacement by drifting out its roll pin toward the right of the bolt. Reassembly is basically the reverse of the above procedures.

Though the Ingram guns have never had any large military sales, the weapons have enjoyed wide popularity among individuals. Therefore, it is possible to encounter this weapon in nearly any part of the world. Unfortunately, the poor stock, heavy weight, high cyclic rate, and crude sights limit usefulness.

MAC-10 (.45) Specifications

Barrel length	5.75 in.
Barrel twist	5 grooves, right-hand twist
Caliber	.45 ACP
Length (stock folded)	10.5 in.
Length (stock extended)	21.5 in.
Length (with silencer, stock folded)	21 in.
Magazine	30-round
Muzzle velocity	900 fps
Cyclic rate	1000 rpm

Weight unloaded, without silencer
  (approx.) . . . . 6.25 lbs.
Weight unloaded, with silencer
  (approx.) . . . . 7.5 lbs.

MAC-10 (9mm) Specifications

Barrel length . . . . 5.75 in.
Caliber . . . . 9mm Luger
Length (stock folded) . . . . 10.5 in.
Length (stock extended) . . . . 21.5 in.
Length (with silencer, stock folded) . . . . 21 in.
Magazine 32-round
Muzzle velocity . . . . 1280 fps
Cyclic rate . . . . 1100 rpm
Weight unloaded, without silencer
  (approx.) . . . . 6.25 lbs.
Weight unloaded, with silencer
  (approx.) . . . . 7.5 lbs.

MAC-11 (.380 ACP/9mm Browning Short) Specifications

Barrel length . . . . 5.25 in.
Caliber . . . . .380 ACP
Length (stock folded) . . . . 9.75 in.
Length (stock extended) . . . . 18.25 in.
Length (with silencer, stock folded) . . . . . . 17.75 in.
Magazine 16-, 32-round
Muzzle velocity . . . . 1040 fps
Cyclic rate . . . . 1200 rpm
Weight unloaded, without silencer
  (approx.) . . . . 3.5 lbs.
Weight unloaded, with silencer
  (approx.) . . . . 4.5 lbs.

M11-9mm Specifications

Barrel length . . . . 5.25 in.
Caliber . . . . 9mm Luger
Length (stock folded) . . . . 13 in.
Length (stock extended) . . . . 23 in.
Length (without stock) . . . . 12.5 in.
Magazine 34-round
Muzzle velocity . . . . 1280 fps
Cyclic rate . . . . 900 rpm
Weight unloaded, without silencer
  (approx.) . . . . 3.75 lbs.

JATI

The JATI is different enough from previous designs to be a prime example of the fourth-generation submachine gun. Through the use of special plastics and a design that cuts down on muzzle climb, the JATI presents a very small, lightweight weapon.

The submachine gun was designed by Jali Timari in 1980 and is manufactured by the Tampereen Aspaja Oy of Finland. The lower receiver, pistol grip, magazine well, rear sight, charging handle, trigger, sear, and disconnector are all made of plastic. Many other parts, including the barrel, are made of stainless steel. The design, coupled with the durable materials, makes a robust gun with only 39 parts!

The weapon works as a standard blow-back, firing from an open bolt. It uses a telescoping bolt that wraps around half the length of the barrel at the moment of firing. Upon firing, the bolt travels at a seven-degree angle from the barrel, moving "up the slope" of the receiver. This causes the weapon to counteract its own recoil forces and places the firer's hand almost directly behind the barrel. Consequently, bursts of fire create backward pushes rather than a climbing muzzle, making the weapon very controllable in full-auto fire. Most shooters will find that one-hand shooting is possible with little or no muzzle climb.

The JATI chambers a wide range of cartridges very reliably for a good reason: there's no feed ramp. The incline the bolt travels over allows the weapon to feed rounds directly into the chamber of the barrel. Rounds also headspace in the barrel; the weapon does not use premature ignition to fire them. While this causes a slight increase in felt recoil, it makes the action much smoother and more controllable in the automatic mode.

Optional threaded barrels are available for use with suppressors made by Tampereen Aspaja Oy. Under-the-jacket carrying "holsters" (actually straps and hooks) are also marketed by the manufacturer; although the JATI seems a little large for concealment, it in fact does well on large-framed users wearing a heavy jacket and using the shorter 20-round magazine.

Magazines are made of extruded aluminum with plastic followers. Only the spring and floor plate are steel. The magazines are very light, sturdy, and quite resistant to rust and corrosion. Interestingly, the 36-round Swedish K magazines also fit the weapon. Smith & Wesson M76 magazines may also work with a little alteration. The magazine release is behind the magazine well; the small dimensions of the JATI allow the user to release it with his trigger finger if he wishes.

The trigger acts as the selector. A slight pull gives the shooter a single shot, while pulling back fully gives automatic fire. The forward grip acts as both the charging handle and safety. When the handle is folded up under the barrel, it locks the bolt and keeps the weapon from firing. When the handle is rotated down at right angles to the barrel, the safety is off and the weapon can be fired. Pulling back on the grip/handle moves the bolt into fire position. While this all works well, it does make one-handed firing hard to initiate; the user must remember to push forward on the foregrip so that the bolt isn't prevented from moving fully forward during its firing cycle.

Another safety feature is the word "Fire" printed on the bolt; this shows at the ejection port when the bolt is back in the fire position. The ejection port remains covered with the bolt in both the cocked and forward positions; dirt has a tough time getting in through it.

The rear sight is a plastic notch molded into the receiver. The front post is adjustable for elevation via two hex nuts and is protected by dog ears.

Cooling holes are located in the receiver cover and the pistol grip. While these holes help prevent heat buildup, the user might be wise to plug them if he expects to fight in a dusty, muddy, or sandy area.

A stock fastens to the lower side of the pistol grip and behind and around the rear sight, thereby giving it protective ears. This accessory would give the JATI much greater accuracy, but many users won't need the stock since the weapon is intended for close-combat defense work. Too, the lack of muzzle climb in full auto makes the stock unnecessary.

Disassembly of the JATI is as follows:

1. Remove the magazine and cycle the weapon to be sure it's empty. Use the charging handle/safety/foregrip to ease the bolt into its forward position while depressing the trigger.

2. Release the cover latch and open it.

3. Push the recoil spring and guide forward and remove them from the receiver.

4. Slide the bolt back and lift it out of the receiver.

5. Remove the barrel by lifting it up and out the front end of the receiver.

The above procedure enables the user to have access to action springs, trigger, etc. Further disassembly is not recommended except for parts repair/replacement. The trigger group can be removed by taking out its retaining screw and pulling it out through the receiver. The bolt head with the fixed firing pin is replaceable and can be removed by first removing the extractor.

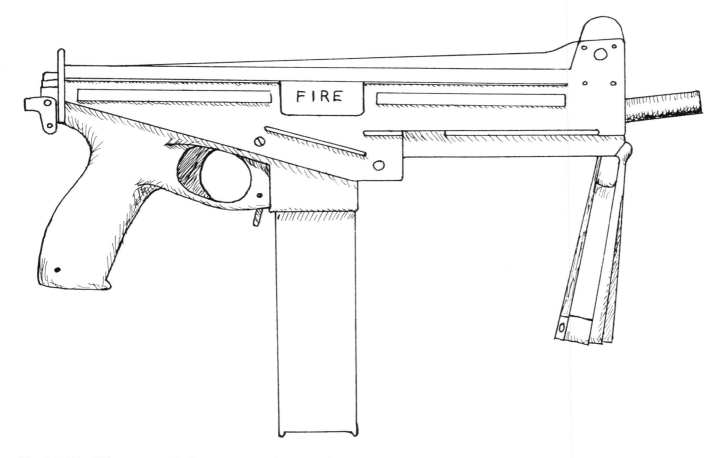

FIRE

The JATI is different enough from previous designs to be a prime candidate as the first of the fourth generation of new submachine guns. Made of special plastics and having a design that cuts down on muzzle climb, the JATI is a very small, lightweight weapon.

Reassembly is basically the reverse of the above procedure. If the trigger group is removed, be sure to keep the disconnector in its forward position when reinstalling it; the trigger spring in the pistol grip must go behind the disconnector.

The JATI is another forward-looking design that greatly erodes the advantages of a pistol on the battlefield due to this submachine gun's small size and heavy firepower. The JATI will be a tough act to follow.

JATI Specifications

Barrel length . . . . 8 in.
Barrel twist . . . . 6 grooves, right-hand twist,
1-in-9.9 turn
Caliber . . . . 9mm Luger
Length (without stock) . . . . 14.8 in.
Magazine 20-, 40-round
Muzzle velocity (approx.) . . . . 1200 fps
Cyclic rate . . . . 650 rpm
Weight unloaded (approx.) . . . . 6.5 lbs.

MADSEN SUBMACHINE GUN

The Madsen Maskinpistols m/50 and m/53 are Danish designs which have been manufactured in Brazil as well as Denmark. Sales were made to a number of countries in Asia and South America, but the weapon has been discontinued by the Madsen firm. The Brazilian weapons were made during the 1950s, before Brazil switched to 9mm, and are nearly identical to the Danish version except that they are chambered in .45 ACP and have the charging handle on the right side of the receiver. The leather cover is generally missing from the stock as well.

The Danish weapons come in two models, the m/50 and the m/53, both of which are descendants of the m/46 model. The m/53 has a curved magazine for better feeding, and the barrel nut screws into the barrel rather than onto the receiver. The bolt is also altered somewhat from that found on the m/50.

The Madsen is fairly conventional in design except that the body and receiver are made of two steel stampings which hinge at the rear. This allows the user to open up the weapon for cleaning by removing the front barrel nut and rotating the weapon's left side back. This greatly simplifies cleaning and maintenance and makes manufacture quite simple.

The charging handle is located at the top of the receiver, the magazine release to the rear of the magazine well, and the safety is a lever at the rear of the magazine housing which is gripped during firing. A safety catch on the frame is also available to lock the bolt back. The front sight blade is adjustable for windage and the rear for elevation. On Danish weapons, the rear of the stock is usually covered in leather.

As one might imagine, field-stripping the weapon is quite simple: Remove the barrel nut, rotate the weapon and half it open, and the inner mechanisms will then be exposed.

The Madsen is a well-designed submachine gun; though the weapon has been discontinued by the Madsen company, it will probably only be a matter of time before other companies start making similar weapons.

Madsen Specifications

Barrel length . . . . 7.8 in.
Barrel twist . . . . 4 grooves, right-hand twist
Caliber . . . . 9mm Luger

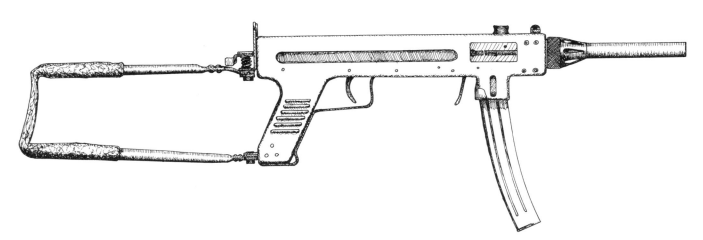

The Danish Madsen Maskinpistol m/50 submachine gun is fairly conventional except that the whole body and receiver are made of two steel stampings which hinge at the rear. This design greatly simplifies cleaning and maintenance and facilitates manufacture as well.

Length (stock folded) .... 20.75 in.
Length (stock extended) .... 31.6 in.
Magazine 32-round
Muzzle velocity .... 1250 fps
Cyclic rate .... 550 rpm
Weight unloaded (approx.) .... 7 lbs.

MARK 45 "COMMANDO"

Though it looks somewhat like a Thompson sub-machine gun, the Mark 45 Commando is a semiauto carbine that is in actuality quite different. The Mark 45 makes extensive use of plastic (General Electric Valux) for the pistol grip, magazine well, and lower receiver as well as the forward grip, which is available either as a standard foregrip or a Thompson-style pistol grip. The Mark 45's stock is a slightly modified Thompson stock complete with the oil trap door butt. The upper receiver is formed from a steel stamping, and the weapon uses the standard blow-back operation.

A 9mm version of the weapon is also marketed. Designated the Mark 9, this weapon may possibly over-shadow the Mark 45 in the United States as the 9mm Luger becomes more popular. A very early version of the Mark 45, designated the Mark III, is readily distinguishable by its alloy grip frame rather than the current plastic. Both the Mark 9 and Mark 45 are available in either the standard blue finish or nickel.

The Mark 45 is not without its shortcomings: the trigger-guard hole is quite small, so that it's nearly im-possible to fire the weapon with gloves on; the charg-ing handle is small and especially hard to work on new, tight guns; trigger pull on many weapons is heavy; ac-curacy is not as good as with other firearms of this type; and new Mark 45s are so tight that they may have func-tioning problems, especially in a dirty environment. Fortunately, many of these problems are curable with a little competent gunsmith work, and the weapons

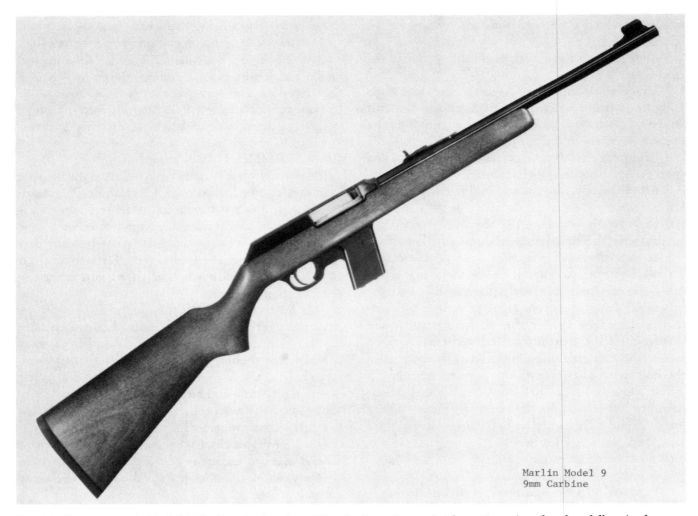

Marlin Model 9
9mm Carbine

The Marlin Company's Model 9 Carbine is chambered for the 9mm Luger (with a .45 version slated to follow in the near future). The carbine fires with a closed bolt and operates with the standard blow-back design. Photo courtesy of Marlin Firearms.

loosen up with use. Added to the weapon's shortcomings is the fact that a Phillips screwdriver, Allen wrench, and standard screwdriver are required for disassembly. If this weapon is to be used in a survival or combat situation, these screws should be replaced by one type and the screwdriver kept in the stock in an enlarged trap.

The charging knob is located on the left side of the receiver and the cross-bolt safety is located well above the pistol grip. The magazine release is to the rear of the magazine well. The rear sight is a fixed aperture with protective ears and the front sight is a ramp blade.

Field-stripping the weapon is complicated but not overly difficult:

1. Remove the magazine and cycle the weapon to be sure it's empty.

2. Pull the trigger to drop the striker.

3. Remove the two screws in the lower forward end of the stock and remove it.

4. Unscrew the large screw at the rear of the receiver's underside which is exposed with the removal of the stock.

5. Slide the grip frame back and rotate it free of the receiver.

6. Unscrew the large screw inside the rear sight wings with an Allen wrench. This will release the rear receiver/buffer cap. Take care, as this part is under pressure from the recoil spring.

7. Remove the receiver cap, buffer, recoil springs, and spring guide from the upper receiver.

8. Move the bolt forward and pull out the charging knob.

9. Remove the bolt from the rear of the receiver.

10. Remove the striker from the rear of the bolt.

This procedure will give you access to the action springs, the trigger, etc. Further disassembly is not recommended except for parts repair/replacement. Reassembly is basically the reverse of the above procedure; take care to place the right side of the receiver cap up when reassembling. If the extractor needs to be replaced, be sure to drive its retaining pin out from the bottom of the bolt to avoid damaging the extractor spring.

The Mark 45 works well but offers little that isn't found on other weapons. Its strong points are a very low price and a Thompson look. Because of its awkward takedown and other shortcomings, it probably is better suited to plinking than combat.

Mark 45 Commando Specifications

Barrel length . . . . 16.5 in.
Barrel twist . . . . right-hand, 1-in-16 twist
Caliber . . . . .45 ACP

Length . . . . 37 in.
Magazine 5-, 15-, 30-round
Muzzle velocity . . . . 960 fps
Weight unloaded (approx.) . . . . 8 lbs.

MARLIN MODEL 9 CARBINE

The Marlin Company has been making firearms since 1888; they've had a lot of experience and have enjoyed large sales of lever, slide, and semiauto rifles. Since many of their rifles are carbines chambered for pistol rounds like the .357 Magnum, .44 Magnum, and the .22 LR, it would seem that the next step would be 9mm and .45 ACP. Enter the Model 9 rifle chambered for the 9mm Luger with a .45 version slated to follow in the near future; this will use magazines similar to those of the Colt .45 pistol.

The Model 9 enjoys the "Micro-Groove" rifling technique developed by Marlin which creates a large number of rifling grooves and gives better stability and velocity. The carbine fires with a closed bolt and operates by blow-back. Though only semiauto versions are available, conversion to automatic fire would be possible.

The rear sight is a simple "U" aperture on a stepped ramp which adjusts for elevation; the front sight is a hooded post. The upper receiver is drilled for a scope mount base. The safety is located inside the front of the trigger guard, which might be of interest to someone wanting to create a "family" of similar operating weapons in the M14/Mini-14/XGI group.

The Model 9 bolt remains open following the last shot and can also be locked open for cleaning. The hardwood stock has a rubber recoil pad. While the pad is hardly needed for the miniscule 9mm recoil on this large a firearm, it does help to keep the weapon steady during extended firing. The receiver is machined steel, which is somewhat of a rarity, especially for a gun in the low end of the price scale.

The major drawbacks at the time of this writing are that the weapon needs to be cleaned *thoroughly* after 250 rounds; takedown for cleaning is rather complex (though not as complex as for some other commercial carbines on the U.S. market), and the plastic buffer seems a bit brittle and breaks easily on some early production guns. Given the company's track record, new models will undoubtedly be produced which will overcome these drawbacks. In the meantime, these problems would seem to eliminate the Model 9 carbine from military use, even though it is suitable for home defense or police use.

Despite this weapon's current shortcomings, it will probably prove a strong contender in the paramilitary market as more improvements are made in its design.

Marlin Model 9 Specifications

Barrel length . . . . 16.5 in.
Barrel twist . . . . Micro-Groove twist
Caliber . . . . 9mm Luger
Length . . . . 35.5 in.
Magazine 12-, 20-round
Muzzle velocity . . . . 1290 fps
Weight unloaded (approx.) . . . . 6.5 lbs.

MAT-49 SUBMACHINE GUN

The MAT (Manufacture d'Armes de Tulle) 49 was created by the French in an effort to manufacture a relatively inexpensive weapon. Made of heavy steel stampings, it has a squared-off look which minimizes assembly work. The weapon works by blow-back and has few design innovations. The weapon was adopted by the French Army in 1949 and was used in Algeria and Indochina. The simple design worked well and was liked by those who used it.

The telescoping wire stock is similar to that of the U.S. M3. The stock can be extended/retracted with the catch located on the left side of the receiver. The ejection-port cover opens automatically with the initial forward or rearward movement of the bolt. The MAT-49 has a grip safety and barrel shroud to protect the user's fingers from the hot barrel. The front sight is hooded, while the two-position 100- and 200-meter rear sight is exposed. The charging handle is located on the left side of the receiver and the magazine release to the bottom rear of the magazine well. A latch located on the bottom of the trigger guard releases the magazine/magazine well to pivot forward. When the magazine well is rotated to a horizontal position, a clip on the underside of the barrel shroud holds the magazine well in place (this clip must be released for the magazine to rotate back down for use).

Large numbers of the MAT-49 were seized by the North Vietnamese and converted from 9mm Luger to 7.62 Tokarev; this caliber is occasionally seen in addition to the original 9mm Luger chambering.

Field-stripping the weapon is quite simple:

1. Remove the magazine and cycle the weapon to be sure it's empty; pull the trigger while holding the bolt and ease it to its forward position. The stock can be removed by pushing in the stock catch on the left side of the receiver and pulling out the stock. Stock removal is not necessary for normal maintenance.

2. Press the upper receiver release located at the rear of the barrel jacket rearward.

3. Remove the barrel, shroud, and receiver assembly by pulling them forward and up. Take care, as the recoil spring is under pressure.

4. Remove the recoil spring and bolt from the rear of the receiver.

You will thus have access to the action springs, trigger, etc. Further disassembly is not recommended except for parts repair/replacement. Reassembly is basically a reverse of the above procedure.

French MAT-49 Specifications

Barrel length . . . . 9 in.
Barrel twist . . . . 4 groove, left-hand twist
Caliber . . . . 9mm Luger
Length (stock retracted) . . . . 21.25 in.
Length (stock extended) . . . . 30.6 in.
Magazine 32-round
Muzzle velocity . . . . 1200 fps
Cyclic rate . . . . 650 rpm
Weight unloaded (approx.) . . . . 7.5 lbs.

MP-38/40/41 SUBMACHINE GUNS

The MP (*Maschinen Pistole*) 38 and the later MP-40 and MP-41 were the first weapons to make extensive use of modern industrial methods to create a cheap but deadly weapon. Often misnamed the "Schmeisser," the weapon was not designed or modified by Hugo Schmeisser. The MP-38 used a plastic receiver housing, an aluminum frame, and a stamped-metal body. The MP-38 and MP-40 both used a single-column magazine which often created jams, especially with poor quality World War II ammunition. The MP-38 also used a number of machining operations which made it relatively expensive to make and was later modified to become the simpler MP-40.

Early MP-38s could fire accidently if dropped so that the bolt was cycled back far enough to chamber and fire a round. To get around this problem, a crude safety was designed consisting of a cutout area in the charging knob channel that allows the bolt to be locked back. (Users must remember that the bolt is safer when locked back than when remaining free and forward when a loaded magazine is in the weapon.) MP-38s that are so modified were designated MP-38/40s.

The MP-40 used a maximum of heavy and often low-grade steel stampings and spot welds to minimize assembly work. Parts were often made in separate factories, and the weapons assembled elsewhere. Over one million MP-40s were made from 1940 until the end of the war.

Some MP-40s have stamped ribs on their magazine well; these are designated the MP-40/I and are more

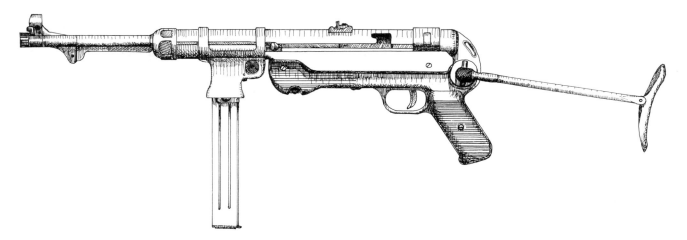

The manufacturers of the German MP (Maschinen Pistole) 40 were among the first to make extensive use of modern industrial methods to create a cheap but deadly weapon. While the MP40 guns are not unique by today's standards, they were very innovative for their time and greatly influenced the design of the STEN and U.S. M3.

common than the nonribbed version. The MP-40/II version had a dual magazine well so that the weapon could feed from two separate magazines; as one might imagine, this action was not overly successful. A later version, the MP-41, had a wooden stock and the trigger mechanism of the MP-28II, though it was otherwise nearly identical to the MP-40; it was developed by Schmeisser.

All versions of the MP-38/40 work by the standard blow-back method. The charging handle is on the left side of the receiver, and the magazine release button is on the left and to the rear of the magazine well. The stock release button is at the pivot point of the stock on the left side of the receiver.

Field-stripping is as follows:
1. Remove the magazine and cycle the weapon to be sure it's empty; pull the trigger while holding the bolt and ease it to its forward position.
2. Pull out the receiver release which is located at the bottom of the frame behind the magazine well. Lock the release open by twisting it.
3. Remove the barrel, magazine well, and receiver tube by holding the pistol grip in one hand and the magazine well in the other. While pulling back on the trigger, rotate the grip and well apart with the grip going to the right about 80 degrees. This will free the upper assembly for removal.
4. Remove the recoil spring, its tube, and the bolt from the rear of the receiver tube by pulling back on the charging handle slightly.

This simple procedure will give access to the action springs, the trigger, etc. Further disassembly is not recommended except for parts repair/replacement. Reassembly is basically a reverse of the above procedure.

While the MP-38/40 guns are not unique by today's standards, they were innovative for their time and greatly influenced the design of the STEN and U.S. M3.

MP-40 Specifications
Barrel length . . . . 9.9 in.
Barrel twist . . . . 6 grooves, right-hand twist
Caliber . . . . 9mm Luger
Length (stock folded) . . . . 24.8 in.
Length (stock extended) . . . . 32.8 in.
Magazine 32-round
Muzzle velocity . . . . 1300 fps
Cyclic rate . . . . 500 rpm
Weight unloaded (approx.) . . . . 8.9 lbs.

MP-83

Bill Holmes has designed the MP-83 pistol based on a conversion unit which adapts the AR-15 lower receiver to 9mm Luger or .45 ACP. The MP-83 was marketed in 1983 and, like Holmes' AR-15 conversion unit, is available in either 9mm Luger or .45 ACP. A slightly different version of the small weapon is also available; this unit, the MP-22, fires .22 LR. The MP-83 uses steel for its receiver, while the MP-22 uses steel and aluminum. Both are available with Zytel plastic pistol grips and foregrips or with surprisingly attractive wooden grips. MP-83 conversion kits allow the owner of one caliber of the weapon to convert it easily to the other caliber.

The MP-83 and MP-22 are available in both semiauto and selective-fire versions. With the selective-fire weapons, a light trigger pull fires single shots, while pulling back fully on the trigger gives full-auto.

At the time of this writing, an experimental version of the MP-83 is being created by adding a stock to the

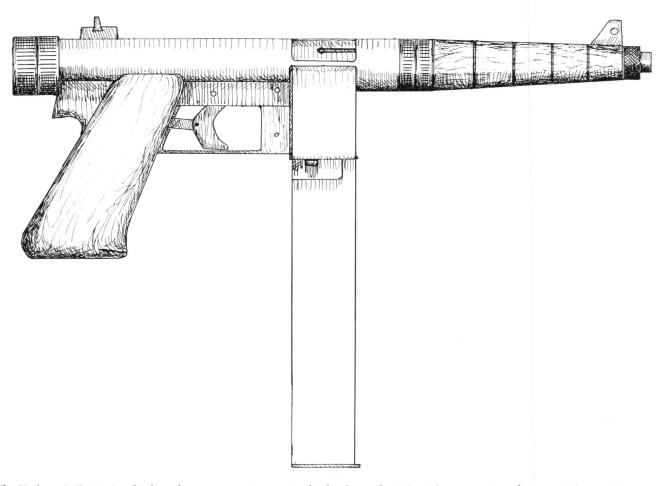

The Holmes MP-83 pistol is based on a conversion unit which adapts the AR-15 lower receiver for use with 9mm Luger or .45 ACP cartridges. The MP-83 is available in either 9mm Luger or .45 ACP. A slightly different version of the weapon, the MP-22, fires .22 LR as its name suggests. The MP-83 uses steel for its receiver, while the MP-22 uses steel and aluminum. Both are available with Zytel plastic pistol grips and foregrips or with surprisingly attractive wooden grips.

unit with the standard length barrel as well as with a 16-inch version—possibly for the semiauto model. Because of the firearm's initial success as well as the open-bolt firing mode of the semiauto version, it's possible that the weapon will soon be offered only in selective-fire. Semiauto versions may become collectors' items.

MP-83 Specifications

Barrel length . . . . 6 in.
Caliber . . . . 9mm Luger/.45 ACP
Cyclic rate (approx.) . . . . 800 rpm
Length . . . . 14.5 in.
Magazine (9mm) 16-, 32-round
Magazine (.45 ACP) 10-, 20-round
Weight unloaded (approx.) . . . . 3.5 lbs.

MP-22 Specifications

Barrel length . . . . 6 in.
Caliber . . . . .22 LR

Cyclic rate (approx.) . . . . 800 rpm
Length . . . . 14.5 in.
Magazine 32-round
Weight unloaded (approx.) . . . . 2.5 lbs.

NIGHTHAWK

This carbine was created by Weaver Arms specifically for U.S. civilian and government agencies and is offered only in semiauto. Though sales have thus far been limited, the Nighthawk did enjoy some free publicity when it was used by security forces at the 1984 Olympics.

The Nighthawk was designed during the early 1980s by George P. Wilson. Its design appears to have borrowed from the modern aircraft industry: lower receiver, grips, sights, charging handle, and other parts are made of glass-filled nylon; investment castings and rivets are noticeable on the receiver. This all adds up to a lightweight and relatively inexpensive weapon, albeit a

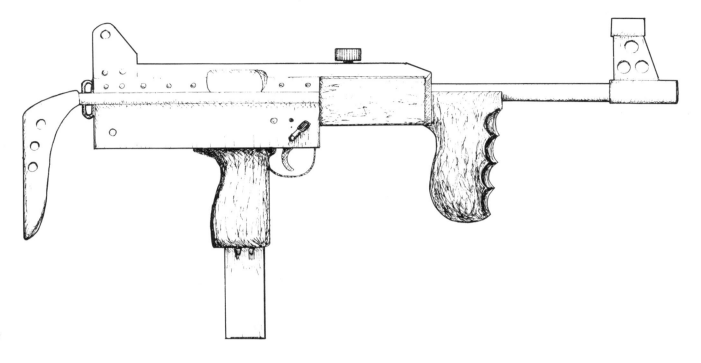

This Nighthawk carbine was created by Weaver Arms specifically for the U.S. civilian and government agencies and is offered only in a semiauto version. The Nighthawk design appears to have borrowed from modern aircraft industrial techniques.

bit unconventional and ugly by most standards.

The Nighthawk uses a closed-bolt, blow-back operation with a separate hammer-operated firing pin. The weapon has ambidextrous selectors located a bit awkwardly on each side of the receiver just above the trigger. The front grip is a Thompson-style pistol grip. The manufacturer claims that it is "human engineered" for comfortable use (shooters will have to decide this for themselves).

The stock is similar to that of the M3 grease gun. Early stocks are steel, while aluminum stocks are slated to replace the steel on newer models to reduce the weight by half a pound. The stock release is located under the rear swivel. The stock mount is riveted to the receiver to prevent its removal, which would shorten the carbine and make it a cut-off rifle in BATF's eyes.

The front sight is a hooded blade; the rear aperture sight is adjustable for both windage and elevation with an Allen wrench. The Nighthawk uses readily available Uzi magazines.

Disassembly of the Nighthawk is as follows:
1. Remove the magazine and cycle the weapon to be sure it's empty.
2. Depress the cover release latch and remove it.

3. Retract the charging handle slightly; pull it up out of the receiver.
4. Remove the recoil spring.
5. Place the selector to the "fire" position.
6. Push the hammer back so that it is engaged by the sear.
7. Remove the recoil-spring guide rod and buffer.
8. Place the selector to the "safe" position.
9. Remove the nylon lower receiver pin.
10. Pivot the lower receiver down and remove it from the upper receiver.

Access is thus provided to the action springs, trigger, etc. Further disassembly is not recommended except for parts repair/replacement. For such disassembly, an Allen wrench is needed. Reassembly is basically a reverse of the above procedure.

The AP-9 (Assault Pistol-9mm) version of the Nighthawk is also made by Weaver and is nearly identical to the carbine except that it has a shorter barrel and lacks the telescoping stock. Magazines and many pistol parts are identical to that of the carbine. Unfortunately, the pistol's weight probably makes it less than ideal as an assault pistol except, perhaps, to Nighthawk owners who would prefer to have a pistol nearly identical to their carbine.

Nighthawk Specifications

Barrel length . . . . 16.1 in.
Barrel twist . . . . 6 grooves, right-hand twist,
1-in-9.8 turn
Caliber . . . . 9mm Luger
Length (stock extended) . . . . 33.5 in.
Length (stock retracted) . . . . 26.5 in.
Magazine 25-, 32-round
Muzzle velocity (approx.) . . . . 1300 fps
Weight unloaded (approx.) . . . . 6.5 lbs.

AP-9 Specifications

Barrel length . . . . 10 in.
Barrel twist . . . . 6 grooves, right-hand twist,
1-in-9.8 turn
Caliber . . . . 9mm Luger
Length . . . . 16.9 in.
Magazine 25-, 32-round
Muzzle velocity (approx.) . . . . 1200 fps
Weight unloaded (approx.) . . . . 5 lbs.

PPSh41 SUBMACHINE GUN

The Soviet PPSh41 (*Pistolet-Pulemyot Shpagina*) was a weapon of desperation. It was created after the Russians had suffered a disastrous defeat in their war with Finland in 1939 and 1940, a war in which the Finns were armed mostly with submachine guns; coupled with this situation was the loss of most Russian small arms and engineering capabilities after the German invasion in 1941. The answer to the Russian situation was a crude weapon which worked well and was cheap and quick to make.

The PPSh41 was designed by Georgii Shpagin. Equipped with rough wooden stocks and the 71-round Suomi drum, the weapon, coupled with good tactics, allowed the Soviets to fight with telling effectiveness against the Germans.

The submachine gun remained in service until the late 1950s and has been manufactured by a number of countries, including China (as the Type 50), Iran, Finland (the m/44 and m/44-46 series), Spain, and Germany (the DUX). The Soviets also manufactured a metal folding-stock version with a pistol grip and box magazine designated the PPSh42 and later the PPSh43; the Chinese copy of this is the Type 54. Because of its high rate of fire, the PPSh41 and Type 50 used by the North Koreans in the Korean War led U.S. troops to give it the crude nickname of "burp gun."

A .22 LR version of the weapon, the PPS-50, is made by Bingham, Limited. The weapon sports a 16-inch barrel and weighs a hefty (for a .22) 6½ pounds. Though the weapon is sometimes converted to selective fire, this mode doesn't work too well due to the "bounce" of the bolt. The weight of the .22 model and the round's lack of punch make it more of an oddity than a combat weapon. Most versions come with a 50-round drum magazine.

The standard PPSh41 is made using extensive steel stampings, welds, and rivets; despite the wooden stock, the weapon is actually a second-generation submachine gun. The selector is located in the trigger guard. Early weapons had a tangent sight, while later models had a two-position flip sight. The barrel shroud is sloped at the muzzle to create a crude muzzle compensator on the PPSh41; the PPSh42 has a circular compensator. The bore and chamber of most Soviet guns are chromed.

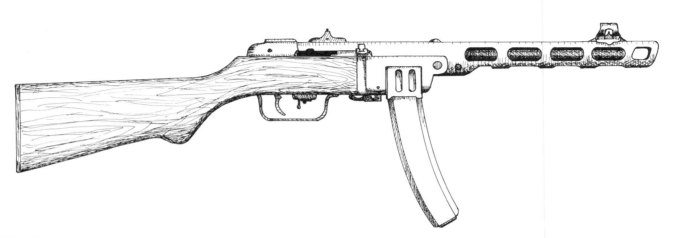

The Chinese Type 50 submachine gun is one of the many copies of the PPSh41. Because of its high rate of fire, the Type 50 used by the North Koreans during the Korean War led to the crude nickname, "burp gun," which was given by the U.S. troops.

Field-stripping the PPSh41 (and most variants) is as follows:

1. Push forward on the receiver catch to release the receiver. Place the bolt in its forward position.

2. Rotate the barrel and receiver cover down to expose the inside of the receiver.

3. Pull back on the charging handle and remove the bolt.

4. Remove the recoil spring and buffer.

5. If necessary, the barrel can be removed from its shroud.

These five steps are generally all the disassembly necessary for maintenance and cleaning. Reassembly is basically the reverse of the above procedure.

Though the weapon has been discontinued and replaced by the assault rifle in the USSR and many other countries, large numbers of the PPSh41 have been made; the Soviets alone are thought to have manufactured over five million. Therefore, the weapons are often seen in use around the world, especially in underdeveloped communist nations.

PPSh41 Specifications

Barrel length . . . . 10.5 in.
Barrel twist . . . . 4 grooves, right-hand twist
Caliber 7.62mm
Length . . . . 33 in.
Magazine . . . . 35-round or 71-round drum
Muzzle velocity . . . . 1600 fps
Cyclic rate . . . . 900 rpm
Weight unloaded (approx.) . . . . 8 lbs.

SMITH & WESSON M-76 SUBMACHINE GUN

The M-76 was developed by Smith & Wesson and marketed in 1967. Though intended for the military market, the weapon saw very little use except by special forces (it was the primary submachine gun for Navy SEAL teams) and a few government and police departments. Though the M-76 is a good weapon, its manufacture was discontinued in 1970 due to lack of interest, as it were. Only a few thousand were made.

With renewed interest in 9mm weapons in the United States, MK Arms, Inc., has started marketing both semiauto and selective-fire versions of the M-76. Designated the MK-760, it is also available in a semiauto "pistol" version which has the dubious distinction of being the heaviest pistol on the U.S. market. The semiauto guns fire from an open bolt and at the time of this writing may be discontinued or modified to meet BATF requirements.

The M-76 and MK-760 bear a slight resemblance to the M3 grease gun and are chambered for the 9mm Luger. Stocks fold to the left side of the weapon, and selectors are ambidextrous. The charging handles are on the upper right side of the receivers and double as safeties (pushing in is the safe position and pulling out puts it into the fire mode). Barrel shrouds on the pistol and submachine gun extend the full length of the barrel. Both front and rear sights are protected by dog ears.

Field-stripping the M-76 is as follows:

1. Remove the magazine and cycle the weapon to be sure it is empty. Place the bolt in its forward position.

2. Push in the barrel collar detent on the front of the receiver just under the barrel. Unscrew the collar and barrel shroud, and remove the shroud.

3. Remove the barrel by pulling it toward the front of the receiver.

4. Hold the receiver cap in place at the rear of the receiver tube and pull the retaining pin up and out. Be careful, as the recoil spring is under pressure.

5. Ease out the endcap, recoil spring, and spring guide from the rear of the receiver.

6. Pull the charging knob back until it lines up with the open point in its track and remove it.

7. Allow the bolt to slide out the rear of the receiver.

8. Fold the stock and use a coin or screwdriver to remove the bolt at the bottom of the pistol grip.

9. Flex the stock away from the pistol grip; pull it down and to the rear of the receiver and remove it.

10. Extend the stock and rotate the trigger assembly down and to the rear to remove it.

The above procedure will give access to the action springs, trigger, etc. Further disassembly is not recommended except for parts repair/replacement. The extractor can be removed by drifting out its pin from the bolt. Ejector replacement requires that the welds on the left of the receiver be ground off and a new ejector welded into place. Reassembly is basically a reverse of the above procedure. To replace the trigger assembly, it is necessary to pull down the magazine release and keep it clear of the assembly.

The M-76/MK-760 is a basically good design but suffered from being marketed before the 9mm became popular with the U.S. military. Now that the 9mm is gaining in popularity, the M-76 is viewed by many as too heavy and large when compared to newer submachine-gun designs. Thus, the weapon may again miss out on the market.

S&W M-76 Specifications
Barrel length . . . . 8 in.
Caliber . . . . 9mm Luger

Length (stock extended) .... 30.5 in.
Length (stock retracted) .... 20.5 in.
Magazine 36-round
Muzzle velocity .... 1150 fps
Cyclic rate .... 750 rpm
Weight unloaded (approx.) .... 7.5 lbs.

MK-760 "Pistol" Specifications

Barrel length .... 8 in.
Caliber .... 9mm Luger
Length .... 20.25 in.
Magazine 36-round
Muzzle velocity .... 1150 fps
Weight unloaded (approx.) .... 7.5 lbs.

STEN SUBMACHINE GUNS

Following World War I, Britain all but disarmed itself. Despite the warnings of Winston Churchill and other leaders, the Spanish Civil War, and the German *blitzkrieg* in Europe, Britain managed to enter the war with a crippled arms industry and no submachine of its own. The British military had turned down the chance to adopt and manufacture the Thompson submachine gun because it was "a gangster gun." Fortunately, the United States sent arms to England (including the Thompson) under the Lend-Lease policy which purchased the time Britain needed to develop a weapon of its own.

The submachine gun chosen for production by the British was the STEN. Its name is derived from the two inventors' last initials, Reginald Vernon Shepperd and Harold John Turpin, and the first two letters of the town where it was designed, Enfield. The first STEN weapons were made at the Royal Small Arms Factory in Enfield, but other manufacturers soon started producing parts and complete guns.

The sheet-metal body and simple design allowed the submachine gun to be stamped out by factories which normally didn't make firearms. The design made use of steel stampings and welds and was extremely simple with a minimum of parts.

Large numbers of STENs were also dropped into Europe during the war for use by resistance fighters. The Germans also copied the STEN design and made small numbers of their version, which was designated the MP3008. Apparently the weapons were to have been used for the defense of Germany by the Volksturm. Finally, the manufacturing techniques and design of the STEN were extensively studied by the United States before it created the M3 grease gun.

Unfortunately, the STEN's crude-looking design did little to inspire confidence, and many of the magazines were poorly built and tended to jam. Consequently, the firearm never was very popular with the troops and was often known as the "stench gun" or "plumber's delight." Nevertheless, the weapons could be built and put into the hands of the troops quickly. The first STEN was adopted in 1941; by 1945, about 3,750,000 STENs had been made and 34,000,000 magazines created! All the STENs were chambered for 9mm Luger, which the English designated as 9mm SAA Ball.

A number of different patterns of the STEN were created. While these tend to break down into six models (marks), there are often variations within each group, particularly in the stock arrangements.

The STEN Mark 1 pattern was often well finished and had a long shroud and a distinctive cone-shaped flash hider. Early Mark 1s had a wooden foregrip that folded down vertically as well as a wooden pistol grip and insert in front of the trigger. The Mark 1 was a simplified model without the foregrip. After 100,000 were made, the STEN pattern was altered for cheaper and faster manufacturing techniques.

Over two million STEN Mark 2 pattern guns were made over a period of three years. The stock was usually a tube with a crude pistol grip and butt welded to it, although a second pattern was made, mainly in Canada, with a folded "U" bar stock and a bayonet mount. The barrel shroud was greatly shortened on both versions of the Mark 2 and the magazine well designed to rotate to close the weapon when it was not in use. A silenced version, the STEN Mark 2-S, was also made in small quantities. The silencer had a very short life but worked well when new and fired in the semiauto mode. Some of these had wooden stocks and pistol grips.

The STEN Mark 3 was similar to the Mark 1 except for its tubular stock. The receiver/barrel jacket was a single sheet steel tube. The barrel and magazine housing were fixed and could not be removed (as could the Mark 2's). Mark 3s were made from 1943 until 1944 in both Canada and Britain and were probably the least expensive of all the models.

The STEN Mark 4 never went beyond the prototype stage. It had a pistol grip and folding stock coupled with a short barrel designed for paratrooper use. Poor performance, excessive weight, and manufacturing difficulties quickly proved that it would not be suitable for issue. There were two models of the Mark 4, "A" and "B." The A model had the pistol grip toward the rear of the receiver, while the B model had the pistol grip toward its middle.

The Mark 5 had a wooden stock, wooden pistol grip, pistol grip handguard, and bayonet mount. Supposedly, it was an attempt to create a Thompson-like weapon

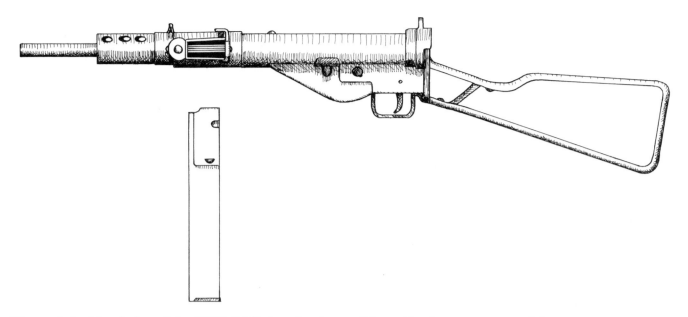

The crude-looking design of the STEN did little to inspire confidence. Furthermore, many of the STEN magazines were poorly built and tended to jam in battlefield conditions. The firearm consequently was never very popular with the troops, who often referred to it as the "stench gun." Shown is the Mark 2.

that would inspire more confidence in the troops using it. The pistol grip on the handguard broke off easily (so much for inspiring the men in the field) and was soon replaced by a more standard foregrip. The magazine still jammed, and the gun weighed more than the standard STEN. The Mark 5 was made after the war and remained in use in the British Army until 1953 when the Sterling was adopted.

The Mark 6 was the Mark 5 mounted with a silencer much like that of the Mark 2-S.

Due to the magazine's heavy spring, the various STEN models were issued with a magazine loader. The magazine is mounted in the well located on the left side of the receiver tube. The magazine release is at the rear of the magazine well.

The charging knob is on the right side of the weapon. The notch in its channel is used to lock the bolt back in its safe position. A button located below the safety slot is the selector. Pushing the button from left to right gives semiauto fire (the "R" on the left face of the button stands for "Repetition"); pushing it from right to left gives automatic fire ("A" for "Automatic").

Sights on the weapon are crude. The rear sight is a fixed aperture; the triangular front sight is unprotected and can be drifted for windage.

It is quite simple to field-strip the STEN:

1. Remove the magazine and cycle the weapon to be sure it's empty. While holding the charging knob, release the bolt by pulling the trigger and ease the bolt to its forward position.

2. Release the stock by pressing in on the stud on the rear of the receiver. Pull the stock out of its slot.

3. Push the release stud again, rotate the recoil spring cap and twist it around so that it unlocks. Carefully ease out the spring housing and recoil spring; they are under pressure, so restrain them.

4. Pull the charging knob back to its safety slot and rotate it so it can be removed from the bolt.

5. Remove the bolt from the rear of the receiver.

Further disassembly is not recommended except for parts repair/replacement. Reassembly is basically the reverse of the above procedure.

New STEN Mark 2-style guns are currently being made and sold in the United States by the Shepperd & Turpin Distributing Company. The company also manufactured a semiauto version of the weapon in an effort to capture the civilian market; to date, U.S. shooters have not taken to the British ugly duckling.

Because of the huge numbers of STEN guns made, it has appeared in virtually every major conflict since World War II. The guns are easily repaired and maintained even though they do not always function with 100 percent reliability.

STEN Mark 1 Specifications
Barrel length . . . . 7.75 in.
Barrel twist . . . . 6 grooves, right-hand twist
Caliber . . . . 9mm Luger
Length . . . . 35.5 in.

Magazine 32-round
Muzzle velocity . . . . 1250 fps
Cyclic rate . . . . 550 rpm
Weight unloaded (approx.) . . . . 7.2 lbs.

STEN Mark 2 Specifications
Barrel length . . . . 7.75 in.
Barrel twist . . . . . . 2 or 6 grooves, right-hand twist
Caliber . . . . 9mm Luger
Length . . . . 30 in.
Magazine 32-round
Muzzle velocity . . . . 1250 fps
Cyclic rate . . . . 550 rpm
Weight unloaded (approx.) . . . . 6.5 lbs.

STEN Mark 3 Specifications
Barrel length . . . . 7.75 in.
Barrel twist . . . . 6 grooves, right-hand twist
Caliber . . . . 9mm Luger
Length . . . . 30 in.
Magazine 32-round
Muzzle velocity . . . . 1250 fps
Cyclic rate . . . . 550 rpm
Weight unloaded (approx.) . . . . 7 lbs.

STEN Mark 4 A and B Specifications
Barrel length . . . . 3.75 in.
Barrel twist . . . . 6 grooves, right-hand twist
Caliber . . . . 9mm Luger
Length (stock folded) . . . . 17.5 in.
Length (stock extended) . . . . 27.5 in.
Magazine 32-round
Muzzle velocity . . . . 1100 fps
Cyclic rate . . . . 570 rpm
Weight unloaded (approx.) . . . . 7.5 lbs.

STEN Mark 5 and 6 Specifications
Barrel length . . . . 7.75 in.
Barrel twist . . . . 6 grooves, right-hand twist
Caliber . . . . 9mm Luger
Length . . . . 30 in.
Magazine 32-round
Muzzle velocity . . . . 1250 fps
Cyclic rate . . . . 600 rpm
Weight unloaded (approx.) . . . . 8.5 lbs.

STERLING

The Sterling submachine gun and its variants are modern classics. The weapon was designed by a team under George W. Patchett working at the Sterling Engineering Company at Dagenham, Essex, toward the end of World War II. The firearm borrows heavily from the STEN design, but is considerably more refined and reliable.

The submachine gun, called the Patchett, was extensively tested by the British military from 1947 through the early 1950s. By 1954, the stock had been altered and the selector moved from the front of the trigger housing to above and behind the trigger. The new gun was added to the British arsenal under the designation of "L2A3" though the weapon is commonly called the Sterling. The Sterling is chambered for 9mm Luger and has the usual blow-back design. The folding stock rotates beneath the weapon's body, and the magazine extends from the left of the tubular receiver in the classic STEN style.

Various models of the Sterling are used by Britain, India, Canada, and New Zealand and by police and special forces units of ninety other countries. The weapon has seen service from the Mau Mau uprising in Kenya to the Falklands War and has proven to be extremely reliable.

The Sterling is designed with reliability in mind but, as a trade-off, it requires a large number of hand operations and machining to manufacture. The gun is made from seamless tubing; only the magazine is stamped sheet metal. Except for the plastic pistol grips, all parts are machined or investment cast, a rarity among modern firearms manufacturing methods. Outside welds and brazing are kept to a minimum, and the weapon is carefully coated with a black crackle epoxy finish.

The bolt has ribs cut into it to catch dirt which allow the weapon to function in extremely dirty environments. The rear sight is two-positioned; one setting gives a 100-meter zero and the second an optimistic 200 meters. The front sight is adjustable. Early weapons did not have protective ears beside the front sight and often had a straight magazine. Most military versions also have a backward-looking bayonet mount.

The safety/selector is located on the left of the receiver, just above the pistol grip; "S" is safe, "R" (for Repeat) is semiauto, and "A" is the full-auto position. The charging handle is on the upper right of the receiver tube, and the magazine release is located at the rear of the magazine well.

The Sterling magazine has a unique design with two rollers on the follower. This allows the magazine to be loaded very easily and makes for reliable functioning, although the magazine has metal lips that are easily bent. The magazine must not be dropped, and the weapon should never be fired while you hold onto the magazine.

Unfortunately, most Sterlings are designed for FMJ bullets; hollow-point or flat-nosed bullets may not feed

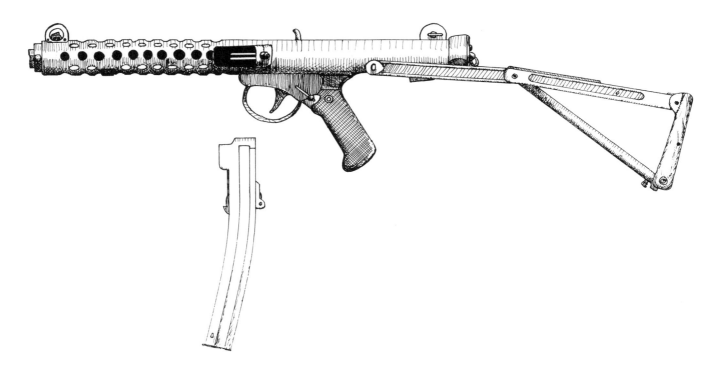

The Sterling submachine gun and its variants are modern classics. The firearm borrows heavily from the STEN design, but is considerably more refined and reliable.

reliably without alteration of the feed ramp.

The firearm is available in several models; the main differences are in barrel length and selective-fire or semiauto-only options. The L2A1 had a grip screw and charging handle that doubled as a screwdriver to dismantle the firearm. The L34A1 (MK-5) has an integral silencer which does not require low-velocity ammunition for ideal performance with the 9mm Luger since the barrel/silencer bleeds off enough gas to lower the bullet's speed. A semiauto version of the L2A1, the Sterling Police Carbine, is offered for police or civilian use; a 16-inch version of this weapon, the MK-6, is available to U.S. citizens.

The MK-7A4 is the Sterling "Para Pistol," a stockless, 4-inch barrel weapon used by the British SAS; a semiauto version of the Para Pistol, the MK-7C4, is also offered. Though the Para Pistol has few advantages over modern, large-capacity pistols, it uses many of the L2A3's standard parts, is selective fire, and operates identically to the submachine gun—major pluses to military users. The Para Pistol is usually offered with a 10-round magazine, though it does accept the standard 34-round magazine and longer barrels as well.

Experimental versions of the weapon include a 7.62 NATO version, which would create yet another "family" of weapons.

Field-stripping the Sterling is fairly simple.

1. Remove the magazine, cycle the weapon to be sure it is empty, and place the weapon in "Safe" (semiauto versions only) or "A" mode (selective-fire weapons). Ease the bolt to its forward position.

2. Move the stock to its folded position.

3. Depress the back-cap catch and rotate it counterclockwise so that the rear locking lugs are clear of the receiver. This will allow the back cap to be removed. (The recoil springs are under slight pressure, so be careful.)

4. Remove the recoil spring, block, and firing pin spring from the rear of the receiver tube.

5. Pull the charging handle completely to the rear. This will allow it to be moved from the side of the weapon and will free the bolt to be removed from the rear of the receiver tube.

6. The firing pin can be removed from the rear of the bolt. These six steps will normally be as far as you need to go in stripping the weapon for maintenance or parts replacement. However, it is possible to strip the weapon further:

7. Set the selector to "Safe," and use a coin or screwdriver to turn the screw on the right side of the pistol grip so that it lines up with "FR" and "EE" ("FREE").

8. Push the pistol-grip retaining pin out with a bullet

tip or the charging handle.

9. Pull the pistol grip back to the rear while depressing the trigger. Pull the front of the trigger group down to remove it from the receiver.

10. The barrel can be removed/replaced by unscrewing the nosecap and disassembling the magazine catch with a screwdriver.

11. The ejector can be removed by loosening the head ejector screw with an Allen wrench and removing the ejector through the ejection port.

12. The various parts of the trigger group can be removed by using a drift punch and screwdriver to release them. Take care to note all positions and to restrain springs.

Reassembly is basically a reversal of the above procedure. Care should be taken not to deform the firing-pin spring and in getting the recoil spring (which will be under a lot of tension) back into place.

Although the Sterling will be removed from the British arsenal as the submachine gun's role is filled by the new service rifle, the Sterling will continue to see use by special forces, police, and citizens well into the twenty-first century.

Sterling L2A3 Specifications

Barrel length . . . . 7.8 in.
Caliber . . . . 9mm Luger
Cyclic rate (approx.) . . . . 550 rpm
Length (stock extended) . . . . 28 in.
Length (stock folded) . . . . 19 in.
Magazine (standard) 34-round
Muzzle velocity (approx.) . . . . 1250 fps
Rifling . . . . 6 grooves, right-hand twist,
1-in-9.84-in. twist
Weight unloaded (approx.) . . . . 6 lbs.

Sterling MK-6 Specifications

Barrel length . . . . 16.1 in.
Caliber . . . . 9mm Luger
Length (stock extended) . . . . 35 in.
Length (stock folded) . . . . 27 in.
Magazine (standard) 34-round
Muzzle velocity (approx.) . . . . 1320 fps
Rifling . . . . 6 grooves, right-hand twist,
1-in-9.84-in. twist
Weight unloaded (approx.) . . . . 7.5 lbs.

Sterling MK-7 (Semiauto Para Pistol) Specifications

Barrel length . . . . 4 in.
Caliber . . . . 9mm Luger
Length . . . . 14 in.

Magazine (standard) 10-round
Muzzle velocity (approx.) . . . . 1050 fps
Rifling . . . . 6 grooves, right-hand twist,
Weight unloaded (approx.) . . . . 3.6 lbs.

SWEDISH K SUBMACHINE GUN

The Carl Gustaf Stads Gevarfaktori of Sweden manufactured the KP m/45 submachine gun, which is a simple but reliable weapon that has changed little since it was introduced in 1945. The weapon was manufactured as the "Port Said" by the Egyptian army and has been used in Indonesia as well. The m/45 (Model 1945) is commonly called the "Carl Gustaf" or "Swedish K." In addition to the standard 9mm Luger, Sweden has developed a special high-velocity round called the "Patron m/39" for use in the m/45.

The Swedish K submachine gun is a fairly conventional submachine gun made of steel stampings. The rear sight is an "L" type and the front a post; both have protective ears. The charging knob is on the right of the receiver and has an old-fashioned safety notch in its channel; the charging knob can be used to lock the bolt in the forward position by pushing it down. The weapon fires only in the full-auto mode, so there is no selector. The stock pivots at the rear of the pistol grip, and the magazine release is at the rear of the receiver.

To field-strip the Swedish K:

1. Remove the magazine and cycle the weapon. Pull the trigger and ease the bolt into its forward position.

2. Depress the catch in the center of the receiver cap at the rear of the receiver tube. Turn the receiver cap slightly counterclockwise (while restraining—it's under pressure).

3. Remove the cap and recoil spring through the rear of the receiver.

4. Remove the bolt from the rear of the receiver tube.

5. Depress the barrel-nut catch with a bullet tip or drift punch, and unscrew the barrel nut. Take off the barrel jacket and barrel.

These steps will give access to the parts of the weapon which need to be cleaned; further disassembly is not recommended. Reassembly is basically the reverse of the above procedure.

Though the Swedish K is not outstanding by modern standards, it works well and is encountered in many parts of the world.

Swedish K Specifications

Barrel length . . . . 8 in.
Barrel twist . . . . 6 grooves, right-hand twist

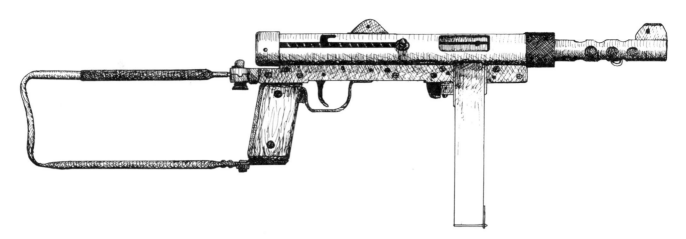

The Swedish KP m/45 submachine gun, commonly called the Carl Gustaf or Swedish K, is a simple but reliable weapon that has changed little since it was introduced in 1945. The Egyptian version is the "Port Said." In addition to the standard 9mm Luger, Sweden has developed a special high-velocity round called the Patron m/39 for use in the m/45.

The TEC-9 is a well-designed "assault pistol" which makes use of modern manufacturing methods to give the purchaser a lot of gun for a relatively small amount of money. This lightweight weapon is probably the "shape of things to come" with its molded plastic lower receiver and simple design.

Caliber .... 9mm Patron/9mm Luger
Length (stock folded) .... 21.75 in.
Length (stock extended) .... 31.75 in.
Magazine 36-, 50-round
Muzzle velocity .... 1250 fps
Cyclic rate .... 600 rpm
Weight unloaded (approx.) .... 7.6 lbs.

TEC-9

The TEC-9 was developed by Interdynamics AB of Sweden. It was originally a selective-fire weapon but was changed to a semiauto, open-bolt fire pistol made in the United States by Interdynamics and marketed by F.I.E. of Hialeah, Florida. The original version, the KG-9, was easily converted to selective fire and was banned for sale except as an automatic weapon by BATF. In a rather odd twist of logic, original, open-bolt KG-9s built before the ban of 1982 are still legal to own, and are not viewed as illegal "easily convertible" weapons by BATF. These often command high prices among those who collect such guns (4,039 of these weapons were made).

The KG-9 was redesigned to fire from a closed bolt and soon returned to the civilian market as the KG-99. In addition to the closed-bolt firing system, a metal serial-number plate was added to the plastic lower receiver to placate BATF. Shortly after this design change, a Hong Kong company bought the rights to the weapon from Interdynamics AB and a new company, Intratec USA, was formed in the United States to manufacture the weapon, redesignated the TEC-9.

Company officials say sales are quite brisk and, consequently, plans for a stocked carbine version were put on the back burner so that demand for the pistol could be met. Several overzealous dealers did advertise the new carbine, however, creating the impression that such a

The TEC-9 enjoys a wide range of accessories offered by Intratec USA. A number of aftermarket accessories are also available for it, as well as for the MAC-10.

unit had been made. As of 1985, no such version of the TEC-9 is offered except for custom-gunsmith modifications. Intratec does plan on introducing the carbine in the near future.

One version of the weapon that is available is the TEC-9M, a shortened, lightened model using the same magazines as the standard model. The TEC-9M lacks the ventilated barrel shroud of the TEC-9 but has a threaded barrel for screw-on accessories. Some shooters may find that the short barrel of the TEC-9M makes it hard to get a safe two-handed grip on the weapon.

A third version of the weapon is the TEC-9B, which is identical to the TEC-9 in size but uses stainless steel for the bolt and other steel parts (these parts are coated with a dull black finish so that the weapon appears the same as the standard model). Because of the heavier weight of stainless steel, the TEC-9B weighs two ounces more than its blued-steel counterpart.

The TEC-9MB is the stainless-steel counterpart of the small TEC-9M. Coated with a nonglare black finish, it looks like its sister gun and weighs only an ounce more.

The TEC-9 has enjoyed great success for two reasons: a low price tag and light weight. Both stem from the use of high-impact plastic for the receiver, magazine well, and pistol grip, coupled with a simple design which cuts down on parts and manufacturing steps as well as the weapon's overall weight; it also adds durability and reliability.

Another point which has helped the weapon's commercial success is the wide range of accessories available for it. The barrel is threaded to the same size as the MAC-10 weapons so that the gun can accept Sionics suppressors, barrel extensions, etc., designed for the 9mm Ingram weapons.

The shroud holes allow a number of accessories to be fastened to the weapon. Grendelite offers a small flashlight and mount which fasten under the barrel to allow users to use the weapon as a flashlight, which can place bullets at the center of its beam if the need arises. For those using the weapon indoors, the Grendelite A-2 flashlight and mount are worthwhile considerations.

The shroud holes make it possible (if a bit awkward) to mount a pistol scope on the weapon. As smaller laser-aiming systems become available, it will probably only be a matter of time before a laser unit is available for the TEC-9 as well.

Intratec USA also offers a wide range of accessories for the TEC-9. Forward pistol grip, 20- or 36-round magazines, Cordura carrying case, recoil compensator/flash suppressor, nylon sling, and (currently in the works) a scope-mount system. Coupled with the low price, these accessories allow the owner of a TEC-9 to create a weapon to suit his needs.

The TEC-9 uses a simple blow-back design with a buffer at the rear of the upper receiver tube soaking up some of the recoil. The charging handle doubles as the safety; after cocking the weapon, pushing in the charging handle locks the bolt closed and blocks the striker. Though the position of the charging handle makes this a bit easier for right-handed users, lefties don't seem to be at much of a disadvantage with this system, especially if they cant the weapon slightly when releasing the safety.

The only drawback with the TEC-9's cocking/safety system is that the charging handle is smooth, which is hard to pull out if the user's hands are wet or oily. While this isn't much of a consideration if the pistol is just a plinking gun, it's an important consideration if the TEC-9 is used for self-defense. A simple solution is to remove the circular handle during field-stripping. Place it in a drill press (or a "fastened down" electric drill) and make grooves into it with a file or hacksaw. Use a little touch-up blue or black spray paint. Now only the safety can be pulled to the "off" position with wet hands. This easy procedure can be done by a gunsmith at nominal expense.

The magazine release is located at the rear of the magazine well and is easily worked. A sling catch is located on each end of the upper receiver tube. These are similar to those on the U.S. grease gun and make it quite handy to carry the weapon on a sling, which can also aid in steadying the weapon during firing.

The ejector also serves as the bolt guide and is attached to the trigger group. The steel extractor (which is not spring-loaded) is held in place with an Allen screw, accessible from the side of the bolt. The TEC-9 pistols don't have hammers; rather, a spring-loaded striker does the work of both hammer and firing pin. All in all, a design that reduces parts and simplifies the weapon.

Field-stripping the weapon is as follows:

1. Remove the magazine and cycle the weapon to be sure it is empty.

2. Push out the assembly pin at the front of the lower receiver (a drift punch may be necessary with new weapons).

3. Lift up the barrel end of the receiver and pull it out and away from the lower receiver. Be careful, as the recoil spring will be under tension.

4. Pull the charging handle back as far as it will go, and pull it out of the bolt through the wide area at the rear of its receiver cut.

5. Remove the bolt from the rear of the upper receiver tube.

Following these steps will give the user access to the action springs, trigger, etc. Further disassembly is not recommended except for parts repair/replacement, but is relatively easy, since the trigger and magazine release are held in place by drift pins. The sear, ejector, and sear spring are also held by a drift pin, but a C-ring must be removed from the pin before trying to drift it out.

Reassembly is basically the reverse of the above procedure. Care must be taken, however, to place the firing pin in the bolt and lock it in place in the upper receiver by pushing in the safety before placing the receiver halves together. Failure to do this makes it impossible to reassemble the TEC-9.

Like most other blow-back weapons, the TEC-9 may have trouble using ammunition with thin brass since the cartridge head won't be supported during the first part of recoil. This feature, coupled with the "radical" use of a plastic lower receiver and an occasional bad magazine, gave early K-99s a bad reputation among some gun writers and users. In fact, the TEC-9 is as good as most other blow-back weapons and more reliable than some since it has a double feed ramp, which allows the chambering of wide-nosed hollow points, etc. In fact, the author has seen TEC-9s that could chamber empty brass from a magazine!

The TEC-9 is a well-designed "assault pistol" which makes use of modern manufacturing methods to give the purchaser a lot of gun for a relatively small amount of money. This lightweight weapon is probably the shape of things to come with its molded plastic lower receiver and simple design.

TEC-9 Specifications
Barrel length . . . . 5 in.
Caliber . . . . 9mm Luger
Length . . . . 12.5 in.
Magazine (9mm) 36-round
Muzzle velocity . . . . 1300 fps
Weight unloaded (approx.) . . . . 3.13 lbs.

TEC-9M (Mini) Specifications
Barrel length . . . . 3 in.
Caliber . . . . 9mm Luger
Length . . . . 10.5 in.
Magazine (9mm) 20-round
Muzzle velocity . . . . 1200 fps
Weight unloaded (approx.) . . . . 2.75 lbs.

U.S. M1/M1A1 "THOMPSON" SUBMACHINE GUN

Although the Thompson submachine gun was invented by retired Army General John T. Thompson during World War I, the U.S. military dragged its feet so much that it failed ever to use the weapon at that time. Civilians in the United States didn't miss the weapon's advantages, however; when the Thompson became available on the commercial market, it became the "gun that made the Twenties roar" on both sides of the law. The caliber chosen by Thompson was the .45 ACP which was also the fodder for the military Colt semiauto pistol. Equipped with a 50-round drum magazine, the Thompson had enormous firepower for its time.

In theory, the Thompson was not a straight blow-back. It had a locking mechanism which worked on the "Blish Principle" that metal faces tend to lock up and resist movement when their surfaces are flat and lubricated. In fact, the submachine gun worked pretty much as a standard blow-back weapon; failure of the locking mechanism made little difference in its operation.

A number of versions of the weapon were available; the most common having ten-inch barrels and a finger-grooved wooden pistol foregrip. Most early Thompsons also had a detachable stock so that the weapon could be used as an assault pistol back before such things were being marketed. Most Thompsons also have a trap door in their stocks for a small container of oil. (Many users enlarge this hole to hold other cleaning equipment and rags, which help prevent rattles.)

The military officially added the weapon to its arsenal as the M1928A1, though apparently the Marines had used it earlier in Nicaragua and the weapon was carried by the Coast Guard before this time. Many of the M1928A1 models appear to be 1921 models which were retrofitted to M1928A1 configuration. The M1928A1 had a removable stock, sling swivels, Cutts muzzle compensator, a leaf-type rear sight calibrated to a fanciful 600 yards, radial cooling fins on the barrel, and usually—but not always—a horizontal foregrip rather than the forward pistol grip. This model was also often called the "Navy" model. By the end of the M1928A1 production, a number of changes had been made, including dropping the compensator and cooling fins and replacing the leaf sight by a simpler rear sight.

With the outbreak of World War II, large numbers of Thompsons were shipped to Britain under the U.S. Lend-Lease program. The British often called the Thompson the "tommy gun," and thus gave it the name it's often known by. As the war stepped up and more weapons were needed quickly, changes were made to the weapon's basic design. Thompsons were hard to mass produce; they required a lot of machining and hand-fitting. The main changes were the removal of the Blish

The semiauto 1927 A-1 Standard model, manufactured by Auto Ordnance, makers of the original Thompson submachine guns. Photo courtesy of Auto Ordnance.

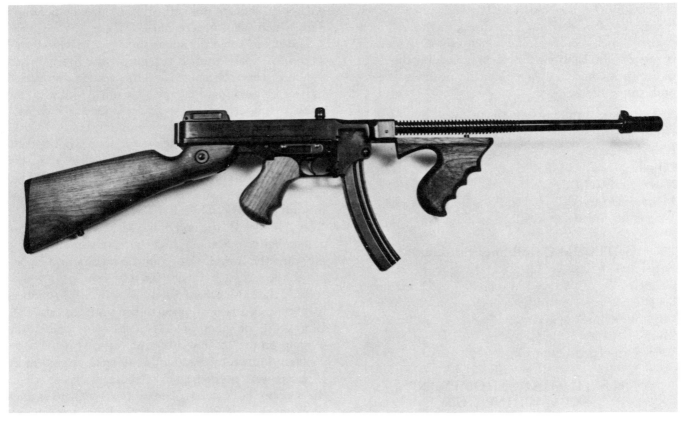

Auto Ordnance's 1927 A-3 model is actually a .22 LR carbine. Photo courtesy of Auto Ordnance.

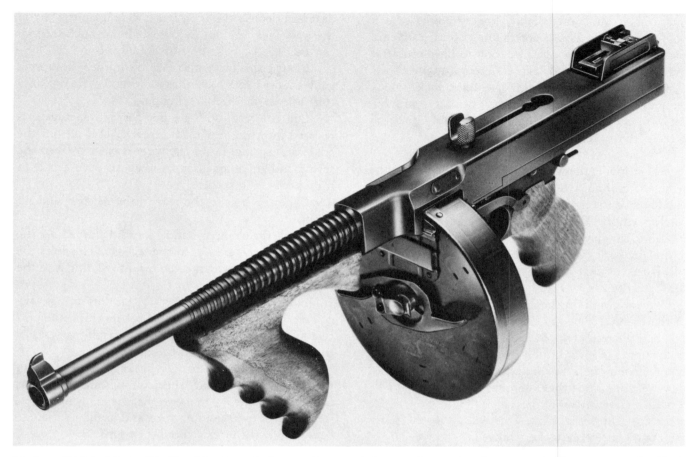

Modern 1927 A-5 "pistol" offered by Auto Ordnance. Because it is manufactured without a stock, this variant is classified by BATF as a pistol. Photo courtesy of Auto Ordnance.

mechanism; the use of a heavier bolt; making the stock nonremovable; moving the bolt handle from the top of the receiver to the right side; simplifying the sights; eliminating the muzzle compensator; and using 20- and 30-round magazines rather than the complex and easily misused drum. These modifications created the M1 variation of the weapon, which is easily recognized by its triangular rear-sight wings. The M1A1 followed and was nearly identical except for eliminating the sight guards on either side of the rear sight aperture and machining a fixed firing pin into the bolt face.

Although officially replaced by the STEN and M3 grease gun, the Thompson was often preferred over the others and production continued in the United States until 1945. The weapon saw use in the Korean War and was given to a number of Asian countries via the U.S. "Offshore Program" up until 1961.

The Nationalist Chinese used the Thompson before and during World War II and also made their own version of the 1928 model. These were chambered for .45 ACP (which the Chinese designated the "11mm"). These weapons continue to be used by the Taiwanese army.

Currently, the Auto Ordnance Corporation, original manufacturers of the Thompson, offers eight versions of the weapon. These include the 1927 A-1 Deluxe (semiauto with leaf sight, barrel ribs, etc.), 1927 A-1 Standard, 1927 A-1C Lightweight (with an alloy frame that makes it 20 percent lighter than other models), 1927 A-3 (in .22 LR), 1927 A-5 "pistol" (stockless, short barrel, semiauto), 1928 (selective fire), and two M1 versions, one in semiauto only and the other selective fire. The selective-fire versions have standard-length barrels while the semiauto carbines have 16-inch barrels. The A-1 series and A-5 are all semiauto and operate as straight blow-back weapons firing from the closed bolt. The inner receiver dimensions of the semiautos prevent the substitution of auto parts, though a few other parts are interchangeable with those of the original selective-fire Thompson. Original Thompson box magazines will not lock into the A-1/A-5 series. New and simplified 39-round drum magazines are available for the weapons, though the firearms will also accept the old 50-round drum magazine. Like standard Thompson submachine guns, these new weapons require the use of FMJ ammunition to function reliably; hollow points or soft points will cause consistent failure-to-feed problems. Excessive oil can also cause the bolt to have problems moving and cause feed failure. Though many of the weapons were designed with the Blish lock, which requires that the surfaces of the bolt be coated with oil, the weapon actually functions more reliably if the oil pads in the system are left dry.

Field-stripping the weapon is slightly different for the semiauto and auto versions. For the semiauto:

1. Remove the magazine and cycle the weapon to be sure it's empty. The stock can be removed on many models to simplify disassembly; release its catch and pull it straight back out of its receiver grooves.

2. Place the bolt forward and put the safety in the "fire" position.

3. Press upward on the frame latch beneath the rear of the frame.

4. Pull the pistol grip/frame assembly toward the rear of the upper receiver until it stops at about the half-off point. (It may be a bit hard to slide the frame off of new weapons since they are often tight.)

5. Use a screwdriver to press in the frame latch at the rear of the upper receiver. This will allow the pistol grip/frame assembly to be removed.

6. Press forward on the recoil-spring guide plate. While depressing the plate, lift the assembly free of the receiver.

7. Remove the firing pin pilot and its spring from the hole at the rear of the upper receiver.

8. Hold the bolt forward and tilt the back of the receiver down so that the striker comes out of the bolt.

9. Remove the bolt handle from the bolt.

10. Remove the bolt.

The above procedure will provide access to the action springs, trigger, etc. Further disassembly is not recommended except for parts repair/replacement. Reassembly is basically the reverse of the above procedure.

For disassembly of selective-fire versions:

1. Remove the magazine and cycle the weapon to be sure it is empty. The stock can be removed on many models to simplify disassembly.

2. Cock the weapon, put the safety in the "fire" position, and place the selector in the "full-auto" position. *Important:* Failure to place the weapon in full-auto position may cause damage during disassembly.

3. Hold the charging handle tightly and pull back on the trigger to release the bolt. Ease the bolt forward.

4. Press upward on the frame latch beneath the rear of the frame.

5. Pull the pistol grip/frame assembly rearward a short distance; depress the trigger and slide it off the rest of the way. Take care not to lose the frame latch button.

6. Pull the bolt to the rear about two inches.

7. Insert a small wire into the hole in the recoil-spring guide (buffer pilot). Note that some models do not have this hole in the recoil-spring guide.

8. Pull the recoil-spring guide forward so that it is released from the rear of the receiver and lift out the guide and spring. Leave the wire in place to keep the spring and guide together on weapons with a hole in the recoil-spring guide.

9. Slide the bolt to the rear of the receiver and lift it out.

10. Slide the charging handle forward and remove the lock through its grooves in the receiver. This frees the charging handle, which is removed by sliding it to the rear.

This process will give access to the action springs, trigger, etc. Further disassembly is not recommended except for parts repair/replacement. Reassembly is basically the reverse of the above procedure.

The Thompson is a first-generation submachine gun that works well. Its only shortcomings are that it has become obsolete due to its weight, the many expensive steps needed in its manufacture, and its failure to function reliably with modern bullet designs. Nevertheless, the weapon continues to be seen in use when newer weapons would be more suitable for combat and it often has a psychological impact far beyond its actual capabilities.

Thompson M1928A1 Specifications
Barrel length . . . . 10.5 in.
Barrel twist . . . . 6 grooves, right-hand twist
Caliber . . . . .45 ACP
Length . . . . 33.75 in.
Length (without stock) . . . . 25 in.
Magazine . . . . . 20-, 30-round, and 50-round drums
Muzzle velocity . . . . 920 fps
Cyclic rate . . . . 700 rpm
Weight unloaded (approx.) . . . . 10.8 lbs.

Thompson M1/M1A1 Specifications
Barrel length . . . . 10.5 in.
Barrel twist . . . . 6 grooves, right-hand twist
Caliber . . . . .45 ACP
Length . . . . 32 in.
Magazine 20-, 30-round
Muzzle velocity . . . . 920 fps
Cyclic rate . . . . 700 rpm
Weight unloaded (approx.) . . . . 10.5 lbs.

Thompson M1927-A1C (Semiauto) Specifications
Barrel length . . . . 16 in.
Barrel twist . . . . 6 grooves, right-hand twist
Caliber . . . . .45 ACP
Length . . . . 39.25 in.
Magazine . . . . . . 20-, 30-round, and 39-round drum
Muzzle velocity . . . . 930 fps
Weight unloaded (approx.) . . . . 8.5 lbs.

U.S. M3/M3A1 SUBMACHINE GUN

The M3 was developed during World War II to replace the Thompson M1. Designed by George Hyde and Frederick Sampson and fielded in 1942, it proved to have a few bugs; modifications were made and the new model, designated the M3A1, was fielded in 1944. The M3 does not have a semiauto mode but has a slow enough cyclic rate that the experienced user can fire single shots. Because of its uncanny resemblance to a grease gun, the weapon is often known by that name rather than by its military designation.

The modifications on the A1 version included removal of the charging lever and replacement with a finger hole which allowed the user to cock the bolt; a larger ejection port cover; modifying the bolt for easier removal; adding a reinforcement bar/magazine charger to the wire stock; moving the ejection-port cover safety backward; and adding a magazine catch so that the magazine couldn't be inadvertently released. An oiling kit was also added which rode inside the pistol grip.

The original submachine gun was designed to fire either .45 ACP or, with another barrel, bolt, magazine and magazine adapter, 9mm Luger with a STEN magazine. While this was a useful feature, few M3s were ever used in this manner. The M3 and M3A1 were plagued with a poorly designed magazine, which often caused the otherwise reliable weapon to be less than ideal in dirty battlefield conditions.

About 1,000 weapons with an extra long barrel and integral silencer were manufactured for the OSS (Office of Strategic Services). A cone-shaped flash hider which attached to the barrel with a wing nut was made available in 1945.

The sheet-metal body and simple design allowed the submachine gun to be built relatively cheaply, and the weapon was kept in the U.S. arsenal following World War II, seeing use in Korea and Vietnam. The M3 and M3A1 as well as a copy, the Type 37, chambered for 9mm, were used by the Chinese during World War II. The weapons continue to be used by the Taiwanese army.

Currently, a semiauto version of the M3A1 is manufactured by the Broadhead Armory. Designated the grease gun M3C, the weapon (with its BATF required 16-inch barrel) is heavy and clumsy compared to other more modern designs and is mainly of interest to collectors. Several versions are produced, including 9mm (with a 32-round magazine) and .45 ACP guns and an "OSS" version with a fake suppressor which helps hide the extra barrel length.

Field-stripping the M3 is quite simple:
1. Remove the magazine and cycle the weapon to be sure it is empty. The stock can be removed by pushing

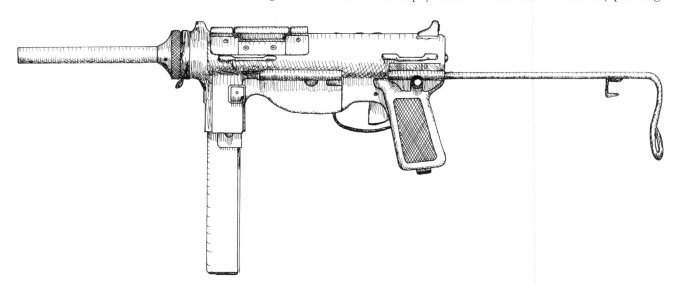

The U.S. M3A1. The M3 was developed during World War II to replace the more expensive, heavier, and harder to produce Thompson (M1). The original M3 was fielded in 1942 but proved to have a few bugs. Modifications were made, and the new model, designated the M3A1, was fielded in 1944. Because of its resemblance to a grease gun, the weapon is often known as the "grease gun" rather than by its actual military designation.

in the stock catch on the left side of the receiver.

2. To remove the housing assembly unit, remove the stock and use its shoulder end to push down on the inside of the trigger guard. This will free it from its slot in the grip and allow it to be rotated toward the front of the gun and removed. The housing assembly unit should be pushed down and then lifted from the rear and removed. This step may be omitted with the M3A1 if only the barrel, bolt, and recoil springs need to be cleaned.

3. Pull the ratchet catch back and unscrew the barrel. This will allow removal of the barrel and its bushing.

4. The bolt, guide rods, and springs can be removed by opening the ejection port cover and tilting the weapon's nose downward.

This will give the user access to the action springs, trigger, etc. Further disassembly is not recommended except for parts repair/replacement. Reassembly is basically the reverse of the above procedure.

The M3 and M3A1 served well in battle but were not as reliable as they could have been, thanks to the poor magazine design. This, coupled with the fielding of the M1 Carbine with its more powerful cartridge, kept the M3A1 from gaining much popularity with American troops. With the adoption of the M16 rifle and pistols chambered for 9mm NATO, the M3A1 will be dropped from the U.S. military arsenal.

U.S. M3 Specifications

Barrel length . . . . 8 in.
Barrel twist . . . . 4 grooves, right-hand twist
Caliber . . . . .45 ACP
Length (stock retracted) . . . . 22.75 in.
Length (stock extended) . . . . 30 in.
Magazine 30-round
Muzzle velocity . . . . 900 fps
Cyclic rate . . . . 450 rpm
Weight unloaded (approx.) . . . . 8.1 lbs.

U.S. M3A1 Specifications

Barrel length . . . . 8 in.
Barrel twist . . . . 4 grooves, right-hand twist
Caliber . . . . .45 ACP
Length (stock retracted) . . . . 22.75 in.
Length (stock extended) . . . . 29.75 in.
Magazine 30-round
Muzzle velocity . . . . 900 fps
Cyclic rate . . . . 400 rpm
Weight unloaded (approx.) . . . . 8.2 lbs.

UZI SUBMACHINE GUN

The Uzi was designed in the early 1950s by Israeli Army Major Uziel Gal when Israel was under pressure to develop weapons for its own defense.

The Uzi's design is based on the Czech 23 series of submachine guns with some modifications. Thoroughly debugged, the weapon is one of the more reliable of its type and is used by many special troops and bodyguards (including the U.S. Secret Service) in addition to the Israeli Army and civilian groups. The militaries of West Germany and the Netherlands have adopted the Uzi, and in addition to those manufactured in Israel by Israel Military Industries (IMI), the weapons are also made in Belgium by Fabrique Nationale.

Like many other modern submachine guns, the Uzi uses steel stampings and a telescoping bolt, which extends part way over the barrel; these features make it inexpensive and compact. The weapon was originally made with a wooden stock, but the folding stock developed for special units became so popular that it is normally found on most modern versions. The weapon has a plastic handguard and pistol grip plates.

The charging knob is located on the top of the receiver, and the somewhat awkward three-position slide selector is located at the top of the pistol grip. The magazine well is inside the pistol grip, which also has a grip safety to prevent the bolt from moving if the weapon is not being held. The magazine release is on the lower left of the pistol grip. While the use of the grip for the magazine well allows for quick reloading, it also creates a less than ideal pistol grip angle; some shooters find that the Uzi points somewhat awkwardly.

The front and rear sight are protected by ears and are adjustable for windage and elevation. All models except the "B" need a special tool for sight adjustment. The rear "L" flip-type sight has 100-meter and 200-meter settings.

In order to reach the civilian and police markets in the United States and elsewhere, a semiauto version has also been marketed. The weapon is nearly identical to the selective-fire Uzi except for its 16-inch barrel (a 10.5-inch barrel is also available where such lengths are legal) and fires from a closed bolt.

A wide range of accessories are available for the weapon. The Choate Machine and Tool Corporation manufactures a fixed Zytel stock to replace the folding metal stock. This gives a much more comfortable cheek rest, especially in very hot or cold weather, and allows the weapon to be used more readily at long ranges. The stock is lightweight but does not fold. Choate also makes a barrel shroud for the 16-inch Uzi; it is easily installed by substituting it for the barrel nut. A .22 LR conversion kit is available from Action Arms and Group Industries for training and practice. Given the cost of 9mm

The Uzi is one of the more reliable submachine guns around and is used by many special troops and bodyguards (including the U.S. Secret Service) in addition to the armies of Israel, West Germany, and the Netherlands. The semiauto carbine version shown here has a big following in the U.S. civilian market. Photo courtesy of Action Arms.

ammunition, this can quickly pay for itself. A .45 ACP version of the Uzi, introduced in 1985, is identical to the 9mm weapon except for the barrel, bolt assembly, and magazine. The use of these three components also allows a weapon to be converted to a second caliber. The .45 magazine holds 16 rounds. Various scope mounts are also available for the Uzi; probably the best is offered by Action Arms and Pars International.

Field-stripping the Uzi is quite simple:

1. Remove the magazine and cycle the weapon to be sure it is empty; pull the trigger while holding the charging handle and ease it to its forward position.

2. Depress the barrel nut retaining catch (located just ahead of the front sight) and unscrew the barrel nut and barrel.

3. Push down on the receiver cover and release its latch (located just ahead of the rear sight). Lift the cover from the rear and remove it.

4. Push the bolt rearward slightly and pull it up and out of the receiver. Be careful, as the recoil spring is under pressure.

5. Remove the recoil spring and striker (on semiauto versions) from the rear of the bolt.

Further disassembly is not recommended except for parts repair/replacement. Reassembly is basically the reverse of the above procedure. Be sure to position the notch cut in the barrel into its proper channel in the receiver bushing when replacing it.

The Uzi is a well-designed and reliable submachine gun. It is little wonder that it has been adopted by a number of governments as well as being a favorite private citizen's defense weapon.

Uzi (Selective-Fire) Specifications
Barrel length . . . . 10.25 in.
Barrel twist . . . . 4 grooves, right-hand twist
Caliber . . . . 9mm Luger
Length (stock folded) . . . . 17 in.
Length (stock extended) . . . . 25 in.
Magazine 25-, 32-round
Muzzle velocity . . . . 1250 fps
Cyclic rate . . . . 600 rpm
Weight unloaded (approx.) . . . . 7.6 lbs.

Uzi (Semiauto Carbine) Specifications
Barrel length . . . . 16.1 in.
Barrel twist . . . . 4 grooves, right-hand twist
Caliber . . . . 9mm Luger
Length (stock folded) . . . . 24.2 in.
Length (stock extended) . . . . 31.5 in.
Magazine 25-, 32-round
Muzzle velocity . . . . 1250 fps
Weight unloaded (approx.) . . . . 8.4 lbs.

Mini-Uzi
The Mini-Uzi is very similar to the full-size weapon but has been considerably shortened. It has a stock which folds to the side of the weapon and is easier to extend than that of the standard Uzi. Many of the parts are interchangeable, as are the magazines. In addition to its smaller size, the Mini-Uzi's sights are more easily

adjusted, and twin cuts in the muzzle help compensate for muzzle climb during automatic firing.

The trade-off for the weapon's size is its high cyclic rate of 1000 to 1200 rpm, which is rather excessive as well as hard to control. Shooters used to setting the standard Uzi to "auto" and using finger touch to fire single shots will find this impossible with the Mini-Uzi.

Assembly and disassembly of the weapon are nearly identical to that of the standard Uzi. Safety, charging handle, magazine release, etc., are all in identical positions.

Mini-Uzi Specifications

Barrel length . . . . 7.9 in.
Barrel twist . . . . 4 grooves, 1-in-10 in.,
                                right-hand twist
Caliber . . . . 9mm Luger

Length (stock folded) . . . . 14.3 in.
Length (stock extended) . . . . 24 in.
Magazine 20-, 25-, 32-round
Muzzle velocity . . . . 1070 fps
Cyclic rate . . . . 1200 rpm
Weight unloaded (approx.) . . . . 5.9 lbs.

Uzi Pistol

Perhaps in an effort to capture the assault pistol market, Israel Military Industries has recently created a pistol version of the Uzi. While the number of parts shared by the two weapons is small, the locations of the safeties, magazine release, charging handle, etc., are identical. Magazines for the Uzi and Mini-Uzi also fit the Uzi Pistol. This makes it very easy to switch from one type to its sister weapon, although someone used to a carbine-style hold on the longer standard Uzi should

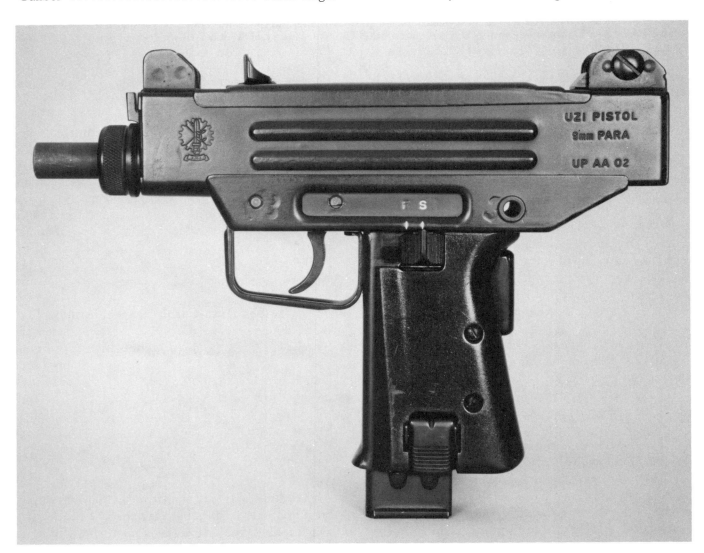

Perhaps in an effort to capture the "assault pistol" market, the Israel Military Industries has recently created a pistol version of the Uzi. Because the cyclic rate of an automatic weapon this size would be excessively high, the Uzi Pistol is generally encountered only in its semiauto form. Photo courtesy of Action Arms.

take care not to get the fingers in front of the barrel.

Because the cyclic rate of an automatic weapon this size would be excessively high, the Uzi Pistol is generally encountered only in its semiauto form. The rear sight is an open sight rather than the peep sight of the Uzi and Mini-Uzi. Field-stripping the weapon is nearly identical to that of the other Uzi weapons.

The Uzi Pistol is a strong contender in the assault pistol market.

Uzi Pistol Specifications

Barrel length . . . . 4.5 in.
Barrel twist . . . . 4 grooves, right-hand twist
Caliber . . . . 9mm Luger
Length . . . . 9.63 in.
Magazine 20-, 25-, 32-round
Muzzle velocity . . . . 1100 fps
Weight unloaded (approx.) . . . . 3.8 lbs.

WALTHER MPL/MPK SUBMACHINE GUNS

The Walther submachine guns were introduced in 1963 but have failed to capture any major market. Most models fire full-auto only, though selective-fire versions are available on special order.

The MPL is the long version of the submachine gun and the MPK, the short. Both are nearly identical, with a steel stock which folds to the left or right, an ambidextrous safety located over the pistol grip, and a charging handle on the upper left of the receiver tube. The weapons are made principally of steel stampings and operate by straight blow-back, with the bolt telescoping over the barrel to cut down on the weapon's overall length. Sights are protected by dog ears; the rear sight has a notch for 75 meters or less and a peep aperture for long-range use.

Thus far, the weapons have captured only a small portion of the police market and have been adopted by the Mexican navy.

Walther MPL Specifications

Barrel length . . . . 10.25 in.
Caliber . . . . 9mm Luger
Length (stock extended) . . . . 29.4 in.
Length (stock folded) . . . . 18.1 in.
Magazine 32-round
Muzzle velocity . . . . 1250 fps
Cyclic rate . . . . 550 rpm
Weight unloaded (approx.) . . . . 6.6 lbs.

Walther MPK Specifications

Barrel length . . . . 6.75 in.

Caliber . . . . 9mm Luger
Length (stock extended) . . . . 25.9 in.
Length (stock folded) . . . . 14.7 in.
Magazine 32-round
Muzzle velocity . . . . 1150 fps
Cyclic rate . . . . 550 rpm
Weight unloaded (approx.) . . . . 6.3 lbs.

WILKINSON TERRY AND LINDA

This carbine/assault pistol design dates back to 1968 when a similar weapon was marketed as the PJK M68. The PJK M68 was not of very high quality, however, and was somewhat different internally. The design was modified by John R. Wilkinson and the two firearms were reintroduced in the late Seventies by Wilkinson Arms. The Terry and Linda weapons are named after Wilkinson's daughters.

The firearms are nearly identical; the Terry has a longer barrel, usually with a cone-shaped flash suppressor, and an integral stock. Because the barrel on either version is easily removed, a conversion kit is available from Wilkinson to turn the Linda into a Terry carbine by adding a longer barrel and stock. Great caution should be used in doing this since a stocked firearm without a 16-inch or longer barrel can quickly get the user into hot water in the United States without a special permit. The long conversion barrel must be mounted first and then the stock mounted; don't even keep the short barrel in the area occupied by the converted Linda and do not carry the short barrel in your pocket when outdoors. Any mistake with this kit could result in a federal offense. Because of federal regulations, it is not legal to convert the Terry rifle into a pistol without a special permit.

The Terry has a maple stock; both firearms have a PVC plastic pistol grip and maple foregrip. Rear sights are Williams adjustables and are protected by dog ears, as is the front post sight. The Terry has a scope base dovetail on top of its receiver. Scope mount systems are available for both weapons.

Both weapons fire from a closed bolt and have a charging handle on the left of the receiver and a spring-loaded dust cover (similar to that of the AR-15) on the ejection port. Each has a cross-bolt safety in the trigger group with the magazine release located below the safety on the left side of the receiver. Care must be taken not to confuse the magazine release and safety!

Disassembly of either firearm is a bit complex:
1. Remove the magazine and cycle the weapon to be sure it is empty.

2. Unscrew the knurled barrel nut and slide it off.

3. Pull off the barrel.

4. Cock the weapon.

5. Remove the two screws that retain the trigger group and remove the assembly.

6. Remove the barrel support screw from the receiver. This is most easily done with the bar tool that comes with the firearm. In a pinch, a large piece of aluminum bar may work. Use a light hammer to tap the sleeve loose if it is tight.

7. Remove the charging handle by unscrewing it with an Allen wrench while restraining the bolt and springs, which will be under tension.

8. Remove the bolt and bolt spring from the front of the receiver tube.

9. If the firing pin needs to be cleaned or replaced, the extractor must first be removed. The extractor is held in place by a drift pin which must be removed to take out the firing-pin retaining bolt which will in turn release the firing pin and its spring.

This procedure will give access to the action springs, trigger, etc. Further disassembly is not recommended except for parts repair/replacement. Reassembly is basically the reverse of the above procedure. Care must be taken to get the twin operating rods into the bolt and line up the barrel collar slot with the barrel sleeve's locator before tightening the retaining nut.

Like most other blow-back weapons, the Wilkinson firearms may have trouble using ammunition with thin brass since the cartridge head is not supported during

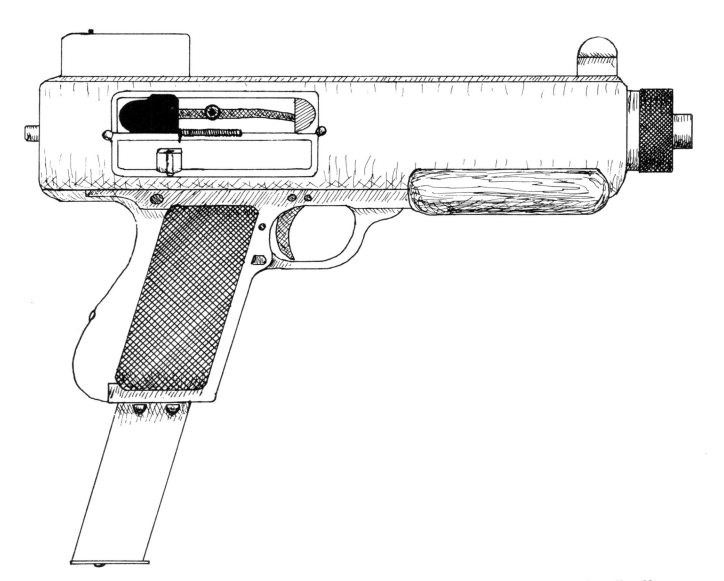

Though a bit complicated to field-strip, the Wilkinson Linda (and its carbine version, the Terry) works well and has most, if not all, of the bugs worked out of its design.

the first part of recoil. Some Wilkinson arms also have trouble digesting hollow-point ammunition; a little feed ramp/throat polishing by a competent gunsmith will take care of this problem.

Though a bit complicated to field-strip, the Terry and Linda work well and have most, if not all, of the bugs worked out of their design.

Wilkinson Terry Specifications
Barrel length .... 16.2 in.
Caliber .... 9mm Luger
Length .... 28.5 in.

Magazine 31-round
Muzzle velocity (approx.) .... 1300 fps
Weight unloaded (approx.) .... 7.1 lbs.

Wilkinson Linda Specifications
Barrel length .... 8.3 in.
Caliber .... 9mm Luger
Length .... 12.25 in.
Magazine 31-round
Muzzle velocity (approx.) .... 1200 fps
Weight unloaded (approx.) .... 4.8 lbs.

3. ASSAULT RIFLES

Assault rifles which are in use today are covered in this chapter. They are alphabetized according to how they are most commonly referred to in the English language.

AR-10

The AR-10 was a weapon ahead of its time, at least as far as the U.S. military was concerned. The Armalite Division of Fairchild Engine and Airplane Corporation developed the AR-10 using manufacturing techniques and a design that departed radically from the U.S. military's standard M1 Garand and M14. Development of the AR-10 began in 1953. The AR-10 was originally chambered for the .30-06 cartridge and was modified two years later for the new .308 Winchester (7.62mm NATO) cartridge.

Several talented workers were involved in the AR-10's final design work. These included Eugene Stoner, L. James Sullivan, who worked as a designer/draftsman, and Robert Fremont, who supervised prototype manufacture and led studies on whether the tolerances needed for rifles would be practical for mass production. These same three men later worked on the AR-15/M16 rifle.

An early version of the AR-10 was submitted to the Springfield Armory in 1956 for testing as a possible replacement for the M1 Garand. Unfortunately, the submitted AR-10 had a titanium barrel surrounded with an aluminum jacket similar to that developed for other Armalite weapons. Although the AR-10, unlike the M14, was able to fire in the automatic mode while remaining easy to control, though recoil was still a bit severe, the barrel burst during testing. The rifle was disqualified, though a number of Armalite people felt that the gun

may have been placed under unreasonable stress in order to create a burst barrel.

Stoner—with the assistance of the Springfield Armory—developed a conventional all-steel barrel for the rifle to replace the alloy barrel. Nevertheless, the U.S. Army chose the M14 rifle, which had been designed by military personnel, over the AR-10 and the FN LAR. Time would prove that they had chosen an inferior weapon.

Though the rifle was still being redesigned by Stoner and others, Fairchild had actively promoted the AR-10. Small numbers of the rifles were sold to Sudan, Burma, and Nicaragua but there were no major sales. Finally, Armalite sold a manufacturing license to the government-owned arsenal of Artillerie-Inrichtingen of Hembrug, Holland, an unfortunate development since the arsenal was not able to tool up in time to meet the demand for the AR-10 which Fairchild's aggressive publicity campaign had created. During this period of turmoil, the AR-10 was tested by the Netherlands, Austria, and Germany (as the G-4 rifle) but never accepted.

Because of the problems created by the tardy Holland arsenal, as well as some political considerations, other rifles such as the FN LAR were adopted by many countries. Only 5,000 AR-10 firearms were manufactured by Artillerie-Inrichtingen; by the time the plant was ready to manufacture large quantities of the rifle, interest had subsided, with only 1,200 being sold to Portugal. Production by the Artillerie-Inrichtingen was finally halted in 1959.

Almost all 5,000 AR-10 rifles (as well as some manufactured by Armalite) were purchased as parts by Paragon Sales and Services. New semiauto receivers were made by Paragon, which rebuilt the rifles into semiauto ver-

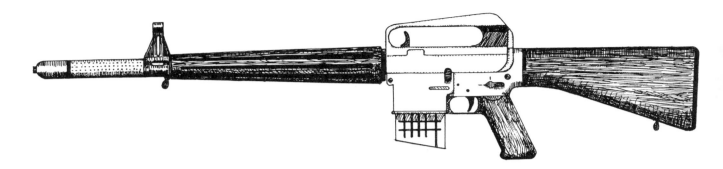

The Armalite Division of Fairchild Engine and Airplane Corporation developed the AR-10 starting in 1953. Originally chambered for the .30-06 cartridge, the AR-10 was modified two years later for the new .308 Winchester (7.62mm NATO) cartridge.

sions for the U.S. civilian market.

Colt's Patent Firearms was licensed to manufacture the improved AR-10, designated the AR-10A. Major improvements were a stronger extractor, a more reliable magazine system, and a cocking handle located toward the rear of the receiver. In an effort to capture part of the military market, Colt created a number of other experimental versions, including a short-barreled carbine and a light machine gun (LMG). The LMG AR-10 had a bipod and was modified to use belt-fed ammunition. Later, the LMG AR-10 was mounted on a tripod, and the gas tube was modified and spring-loaded for use with quick-change barrels. None of the variations attracted much interest among military buyers, however, so Colt decided not to produce the AR-10A and, rather, started marketing the AR-15 after securing the rights to it.

Some of the early AR-10s have a reciprocating charging lever located in the carrying handle. When firing one of these rifles, great care should be taken not to get a finger smashed by the lever during recoil/cycling. Some early AR-10s also did not have a muzzle brake/flash hider. During recoil, these firearms tend to have severe muzzle jump; a suitable muzzle brake will cure this problem.

Most versions of the rifle have a front sight adjustable for elevation and a rear aperture sight adjustable for windage and elevation. On the automatic versions of the rifle, the selector's "safe" position is with the arrow pointing straight up, "auto" is forward, and "semi" is rearward; this is different from the AR-15. Users of the AR-15 should be careful not to get the positions confused during combat!

AR-10 field-stripping procedures are basically identical to those of the AR-15:

1. Remove the magazine and check the chamber to be sure the action is closed; release the bolt carrier so that it is closed.

2. Place the selector into the "safe" position.

3. Push the rear takedown pin outward to the right from the selector side of the lower receiver. This will release the upper receiver so that it can be rotated downward.

4. Pull the charging handle back (the bolt-carrier group will come back with it). Grasp and remove the bolt carrier. The charging handle can be removed by lining it up with the slot in the rear of the upper receiver and pulling it back through the slot.

5. The firing-pin retaining pin can be removed by punching it out from the right side with the tip of a cartridge or small tool.

6. The firing pin can be removed by tilting the carrier up so the bolt faces upward. The firing pin will fall free through the rear of the carrier.

7. Push in the bolt so that the cam pin is clear of the bolt key; rotate the cam and remove it.

8. Pull the bolt assembly from the front of the bolt carrier.

9. To remove the buffer and its spring, depress the buffer retainer plunger while restraining the buffer and its spring.

10. If necessary, the extractor can be removed by pushing out its retainer pin. Take care not to lose the extractor spring.

Assembly of the rifle is basically the reverse of the above procedure. Be sure the cam pin and firing-pin retaining pin are in place, as the rifle would be dangerous to fire without them.

Currently, AR-10 rifles are collector's pieces and command a high price. A number of different versions of the rifle, including some made from AR-10 parts coupled with nonfactory machined receivers, are seen for sale from time to time.

Most authorities feel that the AR-10 is an excellent weapon which missed its place in history because of poor timing and marketing. Very possibly the last has not been seen of the AR-10. The design would be entirely suitable as a hunting/sporting rifle, especially with the huge demand for "assault rifles" in the commercial market. Perhaps a small commercial manufacturer will meet the demand for such a rifle with a semiautomatic AR-10.

AR-10 Specifications

Barrel length . . . . 20 in.
Caliber . . . . 308 Winchester (7.62 NATO)
Cyclic rate (approx.) . . . . 700 rpm
Length (approx.) . . . . 40 in.
Magazine (standard) 20-round
Muzzle velocity (approx.) . . . . 2500 fps
Rifling . . . . 4 grooves, right-hand twist
Weight (approx.) . . . . 7.5 lbs.

AR-15

The AR-15 was developed from 1956 to 1959 by the Armalite Division of Fairchild Engine and Airplane Corporation. Like other Armalite rifles, the AR-15 design was a bold departure for military weapons, with its aluminum receiver, plastic stock, and unique buffer/recoil system. Eugene Stoner was the rifle's main designer.

In 1959, the U.S. Army conducted tests of the AR-15 and Winchester's experimental .224 Lightweight Military Rifle. The test report concluded that the Army should develop a lightweight, reliable rifle "like the AR-15" to replace the M14, but the Army decision makers made no move to adopt the small rounds and rifles for actual use.

Armalite sought to divest itself of the AR-15, and Colt Firearms Corporation purchased the manufacturing rights in 1959. Colt's aggressive sales techniques enabled it to sell a number of the rifles to several small Asian countries, including South Vietnam. As the AR-15 saw use in combat, its lethality became evident. It was only a matter of time before the AR-15 replaced the heavy and awkward M14 rifle. General William Westmoreland, commander of U.S. military forces in Vietnam, ordered more and more of the AR-15s for use by American troops there, and the M14 was phased out.

The new rifle was not without its problems. U.S. troops were often issued rifles without cleaning kits, the magazines weren't too reliable, and the powder used in the military cartridges was different from that specified by the manufacturer. The troubles were further complicated by the calcium carbonate used in the ball powder; it often clogged the gas tube of the rifle, causing it to cease functioning.

Once the source of the problems was determined, the chamber and inside of the bolt carrier were chromed, new magazines fielded, a new type of ball powder used, and troops were trained to clean their rifles. The AR-15 subsequently proved to be a very reliable weapon, and as minor changes continued to be made, its reliability improved; by 1980, the M16A1 proved to be the most reliable weapon used in NATO trials, which included the Galil, FAMAS, and FNC.

A number of variations of the AR-15 have been created. The original model used by the U.S. Army and Air Force was the M16. Later, the Army added a forward bolt assist to the rifle and called for other minor changes, and the new rifle was designated the M16A1. Other variations include a shortened carbine (the "Commando"), as well as HB (Heavy Barrel) weapons, the M231 Port Firing Weapon, SAW (Squad Automatic Weapon) models, LMG (Light Machine Guns), and the like.

The M16A2 model resulted from the 1980 NATO switch to a heavier .223 bullet, which required a change to a 1-in-7 rifling twist. Since this was a major modification, the U.S. military decided to make a number of other changes, including a switch to finger adjustable knobs for elevation and windage on the rear sights; a new pistol grip; a brass deflector; and a three-round burst mode rather than full auto.

The Canadian military has also adopted the M16A2 as the "C7" rifle to replace their FN-C1. Apparently tank and APC crews will have the carbine version of the M16, designated the "C8." Both weapons will retain the full-automatic setting rather than the three-round burst. Scopes will also probably be issued with the rifles, with the iron sights retained for emergency use.

Sources close to the military and Colt have also revealed at the time of this writing that an "A3" model is being developed. The rifle will use a scope for its principle sighting system while an emergency flip-up front sight and a detachable rear sight will be available. The carrying handle will be part of the detachable rear sight so that troops won't normally have the convenient carrying handle. The "if and when" of this rifle design are not known at this time. Another development is an experimental sighting rib, similar to that found on some shotguns, to replace the present sights. This rib is said to greatly enhance a shooter's ability to quickly engage close targets.

Current versions of the Commando-style telescoping stock carbine date back to weapons created during the Vietnam War to fill the need for a weapon that operated as a "submachine gun," even though it used a rifle cartridge rather than a pistol round. The present models of these "submachine guns" are created by combining the rifle receiver and inner parts with a telescoping stock and a 14.5-inch or 16-inch barrel. While the original Commandos had 10- or 11-inch barrels with a special flash suppressor, current Commandos have standard AR-15 rifle flash suppressors. These short carbines enjoy brisk sales worldwide and—though the U.S. military is not currently using the Commando as a standard weapon—it is probable that the Commando will be adopted by U.S. forces as a tanker/weapons crew/commander weapon. Carbines are also being made by Colt for foreign sales with the 14.5-inch barrel and a standard AR-15 rifle stock.

The telescoping stock's release lever is located on its lower side. The rifle can be fired with the stock in the closed position, since the Commando has a shorter buffer tube than the standard AR-15.

It should be noted that the proper name for these carbines is not the "CAR-15." The "CAR-15" designation, used by Colt Firearms when they first started marketing the rifles in the early 1960s, stands for Colt Automatic Rifle-15. Since the Commando was often the first "CAR-15" many users saw, and since the rifle's military designation was "M16," the conclusion is often falsely drawn that the "CAR-15" is the Commando-style carbine. It's a short version of the M16 rifle or an XM177—the experimental designation used by the U.S. military.

A 9mm NATO chambering of the Commando was reintroduced in 1985, drawing on a similar model offered by Colt years back. With the switch by the U.S. military to 9mm ammunition and the greater use of 9mm by law-enforcement and civilian users, the new carbine may be quite successful. A number of companies have also marketed their own 9mm and .45 ACP versions of the AR-15, including Holmes Firearms, Frankford Arsenal, SGW, and A.I.I., Inc.; these companies also offer the upper receiver so that users can use their lower assembly to fire the pistol cartridges. Probably the best of these is the SGW unit since the original magazine release works the unit and no lower receiver inserts are needed: Just snap out the front and rear push pins and exchange the SGW receiver/barrel upper receiver for the .223. Retail cost of the SGW unit is $300.

SGW offers a number of other optional calibers with the same "quick change" upper receiver/barrel assemblies. These all use standard magazines and allow an AR-15 owner to shoot with his choice of 6mm-.223, .17 Remington, or even 7.62×39mm Russian (with only seven rounds per 30-round magazine or ten rounds in the standard 20-round magazine).

It will probably be only a matter of time until AR-15s are created with slightly larger magazine wells and new magazines to accommodate larger calibers. When this is done, things will have gone full circle from the AR-10 to the AR-15 back to the larger caliber. In any event, those who like the AR-15 will be able to own a "family" of the rifles with a wide variety of chamberings.

The M231 Port Firing Weapon has 65 percent of its parts interchangeable with the standard AR-15 and is designed to be fired by troops in armored personnel carriers. Work was started on the modified AR-15 in 1972 when it was needed for the XM723 MICV (Mechanized Infantry Combat Vehicle). The final version has a wire stock but no sights, since it uses all-tracer loads. Though military planners see the rifle as remaining in the APC, it will be interesting to see if the M231 becomes the weapon carried by NCOs and others in actual combat, playing much the same role as the M1 Carbine did in World War II.

Colt has manufactured AR-15s for export, while Singapore, the Philippines, and South Korea have been licensed to manufacture their own AR-15s. Taiwan produces a version which its military has adopted as the Type 68 Rifle. This has lowered sights, altered swivels, a reshaped stock, and redesigned handguards.

Domestically, Colt has marketed the semiautomatic AR-15 Sporter Rifle. The Sporter was originally without the bolt forward assist, but with the switch to the 1-in-7 twist for the M16A2 version, Sporter II was marketed with a new pistol grip and a 1-in-7 twist. As stocks of the old-style receivers ran out, however, new Sporter II versions of the rifle appeared with the forward assist; the rear "finger adjustable" sighting system of the military M16A2 model will soon become available on special target models of the Sporter II.

An AR-15 Sporter Carbine is also available from Colt with the telescoping Commando stock coupled with a 16-inch barrel and a standard AR-15-style flash suppressor. The receiver is identical to the AR-15 Sporter's.

For a more complete history of the AR-15 rifle plus a complete look at available accessories, auto conversions, ammunition, and more, see my book, *The AR-15/M16: A Practical Guide*, available from Paladin Press.

The AR-15 has very good balance since the buffer tube is located in its stock. This feature, coupled with its light weight, makes it a very comfortable weapon. The selector is conveniently located on the left just above the pistol grip; the "safe" position is forward; "semi" fire is up, and "auto" or three-round burst, if either is available, has the selector pointing toward the rear.

A bolt hold-open lever is located on the left of the

A 9mm NATO chambering of the AR-15 Commando was reintroduced in 1985. With the U.S. military switching to 9mm ammunition and the increasing use of 9mm by law enforcement and civilians in the United States, the new 9mm carbine may be quite successful. Photo courtesy of Colt Firearms.

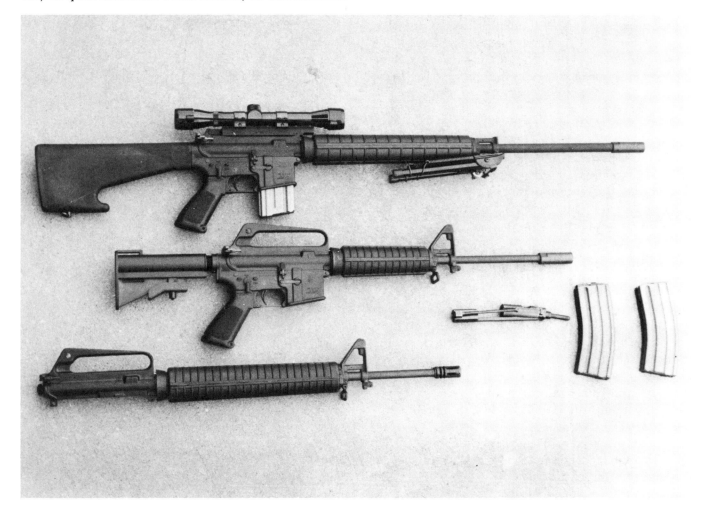

A "family" of AR-15 rifles. At top is a sniper version of the rifle with a Choate E2 stock, Harris bipod, and a 24-inch SGW heavy barrel. At center is a Colt semiauto carbine; a standard barrel/receiver assembly allows the sniper rifle to be turned into a standard rifle. A .22 LR adapter kit allows the shooting of rimfire ammunition.

With bolt-forward assist, 1-in-7 twist, and new pistol grip and handguard, the A2 Sporter II is the semiauto version of the military's M16A2. Photo courtesy of Colt Firearms.

receiver to make reloading quick, and the magazine release is located just ahead of the trigger on the right side of the receiver. The bolt can be released after replacing the magazine by pulling the charging lever or by pressing the bolt release. The nonreciprocating charging lever is located at the rear of the upper receiver below the rear sight; care should be taken to release its lock on the left side of the lever when pulling it back.

The excellent design is rounded out with its easy field-stripping, which is carried out as follows:

1. Remove the magazine from the AR-15 and check the chamber to be sure the action is closed; release the bolt carrier so that it is closed.

2. Place the selector into the "safe" position.

3. Push out the rear takedown pin from the selector side of the lower receiver. This will release the upper receiver so that it can be rotated downward.

4. Pull the charging handle back (the bolt carrier group will come back with it). Grasp and remove the bolt carrier. The charging handle can be removed by pulling it back and downward through the slot in the key channel.

5. The firing-pin retaining pin can be removed by punching it out from the right side with a tip of a cartridge or small tool.

6. The firing pin can be removed by tilting the carrier up so the bolt faces upward. The firing pin will fall free through the rear of the carrier.

7. Push in the bolt so that the cam pin is clear of the bolt key; rotate the cam and remove it.

8. Pull the bolt assembly from the front of the bolt carrier.

9. To remove the buffer and its spring, depress the buffer retainer plunger while restraining the buffer and its spring.

10. If necessary, the extractor can be removed by pushing out its retaining pin. Take care not to lose the extractor spring or the small nylon buffer that is nestled inside most extractor springs.

Assembly of the rifle is basically the reverse of all the above procedures. Be sure the cam pin and firing-pin retaining pin are in place, as the rifle would be dangerous to fire without them.

An endless array of accessories is available for the AR-15 from both military and commercial sources. Probably of the greatest use are the new plastic magazines.

The AR-15 is capable of very good accuracy, provided pressure is not placed on its barrel by a sling; bipod use will also change the point of impact. Because of the rifle's inherent accuracy, a scope mount makes a lot of sense. Probably the best is the new A.R.M.S. mount. It has a see-through base to allow the user to quickly use the iron sights if necessary and will accept Weaver rings as well as NATO standard scopes and night-vision equipment. The milled base is available directly from A.R.M.S. for $39. A similar, but considerably less expensive base is also available from SGW for $10. Though its fit is not quite as good, it is considerably less expensive if you won't be using other than Weaver-ring mounts.

My favorite sling system for the AR-15, the Redi-Tac II, is marketed by JFS, Inc. One end of the Redi-Tac II attaches to the handguard with two nylon loops and the other end to the rear swivel. The top screw on the butt of the stock is replaced with a snap which locks into a snap on the one-inch nylon sling. Once in place, the rifle is well balanced and can be comfortably carried in the assault position. Shouldering the rifle places enough pressure on the strap to unsnap the sling on the stock (the end still stays in the swivel). The Redi-Tac II is available from JFS, Inc., for $21.

JFS, Inc., also markets the Redi-Mag, which allows you to carry a spare magazine on the selector side of the rifle. It has one real plus: Fresh magazines can be placed in it easily so that regular web gear can be used to carry the spares. The Redi-Mag weighs eight ounces and attaches with two clamp screws. It's very quick and simple to exchange a spare magazine for the empty magazine in the rifle; when the full magazine has been placed into the rifle, the shooter can slip a new spare magazine into the holder by just pushing it into place. The Redi-Mag is available from JFS, Inc., for $40.

Many tall shooters find the stock of the AR-15 A1 models about an inch too short for comfort (the A2 model is three-quarters of an inch longer). There are three solutions to this problem. One is the Choate Machine and Tool Zytel "E2" stock which is three-quarters of an inch longer than the standard stock; cost is $30. The second is the Choate extended butt plate which replaces the trap door of the AR-15; it costs $15. If you have an AR-15, you'd do well to get a copy of Choate's catalog. They have a wealth of accessories like flash suppressors and gadgets for a number of rifles including the AR-15.

The third way to extend the stock is to use an SGW stock spacer kit. This allows the standard stock to be used while a spacer fills the space between the stock and the receiver, and a longer screw and internal spacer take up the slack at the rear of the buffer tube. Cost is $9.

A commercial trap-door pistol grip is nice to have, especially with Commando-style rifles. A good one is the Stow-Away Grip, available from Lone Star Ordnance for $9.95. SGW has a slightly different grip that has the A-2 styling with a finger swell for $10, and the "Laser" from Ram-Line is yet another which also has the A2-style finger ridge ($7).

For teaching beginners how to shoot, or for cheap plinking, a .22 LR conversion unit is hard to beat. The M16 military surplus adapter is easily installed by just opening up the rifle, pulling out the bolt carrier, pushing in the adapter, and placing a full .22 adapter/magazine into the magazine well. With its 20-round magazine and low retort and recoil, the .22 conversion is perfect for cheap practice with the rifle. CCI's CB Long Caps can be used in the adapter for nearly silent practice or training; the rounds don't cycle the action (standard .22 LRs will) so that the AR-15 becomes a "bolt-action" rifle—a definite plus in teaching beginners. The conversion unit can be ordered from Numrich Arms Corp. for $150.

Though there has been some concern about the lethality of the new 1-in-7 twist, recent findings indicate that FMJ bullets are more lethal than they were before their new twist. Where the 1-in-12 twist achieved large wounds by tumbling, the centrifugal force created on the jacket by the faster twist makes it shatter on impact. This, coupled with the greater long-range accuracy of the new twist, makes it better than ever (nevertheless, expanding bullets are preferable if conventions of war don't prohibit your use of them).

The new twist also makes the AR-15 as accurate as many bolt-action rifles. Most AR-15s can shoot one-inch or smaller groups with good ammunition. (Care must be taken not to place extra stress on the handguard, for to do so can cause the bullet impact to shift.)

Probably the optimum accuracy is created by the new Insight upper receiver/barrel assembly. Using a heavy barrel which is "free floated" inside the handguard so that stress placed on the handguard with a tight sling or bipod won't change the point of impact, the assembly uses the original weapon's bolt, carrier, and charging handle. Accuracy? Some good shooters can cover a five-shot, 100-yard group with a pattern the size of a dime with the Insight barrel/receiver!

Two models are available. Model I has a Weaver sight base mounted on it, while the Model II has the standard carrying handle and sight system. Both models retail for $385. Despite almost no advertising on the part of the company, a number of SWAT units are now using these models; the days of the bolt-action sniper rifle are probably numbered.

Huge numbers of the AR-15 have been sold or given to military users worldwide. In addition, the civilian success of the rifle and the number of accessories for it guarantee that the AR-15—like the Mauser bolt-action "combat" rifle at the turn of the century—will probably span several centuries of civilian use before ever being retired as an antique.

AR-15/M16A1 Specifications
Barrel length . . . . 20 in.
Caliber . . . . .223 Remington
Cyclic rate (approx.) . . . . 800 rpm
Length . . . . 39 in.
Magazine (standard) 30-round
Muzzle velocity (approx.) . . . . 3250 fps
Rifling . . . . . 4 grooves, 1-in-12 in., right-hand twist
Weight unloaded (approx.) . . . . 6.3 lbs.

AR-15 "Commando" Specifications
Barrel length . . . . 11 in.
Caliber . . . . .223 Remington

The accuracy of the AR-15 rifle is probably most effectively increased by replacing the standard upper barrel and receiver with the new Insight upper receiver/barrel assembly. The heavy barrel is free-floated inside the handguard so that stress placed on the handguard won't change the point of impact. Photo courtesy of Insight Systems.

Cyclic rate (approx.) . . . . 750 rpm
Length (stock extended) . . . . 31 in.
Length (stock folded) . . . . 28 in.
Magazine (standard) 30-round
Muzzle velocity (approx.) . . . . 3000 fps
Rifling . . . . . 6 grooves, 1-in-12 in., right-hand twist
Weight unloaded (approx.) . . . . 6.6 lbs.

AR-15 9mm Carbine Specifications
Barrel length . . . . 16 in.
Caliber . . . . 9mm NATO
Length (stock extended) . . . . 34 in.
Length (stock folded) . . . . 30.5 in.
Magazine (standard) 20-round
Muzzle velocity (approx.) . . . . 1000 fps
Weight unloaded (approx.) . . . . 6.6 lbs.

AR-15 A2 (Match Grade)/M16A2 Specifications
Barrel length . . . . 20 in.

Caliber . . . . 5.56mm NATO
Cyclic rate (approx.) . . . . 800 rpm
Length . . . . 39.7 in.
Magazine (standard) 30-round
Muzzle velocity (approx.) . . . . 3250 fps
Rifling . . . . . . 4 grooves, 1-in-7 in., right-hand twist
Weight unloaded (approx.) . . . . 7.2 lbs.

M231 Specifications
Barrel length . . . . 11 in.
Caliber . . . . 5.56mm NATO
Cyclic rate (approx.) . . . . 1100 rpm
Length (stock extended) . . . . 33 in.
Length (stock folded) . . . . 28.5 in.
Magazine (standard) 30-round
Muzzle velocity (approx.) . . . . 3000 fps
Rifling . . . . . . 4 grooves, 1-in-7 in., right-hand twist
Weight unloaded (approx.) . . . . 8.5 lbs.

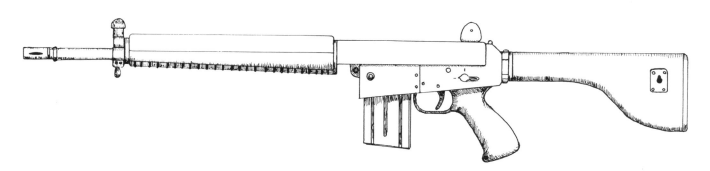

Because of political quagmire, poor timing, and poor work done by subcontractors, Armalite's AR-18 never enjoyed the success it probably deserved.

AR-18/180

The AR-18 was developed from 1962 to 1964 and was chambered for the .223 Remington (5.56mm). Principal work on the rifle was done by Charles Dorchester (who later became the chairman of the board at Armalite). According to Burton T. Miller, who was vice president of Armalite during this period, Eugene Stoner also worked on the AR-18, although the rifle was marketed after Stoner left the company.

Armalite sold the manufacturing rights for the AR-18 to the Howa Machinery Company of Nagoya, Japan. At the time, the Japanese government was applying political pressure to end the war in Vietnam. In an effort to put the heat on the United States, Japan would not grant Howa a license to export the AR-18 to any country even remotely involved with the war. Thus, when the U.S. Army tried to secure some AR-18s for testing, the Japanese government refused to allow the rifles out of the country. This might well have caused the Army to continue to use the more expensive, but readily available, AR-15.

Because of this political quagmire, Armalite set up its own small production plant in 1968 to produce limited numbers of the AR-18 as well as a semiauto version, the AR-180, aimed at the U.S. civilian market. Production was halted in 1970 when Japan agreed to ship civilian models of the rifle to the United States. The Japanese manufacturing license was revoked by Armalite in 1973 and a new license granted to Sterling Arms of England in 1976. Because of excessive overhead and quality-control problems, Armalite, which had been purchased by a Philippine-based conglomerate, shifted the production of the rifle from Sterling Arms to the Philippines.

The AR-18 was designed to be produced with simple machinery and at a lower price than rifles like the AR-15 or M14. Its design does do away with some of the potential problems of the AR-15. The AR-18/180 has two recoil springs inside its receiver rather than a buffer tube in the stock like the AR-15. This allows for a folding stock and lower front and rear sights. Another plus in the eyes of many users is the use of a gas piston system rather than the gas tube found in the AR-15, which tends to become clogged with poor ammunition. The design also opens up the possibility of modifying the weapon into a bullpup. Finally, the design makes extensive use of steel stampings so that a minimum of complex tooling is necessary; this would allow Third World countries to produce the AR-18 with a minimum of fuss. According to Armalite, the AR-18 can be produced with only 14 steel stampings, 28 automatic screw machine operations, three machined castings, six moldings, and only four machining operations (the barrel, bolt carrier, extractor, and barrel extension).

The AR-18's charging handle has a crook in it so that left-handed shooters can reach over its top and cock it; the safety is likewise ambidextrous. Interestingly, the charging handle moves with the bolt so that the handle can be used as a forward assist; this design is a lot simpler than the AR-15's charging handle and forward assist. The ejection port has a dust cover similar to that of the AR-15, and the magazine release is just ahead of the trigger on the right side of the rifle. The firing pin is spring loaded so that it will not strike the primer of a round during chambering; this is safer than a floating firing pin.

A metal dovetail base is welded to the top of the receiver so that a 3X scope designed specifically for the rifle can be quickly mounted; it is held on the mount with a spring-loaded rod. A mount which allows the use of standard one-inch diameter scopes is also available. The front sight is a post adjustable for elevation; the rear sight is adjustable for windage and flips to either a 200-yard or 400-yard zero. (These settings are approximate; different types of ammunition may or may not maintain a zero from one setting to the other.)

Many AR-18s have a front flash suppressor with slots only in the top and sides to help reduce muzzle climb. The threads on the barrel allow the AR-18 to use any muzzle brake or flash suppressor designed for the AR-15 or similar rifles.

Field-stripping is quite simple and requires no special tools other than a blunt punch or cartridge tip. After removing the magazine and cycling the weapon to be sure it is empty, set the selector to the "safe" position. Then proceed as follows:

1. Release the receiver latch and push it forward to free the rear of the upper receiver.

2. While keeping the receiver latch depressed, pivot the top and lower receiver halves apart (be careful; the recoil spring assembly is under pressure).

3. Slowly let the recoil springs and their guides out of the rear of the upper receiver. Pull them out of the rear of the receiver once spring tension is released.

4. Pull the charging handle all the way to the rear of its track and remove it by pulling it out to the right.

5. Turn the receiver so that the bolt carrier/bolt slides out the rear end of the open receiver.

6. Push the spring-loaded firing pin from its rear side so that the cross-pin that retains it can be pulled out the left side of the bolt carrier. This will free the firing pin and its spring.

7. With the firing pin removed, the cam pin can be pulled out to the left of the bolt carrier. This will free the bolt, which can be pulled from the front of the bolt carrier.

8. The upper handguard half is released when the recoil spring assembly is removed. Pull it up at its rear end and pivot it up and off the barrel.

9. Move the piston rod toward the receiver and tilt the connector toward the rear as well. Free it by tilting it to one side.

10. After removing the connector, release the piston rod and tilt it to one side and remove it and its spring.

11. Remove the gas piston to expose the gas tube.

This is all that normally needs to be done to clean and maintain the AR-18/180. Reassembly is basically the reverse of the above procedure. When putting the bolt back into the carrier, be sure to point the extractor to the right and get the cam pin right side in so that the firing pin can go through it.

The plastic stock is folded by depressing two buttons, one above and one below, at the rear of the receiver. This allows the stock to be folded to the left where it locks on a short pin on the side of the rifle. A light pull on the stock releases it and allows it to be extended and locked into place.

The barrel is attached to the receiver only at its front. The handguards are attached to the barrel rather than the receiver, so that pressure on the front handguard or barrel can displace the point of impact somewhat. If a shooter uses a tight sling or bipod to steady the rifle, the point of impact may move several inches at 200 yards.

At one time, a short-barreled version of the AR-18 was also available. It was identical to the standard model except that it had a 10-inch barrel and a shorter handguard, operating rod, etc. A pistol grip was mounted on the lower side of the handguard. Most models had a cone-type flash suppressor rather than the standard slotted type. This model was designated the "AR-18 S" and was designed to fill the submachine gun role in much the same way the AR-15 Commando did.

The AR-18/180 will accept many of the accessories designed for the AR-15/M16. Military M16 magazines can theoretically be adapted for use in the AR-18 by filing off some metal. In practice, though, this isn't too reliable. Although the original magazines for the AR-18 had a 20-round capacity, after-market magazines are available with 30- and 40-round capacities, as is a 40-round magazine sold by Armalite.

AR-18/180 Specifications

Barrel length . . . . 18.25 in.
Caliber . . . . .223 Remington
Cyclic rate (approx.) . . . . 750 rpm
Length (stock extended) . . . . 38 in.
Length (stock folded) . . . . 28.75 in.
Magazine (standard) 20-round
Muzzle velocity (approx.) . . . . 3200 fps
Rifling . . . . . 4 grooves, 1-in-12 in., right-hand twist
Weight unloaded (approx.) . . . . 6.6 lbs.

AR-18 S Specifications

Barrel length . . . . 10 in.
Caliber . . . . .223 Remington
Cyclic rate (approx.) . . . . 750 rpm
Length (stock extended) . . . . 30 in.
Length (stock folded) . . . . 20.75 in.
Magazine (standard) 20-round
Muzzle velocity (approx.) . . . . 2900 fps
Rifling . . . . . 4 grooves, 1-in-12 in., right-hand twist
Weight unloaded (approx.) . . . . 6.6 lbs.

AR70

The AR70 is manufactured by the Pietro Beretta Company of Italy in four models: the selective-fire infantry AR70; the "special troops" carbine SC70 with folding stock and varying barrel length; the AR70/78 SAW (Squad Automatic Weapon) with bipod and quick-change barrel (weighing about a pound more than the other versions); and a semiauto AR70/SPORT version without grenade-launching sight and lever, and without a bayonet lug under the front sight assembly. All versions have chrome-lined barrels and a black epoxy finish.

The AR70 resembles the SIG rifles for good reason; in 1963, SIG and Beretta undertook joint research and development for a new .223 assault rifle. The two companies terminated their joint efforts and went on to create two similar rifles. Work on the AR70 began in 1968 under the direction of Vittorio Valle; the rifle was completed in 1970. The rifle is made with a large number of steel stampings and has plastic furniture. The gas piston rod, with its recoil spring wrapped around it, is above the barrel. Locking recesses for the bolt are welded into the forward end of the upper receiver (similar to the Soviet AKM). The AR70 has a twin-lugged bolt (similar to that of the AKM or M1 Carbine) and a bolt hold-open lever like the M16. Certainly Beretta took the best of all worlds to create their rifle.

The charging handle is a bolt which sticks out of the right side of the weapon and also serves as the pin that holds the bolt carrier and piston rod together. The handle is bent upward on the military weapons and straight out on the AR70/SPORT. The slot in the rear

The AR70 is well designed and makes extensive use of steel stampings and plastic furniture. Beretta certainly took the best of all worlds to create its rifle! Photo courtesy of Beretta Firearms.

of the upper receiver where the bolt travels has a spring-loaded metal dust cover that opens when the weapon is fired or cocked. The bolt-carrier guide rails and stationary ejector are welded to the sheet-metal upper receiver.

The safety is located on the left of the lower receiver and operates "backwards" from many other assault rifles; the selector does not actually point toward the "S" (Safe) position. Shooters used to other types of rifles may find this a bit confusing until they become accustomed to the firearm.

The pistol grip has a sliding trapdoor on its bottom. This holds the cleaning kit, which consists of a pull-through chain/patch tip, brush, and oiler. Sling mounts are on the left of the stock and to the left of the gas vent on the barrel, making the rifle comfortable to carry with the sling. The folding and rigid stocks are interchangeable so that the AR70 can quickly be "changed" into a long-barreled SC70 or the SC70 to a short-barreled AR70. The original SC70 stocks were made of heavy wire; these proved fragile and have since been replaced with an FN LAR-style stock.

The grenade launcher spindle-valve lever is located in front of the front sight assembly on the military rifles. It is normally folded down; when grenades are to be launched, the lever is pulled up over the front sight perpendicular to the barrel. The grenade sight is normally folded down behind the rear sight; when needed, it folds up and has peep holes for 50, 75, and 100 meters. The front flash-suppressor assembly is designed for use with 40mm grenades.

Barrel lengths of the SC70 version may vary accord-ing to user specifications. Currently, the SC70/SHORT is the shortest offering of the AR70 rifles. This short barrel coupled with the folding stock makes the SC70/SHORT a very handy, compact weapon. In addition to the shortened barrel, the SC70/SHORT has a short flash suppressor and a gas piston and cylinder which have had two inches lopped off. The SC70/SHORT will not accept the AR70 bayonet nor can it launch rifle grenades. Velocity of bullets fired from the SC70/SHORT is lower and muzzle blast greater because of its shorter barrel.

The original version of the AR70/78SAW was the LMG70, which was bascially a standard AR70 with a heavy quick-change barrel. The new AR70/78SAW has eight cooling fins milled into the receiver end of the barrel. The new rifle has a barrel extension, rather than a sleeve, welded to the upper receiver with a notch to match the barrel's catch. Since the bipod is attached to the gas rod assembly, the barrel may be changed very quickly. A mounting on the barrel catch is designed for tripod or vehicle use, and a carrying handle and 40-round magazine are available. At first glance, the flash suppressor resembles that of the AR-15, but in fact has a five-inch extension that slips down over the barrel and holds the gas block in position.

Steel scope blocks are welded to the receiver top so that a scope is easily mounted. Beretta currently sells a scope sight for the rifle as well as a night-vision scope. The front sight is adjustable for elevation and the rear peep sight for windage with either a screwdriver or bullet tip. The rear sight has a flip-up, double-position aperture with realistic ranges of 150 and 300 meters.

The AR70/SPORT has an eight-round magazine as well as the standard 30-round steel model. The magazine release lever on all models is located behind the magazine well. The magazine must be rotated on the front of the well and moved up and down when loading.

Field-stripping an AR70 is quite simple and requires no tools other than a small punch or the tip of a cartridge:

1. Remove the magazine and cycle the action to be sure it is empty.

2. Push in the push pin on the left side of the receiver and pull it to its release position. This allows the receiver halves to be rotated open.

3. Remove the charging handle by pushing back on the hole in the sheet metal just to its rear and pulling out on the handle.

4. Remove the bolt and bolt carrier from the upper receiver.

5. Remove the bolt by twisting it and pulling it out of the front of the carrier (note its position in the bolt carrier for reassembly).

6. Remove the firing pin by pushing out the retaining pin from the left of the carrier with a cartridge tip (there is no firing pin spring).

7. Remove the handguard by pulling down at its front and rotating it down and forward.

8. Depress the release lever on the front of the front sight and unscrew the flash suppressor. This releases the gas cylinder block, which can also be removed.

9. The gas piston, rod, and spring can be removed by pushing them into the receiver slightly and rotating them 180 degrees, then pulling them forward and out.

Reassembly is simply the reverse of the above procedure. If trouble is experienced in pushing the bolt carrier back into the upper receiver, the bolt is probably backwards or not pulled out.

The AR70 has fewer parts than many other rifles and is noted for its reliability and accuracy.

AR70 (SC70) Specifications

Barrel length	17.8 in.
Caliber	.223 Remington
Cyclic rate (approx.)	650 rpm
Length (stock extended)	37.6 in.
Length (stock folded, SC70 version only)	28.8 in.
Magazine (standard)	30-round
Muzzle velocity (approx.)	3180 fps
Rifling	4 grooves, 1-in-12 in., right-hand twist
Weight unloaded (approx.)	7.8 lbs.

SC70/SHORT Specifications

Barrel length	12.6 in.
Caliber	.223 Remington
Cyclic rate (approx.)	600 rpm
Length (stock extended)	32.4 in.
Length (stock folded)	23.6 in.
Magazine (standard)	30-round
Muzzle velocity (approx.)	2900 fps
Rifling	4 (or 6) grooves, 1-in-12 in., right-hand twist
Weight unloaded (approx.)	7.6 lbs.

AUG

The AUG (*Armee Universal Gewehr*) is manufactured by Steyr-Daimler-Puch, AG, of Austria. The rifle was developed during the late 1960s by the Austrian Office of Military Technology under the direction of Colonel Walter Stoll.

The AUG is a state-of-the-art rifle that makes use of plastic for a wide array of parts normally made of steel. Added to this is the futuristic appearance of the rifle, its bullpup design, and the use of an integral scope/carrying handle.

There were originally two models of the AUG: Type 12 and Type 13. The Type 13 had iron sights and is no longer made. The Type 12 is available in four barrel lengths which allow the rifle to be deployed as anything from a "submachine gun" to an SAW or LMG. The 24.4-inch barrel is used to create the HBAR (Heavy Barrel Automatic Rifle). The barrel is often used with a special flash suppressor and usually has a telescoping bipod. The HBAR-T model is also available and would be suitable as a sniper rifle. It has a special receiver which can use removable scopes or night-vision equipment and usually has a special carrying handle which mounts on the upper scope ring halves. A third version of the AUG is the LSW. It is much the same as the HBAR but fires from an open bolt and has a different charging mechanism.

The quick-change barrel, which is connected to the receiver assembly with an interrupted thread, coupled with a forward grip that allows a hot barrel to be easily handled, makes it easy to change a barrel. Barrel lengths include 13.75, 16, 20, and 24.5 inches. The barrel assembly includes the barrel, gas port, cylinder, regulator, and hand grip. All barrels and chambers are chrome-lined. A flash suppressor is fitted to the muzzle; internal threads in the suppressor and a special threaded insert allow the use of blanks on all but the 24.5-inch flash suppressors, which have external threads. The 13.75-inch barrel's four-pronged flash suppressor is overcome by the muzzle flash; there is no way to prevent this, since so much unburned powder leaves the barrel. The flash suppressors on the 16- and 20-inch barrels are open-pronged like the 13.75 suppressor, but have two slots on the side and one on the top; the top slot acts as a muzzle compensator while the absence of a bottom slot keeps the muzzle blast from kicking up dust during prone shooting. The 24.5-inch flash suppressor also acts as a muzzle brake and compensator. It has two large ports on each side and three smaller holes drilled into its front (the unit is machined steel). In addition to these three styles of flash suppressor, the M16-style birdcage suppressor is available as an option.

The foregrip can be placed in one of two positions, parallel to the barrel or rotated forward to a vertical position for a "submachine gun" hold. On the short barrel model, the grip is locked into its vertical position to protect the shooter's fingers since the end of the grip would extend past the muzzle in the folded position.

The gas regulator has three settings, one for regular ammunition (position 1, small dot on the gas cylinder); a second for underpowered ammunition or times when the weapon is dirty or the gas system fouled (position 2, large dot); and the third (marked "GR") for the use of ballistic grenade firing blanks. The adjustments are made by pulling on the top of the gas plug and then rotating the assembly until the detent is lined up in the correct position.

The receiver assembly is made from a pressure-die aluminum casting. The handle/optical sight is part of the receiver; the optics are made by Swarovski Optik of Tyrol, Austria. The scope is designed for combat within 300 meters and comes in several versions. The military scope has a black ring-reticle which doubles as

a range finder; a standing man just fills the inner diameter of the reticle at 300 meters. The law-enforcement version has a small dot at the center of its picture. Emergency sights are located on top of the integral scope and consist of a rear notch and a front blade. Most models have luminous dots on the blade and notch.

A locking collar is enclosed in the receiver in which the bolt assembly locks, and steel guides and inserts for the bolt and barrel are permanently installed. The charging handle is located on the left side of the receiver.

The stock and pistol grip are made of a single plastic molding and are available in a wide array of colors. Currently, the AUG is made in sand tan, olive green, and black. An "E2" hook located at the lower end of the stock allows shooters using a bipod to steady the stock against the shoulder with the free hand.

The pistol grip/trigger guard wraps around the entire hand so that the rifle can be operated with mittens. Trigger pull is heavy, a crisp nine pounds on the average. The magazine release is a plastic lever just behind the magazine well. Because of its central position, it can be reached by left- or right-handed shooters.

The trigger group is largely plastic; the only steel is in the springs and pins. The trigger itself controls the type of fire: the first-stage fires the weapon in the semiauto mode; pulling back further gives automatic fire. The trigger is permanently mounted in the stock and has two steel rods connecting it to the trigger group.

Just behind the trigger is the square plastic safety. Pushing the safety from the right to left will expose a red dot and put the rifle in the "fire" mode; pushing to the right places the safety in the white dot, "safe" position. To the rear of the safety is the receiver lock-

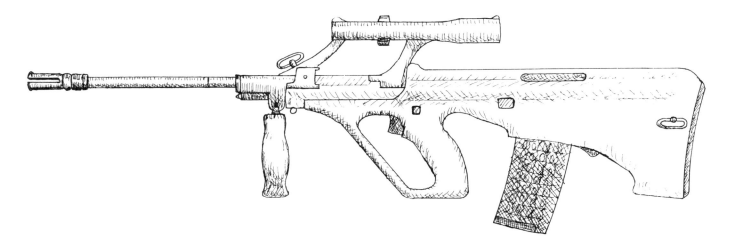

The Steyr AUG is a state-of-the-art rifle that makes use of plastic in a wide array of parts normally made of steel. Other distinctive features of this rifle are its futuristic appearance, bullpup design, and integral scope/carrying handle.

ing pin; depressing this will free the stock from the receiver group.

Two guide rods are located on either side of the receiver/barrel assemblies. The right guide rod doubles as the gas piston/gas rod while the left doubles as the charging rod. The piston rod has three split gas rings which act as a seal; care must be taken that the gaps in the rings are not lined up. The charging lever is normally nonreciprocating when the weapon is fired, but it can be locked to the rod for a forward assist by depressing a button on top of the charging lever. Each rod has a spring for cycling the action and each is brazed to the bolt carrier. The 7-lug bolt (the eighth position is occupied by the extractor) is cam-locked by a steel insert in the receiver. A left-hand bolt is available for left-handed users. When the left-handed bolt is used, brass is ejected out the left side of the receiver and the right ejection port is covered by the plastic insert normally kept over the left port.

The integral optical sight is generally 1.5 power. It has a dot reticle which gives very quick sighting under battle conditions. A small tool is needed for windage and elevation adjustments. Because the optics are mounted in the handle of the rifle, the system normally needs little adjustment and is quite tough.

Special clear plastic magazines allow the user to visually check the ammunition supply. The 30-round magazine is more suitable than the 42-round model for use with the bipod; the 42-round will get hung up when firing from a low bipod position.

Field-stripping the rifle is simple:

1. Remove the magazine and pull the charging handle back to clear the chamber.

2. Lock the handle in its receiver detent and place the safety into the "safe" position.

3. Push the barrel release button behind the foregrip on the left side of the receiver; rotate the foregrip from the bottom of the barrel toward the left of the rifle.

4. Pull out the barrel assembly.

5. Push the receiver release in on the left side of the stock; remove the receiver group.

6. The bolt assembly can now be removed from the rear of the receiver; remove the bolt by turning the firing pin counterclockwise to release it and the bolt.

7. The butt plate is removed by pushing in the indentation on it while pulling out the rear swivel. Pop off the plate; pull out the trigger group or remove the cleaning kit.

Spare firing pins are usually located in a small space in the stock just above the trigger guard; these are held in place by a screw retainer. Reassembly is basically the reverse of the above procedure.

In addition to the selective-fire rifle, a semiauto version is also available commercially. This model is imported to the United States by Interarms.

The AUG is a very forward-looking design whose innovative use of plastic and aluminum has developed a versatile, tough, and relatively light rifle that is easily repaired. It has been adopted by a number of armed forces, including Austria (designated the Stg 77), Malaysia, Morocco, Oman, Saudia Arabia, and Tunisia and is being used by elite units such as the U.S. Navy SEALS and the British SAS. At the time of this writing, the AUG is also undergoing trials for possible adoption by the Australian armed forces.

AUG Submachine Gun Specifications

Barrel length .... 13.8 in.
Caliber .... .223 Remington
Cyclic rate (approx.) .... 725 rpm
Length .... 25 in.
Magazine (standard) .... 30- or 42-round
Muzzle velocity (approx.) .... 3085 fps
Rifling ...... 6 grooves, 1-in-9 in., right-hand twist
Weight unloaded (approx.) .... 6.7 lbs.

AUG Carbine Specifications

Barrel length .... 16 in.
Caliber .... .223 Remington
Cyclic rate (approx.) .... 725 rpm
Length .... 27 in.
Magazine (standard) .... 30- or 42-round
Muzzle velocity (approx.) .... 3182 fps
Rifling ...... 6 grooves, 1-in-9 in., right-hand twist
Weight unloaded (approx.) .... 7.3 lbs.

AUG Rifle Specifications

Barrel length .... 20 in.
Caliber .... .223 Remington
Cyclic rate (approx.) .... 725 rpm
Length .... 31 in.
Magazine (standard) .... 30- or 42-round
Muzzle velocity (approx.) .... 3208 fps
Rifling ...... 6 grooves, 1-in-9 in., right-hand twist
Weight unloaded (approx.) .... 7.9 lbs.

AUG Light Machine Gun Specifications

Barrel length .... 24.5 in.
Caliber .... .223 Remington
Cyclic rate (approx.) .... 725 rpm
Length .... 35 in.
Magazine (standard) .... 30- or 42-round
Muzzle velocity (approx.) .... 3245 fps

Rifling ..... 6 grooves, 1-in-7 in., right-hand twist
Weight unloaded (approx.) .... 10.8 lbs.

BUSHMASTER

In the late 1960s, Colt started work on a weapon which falls neither into the rifle nor pistol category. This weapon made use of many AR-15 parts but its pistol grip was mounted in front of the magazine and it lacked the recoil spring/buffer assembly. In effect, the weapon was a stockless "bullpup" rifle. Those working on the rifle called it an "arm gun," and it was described in Colt's literature as a "lightweight rifle/submachine gun."

The stockless arm gun was aimed by holding the weapon straight out in front of the firer with the shooter's free hand holding the "butt" of the weapon against his upper arm. The shooter rested his head against the upper part of the arm holding the weapon while he sighted down a small scope or an iron sight, which swiveled to accommodate right- or left-handed users.

The arm gun was originally chambered for pistol ammunition, but the recoil was so mild that the 5.5-pound weapon was chambered for rifle ammunition. According to users, the recoil, even with 7.62mm NATO ammunition, was minimal because the shooter's arm soaked up the recoil rather than his shoulder; this causes felt recoil to be considerably lighter.

The Air Force conducted a number of tests with the arm rifle for possible use as a survival weapon or a 5.56mm "submachine gun" in 1969. The rifle used in the tests was chambered for the .221 IMP cartridge, so that the weapon is sometimes called the "IMP." To date, no other real interest has been shown by the U.S. military in the arm rifle, but an interesting commercial "pistol" and rifle have grown out of the design.

The new commercial "pistol" was designed by Mack Gwinn. Called the Bushmaster, his weapon uses many of the design features of Colt's arm rifle. Perhaps its greatest plus is that it uses even more AR-15 parts than the original arm gun, thereby keeping the cost of manufacturing down since many of the AR-15 parts are easily fabricated or are mass-produced at a very low price. The pistol's grip pivots to the right or left to accommodate left- or right-handed shooters, and the ejection port at the top of the receiver is "closed" by the bolt carrier except during ejection of spent cartridges.

Because the firearm lacks a conventional stock, it is considered to be a pistol by the BATF. Thus, the semiauto version of the arm rifle is one of the few rifles which can have a barrel length less than 16 inches and remain within the limits of BATF regulations for a personally owned firearm. Early Bushmasters suffered from poor quality control and the original manufacturer went bankrupt. A new company, Bushmaster Firearms, Inc., has been set up and quality has improved. A rifle model of the Bushmaster has also been made; it brings the weapon full circle since it started as a pistol, which was a spin-off of the "IMP," created from the AR-15 rifle. The Bushmaster rifle, like the pistol, has a stamped-steel upper receiver.

The piston/recoil spring assembly is over the barrel, which is welded to the upper receiver. On the original pistols, the safety was located on the left rear of the receiver similar to the AR-15 rifle; early production models of the pistol had the safety in the trigger guard. This arrangement proved unsatisfactory, however, and current models of the pistol and the rifle have the safety in its original location. On the Bushmaster rifle, this location is convenient; on the pistol, it is far from the trigger finger and requires the use of the off hand to switch it to or from "safe."

Since the Bushmaster rifle doesn't have the AR-15's

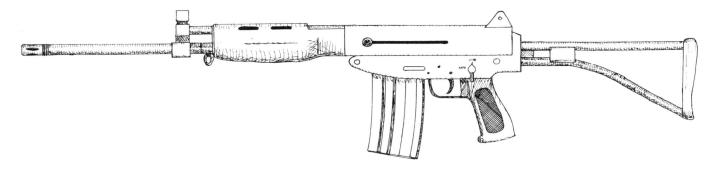

The Bushmaster started out as a design based on Colt's "arm rifle." Coming full circle, it was made into a rifle which uses a number of AR-15 rifle parts.

buffer system in the stock, a folding-stock model is available as well as the standard wooden stock. Like the wooden handguard, the wooden stock is painted black. There is no bolt hold-open lever on either the rifle or pistol; when the last shot is fired from a magazine, the bolt closes on an empty chamber. The rifle's ejection port is located on its right side. The magazine release is on the right side of the receiver toward the rear of the magazine well.

The phosphate finish on Bushmasters is far from pretty, and spot welds are not ground down completely or polished. The rifle and pistol have all the beauty of a wartime production STEN, but the rifle is inexpensive to build and its price is probably the lowest on the market. (Critics of the finish should recall that these weapons are designed for combat, not beauty contests.)

Currently, the semiauto Bushmaster is sold to the civilian market, though selective-fire versions are available, as is a nickel-plated model. Bayonet lug kits are also available for the rifle. (Unless these are very tightly anchored in place, they have a tendency to work loose with continued firing.)

To field-strip the Bushmaster:
1. Remove the magazine and cycle the action to clear the chamber; check to be sure the weapon is empty.
2. Remove the pin from the rear of the receiver halves and rotate the action open (the front pin is also removable so the rifle can be broken down for storage).
3. To remove the bolt carrier and bolt, move the bolt carrier fully back so that the charging knob can be pulled out (care should be taken not to lose the small handle).
4. Remove the firing-pin retaining pin and allow the firing pin to fall out the back of the bolt.
5. Remove the cam pin.
6. Remove the bolt.
Reassembly is basically the reverse of the above procedure.

Because of the poor quality of early production models and the lackluster finish of the current firearms, Bushmasters are either sworn by or sworn at depending on the weapon's origin and the user's expectations of how a gun should look. The Bushmaster is a basically good, if Spartan, design, and it is hoped that improved quality control will keep the firearm in the marketplace.

Rifles and pistols made before the quality-control improvements did not have a "J" prefix on the pistol's serial number or an "F" prefix on the rifle; if you purchase one of these weapons, try it out and look for the "J" or "F" prefix. Generally a firing-in-period is required to smooth out the action for optimum functioning.

Bushmaster Pistol Specifications
Barrel length . . . . 11.5 in.
Caliber . . . . .223 Remington
Cyclic rate (approx.) . . . . 750 rpm
Length . . . . 20.5 in.
Magazine (standard) 30-round
Muzzle velocity (approx.) . . . . 3000 fps
Rifling . . . . 1-in-10 in., right-hand twist
Weight unloaded (approx.) . . . . 5.25 lbs.

Bushmaster Rifle Specifications
Barrel length . . . . 18.5 in.
Caliber . . . . .223 Remington
Cyclic rate (approx.) . . . . 750 rpm
Length . . . . 37.5 in.
Length (stock folded) . . . . 27.5 in.
Magazine (standard) 30-round
Muzzle velocity (approx.) . . . . 3200 fps
Rifling . . . . 1-in-10 in., right-hand twist
Weight unloaded (approx.) . . . . 7.5 lbs.

CETME MODEL 58 AND L

The CETME rifles are nearly identical to the 7.62mm NATO versions of the Heckler & Koch rifles; this stands to reason since the HK-G3 is based on the CETME. The CETME can be traced back to experiments conducted at the Mauser Werke in Germany at the close of World War II. The experimental rifle never saw combat and only one known model of it was assembled, though it had been designated the StG45. At the close of the war, the three engineers involved with the rifle, Edmund Heckler, Theodor Koch, and Alexis Seidel, founded a firm in Spain to manufacture precision machinery. The company shortly won the contract to design a battle rifle for the Spanish army. Their work was carried out at CETME (*Centro de Estudios Tecnicos de Materials Especiales*, a government research establishment) whose name was given to the rifle in the 1950s. The design of the CETME rifle was based in large part on the internal workings of the StG45 but was chambered for the larger 7.62mm NATO as well as the 7.9×40mm cartridge developed by CETME.

Heckler and Koch had established their own firearms company in West Germany in 1949 so when the Spanish factory was ready to start manufacturing the rifles, Heckler and Koch were consulted to help with setting up the Spanish plants. At about the same time, West Germany adopted the CETME as its standard rifle, designated the G1. Later, the German military switched to the FN LAR, which became the G2, but couldn't reach a satisfactory manufacturing agreement with

Fabrique Nationale. In 1954 the Germans purchased a license to manufacture the CETME in Germany; the German-modified CETME rifle design became the G3.

The G3 rifle proved to be very tough and reliable. In the meantime, CETME continued to manufacture its own weapons and tried to compete on the international scene but was largely unsuccessful, especially as the Germans created a whole family of weapons based on their version of the rifle. The rifle did meet with the approval of the Spanish military, however, and was adopted as the Model 58 in 1958.

The CETME rifles differ from those of Heckler & Koch in only a few minor areas, such as the rear sights and the use of an integral bipod which folded up to become the handguard on early versions. Like the H&K rifles, the CETME has a reputation for reliability. The CETME is also simpler than many other rifles since the roller-locking system does away with the gas tube, piston, etc. The locking system also allows a wider power range of ammunition to be used without failure to cycle the weapon. Like the H&K rifles, the CETME also has a

fluted chamber to allow the brass to "float" on a gas jet during firing and create positive extraction. One major difference between the rifles occurs during automatic fire: The CETME fires from an open bolt in the auto mode so that a hot chamber can't cause rounds to "cook off" and fire prematurely. Magazine release, selector, charging handle, etc., are all located in the same places as on the H&K rifles. Field-stripping is nearly identical.

Several models of the CETME were developed to try to reach an international market. These include models with wooden furniture, semiauto-only models, and sporting rifles as well as the stockless, sightless Model R for use as a port-firing weapon.

CETME Model 58 Specifications
Barrel length	17.7 in.
Caliber	7.62mm NATO
Cyclic rate (approx.)	600 rpm
Length	40 in.
Magazine (standard)	20-round

The CETME has a reputation for reliability. The CETME is also simpler than many other rifles, since the roller-locking system does away with the gas tube, gas pistons, etc. The CETME fires from an open bolt in the auto mode.

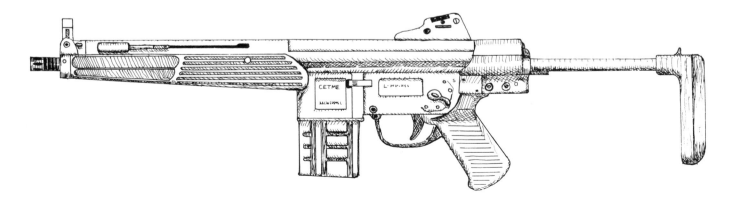

In an effort to gain a portion of the new international market in which the .223 Remington round achieved such success, CETME created the Model L. Shown here is the folding stock, short-barrel version.

Muzzle velocity (approx.) .... 2580 fps
Rifling ..... 4 grooves, 1-in-12 in., right-hand twist
Weight unloaded (approx.) .... 10 lbs.

With the introduction of the .223 Remington round, CETME has tried to gain a portion of this new market by creating its own .223 rifle. The results of this work are two versions of the Model L; one has a standard stock and the other a folding stock with a shorter barrel.

Internally the rifles are very similar to the Model 58 with the roller-locking system, with a spring-loaded charging lever being added. A ratchet mechanism has been added to create a three-round burst capability as well as full-auto and semiauto fire. Field-stripping is nearly identical to that of the Model 58.

Model L Rifle Specifications

Barrel length .... 15.7 in.
Caliber .... .223 Remington
Cyclic rate (approx.) .... 750 rpm
Length .... 36.4 in.
Magazine .... 10-, 20-, or 30-round
Muzzle velocity (approx.) .... 3020 fps
Rifling .... 6 grooves, right-hand twist
Weight unloaded (approx.) .... 7.5 lbs.

Model L Carbine Specifications

Barrel length .... 12.6 in.
Caliber .... .223 Remington
Cyclic rate (approx.) .... 750 rpm
Length .... 33.8 in.
Length (stock retracted) .... 26.2 in.
Magazine .... 10-, 20-, or 30-round
Muzzle velocity (approx.) .... 2800 fps
Rifling .... 6 grooves, right-hand twist
Weight unloaded (approx.) .... 7.5 lbs.

DAEWOO K1A1 AND K2

South Korea is another country that first manufactured the AR-15 and then went on to produce its own rifles—comprised of a lot of ideas "borrowed" from other designs. The rifles are being made by the Daewoo Company, which also produces automobiles and a wide range of other products.

Like many other modern rifles, the Daewoo rifles are a lot of different ideas put together to form composites: the trigger group, sights, and lower receiver are all AR-15 in origin (as is the gas system on the K1A1); the recoil/gas system of the K2 is similar to that of the AK-47; the cleaning-kit storage compartment in the pistol grip is "borrowed" from the FN LAR; and the

folding stock of the K2 is quite similar to the Galil. As might be expected, the rifle uses the AR-15 magazines, which are becoming the standard magazine for the free world.

The selector is located on the left side of the lower receiver just above the pistol grip; semiauto, full-auto, three-round burst, and safe positions are to be found on the selective-fire versions of the rifles. The magazine release—like the AR-15's—is located in front of the trigger on the right side of the receiver. The reciprocating charging handle is located on the right side of the receiver just above the ejection port.

The K1A1 and K2 are different rifles rather than different versions of the same rifle, though many parts are interchangeable. The K1A1 has a telescoping stock similar to that of the U.S. grease gun with two extended positions to accommodate large and small shooters. Depressing the stock release an extra time after it is fully extended allows the stock to be removed. The K1A1 has a 10-inch barrel with an XM177E2 Commando-style flash suppressor, while the semiauto version has a 17-inch barrel to meet BATF requirements.

The K2 has a conventional folding stock which allows the rifle to be stored in a smaller space. The lockup of the stock is patterned after that of the Galil; it is released by pushing the stock down. While this gives a very tight lockup in the extended position, it also makes the stock awkward to fold back up. Another poor design feature is that the stock, when folded, covers the magazine release.

Both rifles are quickly field-stripped by depressing forward on the release located at the end of the guide rod(s), rotating the receiver halves apart, and removing the recoil springs/guides. This allows the charging handle to be pulled back and out the side of the receiver, similar to the method used on another Armalite rifle, the AR-7, and the bolt/carrier can then be removed.

Both the K1A1 and K2 are lighter than many other assault rifles and are quite competitively priced. Accuracy is not as good as that of the AR-15, however, and the rifle offers little that can't be found with the AR-18 or AR-15. The rifles are simple and robust and have been adopted by the South Korean military. At the time of this writing, Stoeger Industries is importing semiauto versions of both rifles; the semiauto K1A1 is designated the "MAX I" by the company and the K2, the "MAX II."

Daewoo K1A1 Specifications

Barrel length .... 10 in.
Caliber .... .223 Remington
Cyclic rate (approx.) .... 750 rpm
Length .... 33 in.

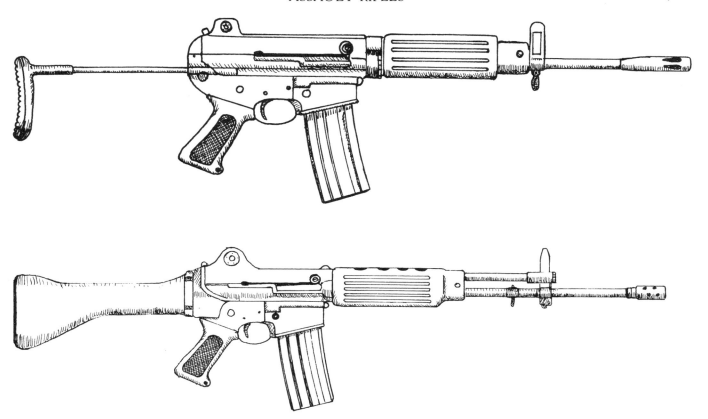

Like many other modern rifles, the Daewoo rifle is a new weapon created from a combination of a lot of ideas. The K1A1 and K2 are different rifles rather than different versions of the same rifle; though many parts are interchangeable, they are not consistently so. Top: the MAX I/K1A1; bottom: the MAX II/K2.

Length (stock folded) . . . . 26 in.
Magazine (standard) 30-round
Muzzle velocity (approx.) . . . . 3050 fps
Rifling . . . . . 6 grooves, 1-in-12 in., right-hand twist
Weight unloaded (approx.) . . . . 6.4 lbs.

Daewoo K2 Specifications

Barrel length . . . . 18.3 in.
Caliber . . . . .223 Remington
Cyclic rate (approx.) . . . . 700 rpm
Length . . . . 38.4 in.
Length (stock folded) . . . . 28.7 in.
Magazine (standard) 30-round
Muzzle velocity (approx.) . . . . 3200 fps
Rifling . . . . . 6 grooves, 1-in-12 in., right-hand twist
Weight unloaded (approx.) . . . . 7.5 lbs.

THE ENFIELD IW

Following World War II, the British started work on a rifle that would use a "reduced" caliber and charge since studies indicated that the .303 rifle cartridge was too powerful for normal combat ranges and the bolt-action rifles used by the British had become obsolete. The EM2 (7mm Number 9, Mark 1) rifle, the forebear of the Individual Weapon (IW), was thus created in the late 1940s.

7mm Number 9, Mark 1 (EM2)

The EM2 had a bullpup design and was chambered for a short-brass, .280-caliber round. The rifle was selective fire and is said to have functioned very reliably. The sight was a small scope mounted in a carrying handle. All in all, this rifle was about three decades ahead of its time.

Why wasn't it accepted? A number of reasons. The political sentiment in England was against spending money on armaments, especially a rifle that would make obsolete the large stocks of ammunition on hand following World War II. The United States was trying to get its 7.62mm round accepted by the NATO forces. Efforts were made to revive the rifle, but the acceptance of the 7.62mm NATO and then the 5.56mm NATO rounds

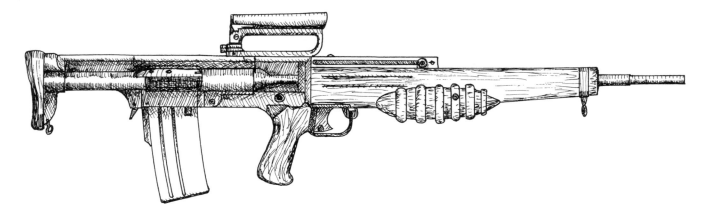

The EM2 rifle was created in the late 1940s. All in all, this rifle's forward-looking design was about three decades ahead of its time.

sealed the EM2's fate. Nevertheless, the basic design of the EM2 has risen like a phoenix in the form of the Enfield IW.

EM2 Specifications

Barrel length . . . . 24.5 in.
Caliber 280/7mm
Length . . . . 35 in.
Magazine (standard) 20-round
Muzzle velocity (approx.) . . . . 2530 fps
Rifling . . . . 4 grooves, right-hand twist
Weight unloaded (approx.) . . . . 7.6 lbs.

Individual Weapon

Following the acceptance of the 7.62mm NATO round, Britain adopted the FN LAR as its infantry weapon. This rifle became the L1A1 and remained in service for over 25 years. A number of minor changes were made to the FN LAR design, though the weapon remains nearly identical to other FN LAR variations. One major change was made in the dimensions of the rifle; they were changed to "Imperial Measurements" to accommodate manufacturing the rifle at the Royal Small Arms Factory in Middlesex. Thus, though the rifle is nearly identical to its metric counterparts, the parts are not always interchangeable.

The British continued experimenting with a bullpup design, probably a variation of the EM2, following their acceptance of the L1A1. They also worked on developing a smaller, high-velocity caliber to use in it.

The outgrowth of this research was the IW and the LSW (Light Support Weapon), which were originally designated the XL64 and XL65, respectively. Almost 80 percent of the weapons' parts are interchangeable, with

the IW designed to replace the submachine gun, rifle, and grenade launcher and the LSW taking on the LMG role. The major differences between the two are barrel size, magazine capacity (though magazines are interchangeable), and the use of a bipod on the LSW. Originally there were left-handed models of the two weapons, but it was decided that it was easier to train lefties to shoot as right-handers than to face the supply complications of fielding four different rifles rather than two.

The original round for the rifles was 4.85mm in diameter and slightly longer than the 5.56mm NATO cartridge. This round and the rifle were submitted for testing during the 1977 to 1979 NATO ammunition trials. By the early 1980s, NATO decided to use the SS109 as the standard round; it has been designated the 5.56mm NATO.

Rather than scrap all their work on the IW and LSW, the British decided to rechamber and modify their experimental bullpups for the new NATO standard and to use the M16 magazine so that their rifles could swap magazines with those of the United States. The model designation was changed to the XL70E3 series. Currently, there are also tentative plans to produce a semiauto version of the rifle for the civilian/police market; this will probably be marketed in the United States by Sage International.

The IW makes use of steel stampings and plastic furniture. While stampings are heavier than aluminum castings, one of the prime considerations for the British design is that it be easy to mass-produce. The weapon's weight does make it more controllable in automatic fire and makes the recoil of the 5.56mm round nearly insignificant.

The IW has been designed to use an optical sighting

system known as the SUIT (Sight Unit Infantry Trilux) on early units and, in a modified version, as the SUSAT (Sight Unit Small Arms Trilux). All combat units will have this scope mounted on their weapons, while rear units and support personnel will use weapons with metal sights (during time of war, the scope units might be quickly dispensed with for economic reasons). On the off chance that the tough SUSAT might become damaged, a flip-up metal sight is located on the top of the handguard, and the emergency rear sight is stored in the pistol grip. The scope itself is four power and adjustable for minor differences in individual eyesight. Leaving nothing to chance, the scope tube has been designed with battle sights on its top, consisting of a blade at the front and a notch at the rear. The SUSAT is mounted on a bracket which is used to make windage and elevation adjustments. The bracket and scope are mounted on a dovetail welded to the top of the rifle's receiver. The bracket/scope assembly is held in place with two wing nuts and a detent.

The charging handle is located on the right side of the receiver, which makes it a little awkward to use. This position, coupled with the right-side ejection port, would make the rifle dangerous if fired left-handed. The magazine release is located just behind the magazine well on early IW models; the release is currently on the left side of the receiver above the magazine.

The safety is on the left side just above the pistol grip with its upward position, "S," being safe and the lower "F" being the fire position. This is not a safety/selector, however. The selector switch is located in a rather unhandy position to the rear of the lower left side of the receiver/stock. Semiauto is "S," and "A" is automatic on the selective-fire models; "S" is not the safe position!

The gas system on the IW can be adjusted for normal loads, shut off for ballistic cartridges, or increased for dirty conditions or low-powered or defective ammunition. The gas system is similar to that of the AR-18, and the flash suppressor is a birdcage style. Early models had open rings on the top rear of the stock and at the front folding sight for attachment of a sling for an assault carry; current models have the sling mounts on the side of the stock and handguard.

The weapon also has a knife bayonet which incorporates wire cutters, whetstone, saw (in the sheath), bottle opener, and a modified serrated blade. The handle is hollow and offset and fits over the muzzle of the rifle.

The IW is internally very similar to the AR-18 and takedown for the two rifles is nearly identical. To field-strip the IW:

1. Remove the magazine and cycle the action to clear the chamber.

2. Remove the scope (if necessary) by loosening the wing nuts, lifting up the spring latch detent under the scope, and sliding it off.

3. Pull the captive pin at the rear of the cheek rest to the left to its first release position.

4. Pull the lower receiver captive pin behind the pistol grip out of its release position.

5. Rotate the trigger group out and remove it.

6. Hold the recoil spring assembly in the receiver and pull the captive pin at the rear of the cheek rest to the left and to its second release position.

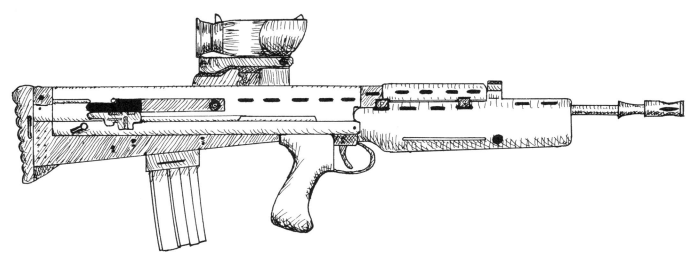

Though the Enfield IW doesn't break any new technological ground, it appears to be very reliable and tough and will see a lot of use before it is replaced by another family of weapons.

7. Remove the recoil rod assembly.

8. Slide the bolt carrier as far as it will go to the rear of the receiver and pull out the charging handle.

9. Slide out the bolt carrier.

10. To disassemble the bolt carrier, remove the bolt firing-pin retaining pin and slide out the firing pin and bolt cam. This will free the bolt for removal from the carrier.

11. Access to the gas system can be gained by removing the handguard.

Reassembly is basically the reverse of the above procedure.

The EM2 was a forward-looking rifle that led to the development of the IW. Yet, by the time this rifle was finally fielded, it was "just another bullpup." Though the IW and LSW don't break any new technological ground, they appear to be very reliable and tough weapons, and both will probably see a lot of use before being replaced.

IW XL64 Specifications

Barrel length . . . . 20.4 in.
Caliber . . . . 4.85mm NATO
Length . . . . 30.3 in.
Magazine (standard) 20-round
Muzzle velocity (approx.) . . . . 2950 fps
Rifling . . . . . . 4 grooves, 1-in-5 in., right-hand twist
Weight unloaded (approx.) . . . . 8.5 lbs.

IW XL70 Specifications

Barrel length . . . . 20.4 in.
Caliber . . . . 5.56mm NATO
Cyclic rate (approx.) . . . . 750 rpm
Length . . . . 33 in.
Magazine (standard) . . . . 20-, or 30-round
Muzzle velocity (approx.) . . . . 2750 fps
Rifling . . . . . . 4 grooves, 1-in-9 in., right-hand twist
Weight unloaded (approx.) . . . . 10 lbs.

LSW (5.56mm NATO) Specifications

Barrel length . . . . 25.4 in.
Caliber . . . . 5.56mm NATO
Cyclic rate (approx.) . . . . 750 rpm
Length . . . . 35.4 in.
Magazine (standard) 30-round
Muzzle velocity (approx.) . . . . 2880 fps
Rifling . . . . . . 4 grooves, 1-in-9 in., right-hand twist
Weight unloaded (approx.) . . . . 11.9 lbs.

FAMAS

The Fusil Automatique MAS, or FAMAS, was designed by the French Arsenal at Saint Etienne, which is part of the industrial combine GIAT, and went into production in 1975. Those involved in designing the rifle are also said to have worked on the HK-33; the influence of the Heckler & Koch designs can be seen in the internal workings of the FAMAS, especially the locking system.

Because specifications called for the power of the 5.56mm round coupled with the handiness of a submachine gun, it was essential that the bullpup design be used. The locking system is a delayed blow-back; a delay lever locks the bolt against the receiver walls until the pressure drops to safe levels, and the bolt then travels rearward, extracting the empty cartridge and cycling the action. Like the Heckler & Koch weapons, the FAMAS has a fluted chamber so that the round is extracted while it floats on a layer of hot gas. The system makes for greater reliability with a wide range of ammunition and also does away with the fouling a gas mechanism can create.

One problem of the delay lever lockup is that the cyclic rate is very high. Therefore, a three-round burst mechanism is included; the shooter has the option of using semiauto, full-automatic, or three-round burst fire.

The carrying handle contains the front and rear sights and the charging lever. The plastic cheekpiece fits over one of two ejection ports and is reversible, as is the bolt; the rifle can be changed from left- to right-handed use in a manner of minutes.

The barrel has a more or less standard flash suppressor which, coupled with rings on the barrel, allows the rifle to fire grenades. Since the current French military trend seems to be toward grenades with bullet traps, which can be fired with rounds, it would appear that the time when every rifle-armed infantryman is a grenadier is fast approaching.

The rifle also has a bayonet and sling, specifically designed for it, and an integral bipod folds up along the upper receiver just below the carrying handle.

To field-strip the weapon:

1. Remove the magazine and cycle the action. Check to be sure the weapon is empty.

2. Pull out the pins that hold the plastic stock and carrying handle assembly in place.

3. Remove the stock and carrying handle (which must be pulled forward and up).

4. Pull out the hammer-assembly pin, and remove the assembly and lower receiver from the upper receiver.

5. Pull out the bolt carrier and disassemble it.

A semiauto version of the rifle chambered in .222 Remington is made for civilian use in France (different

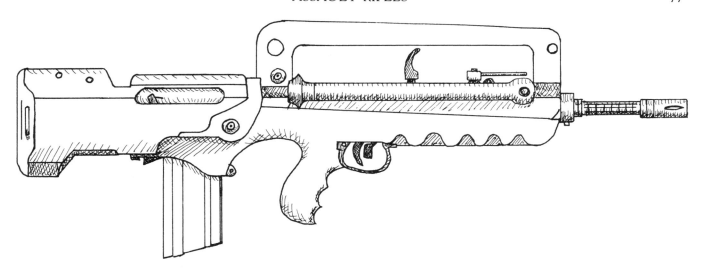

The Fusil Automatique MAS—or FAMAS—was designed to conform to French specifications for a new rifle the size of a submachine gun which fired the 5.56mm.

chambering is required by French law), an export version is made without grenade-firing "fins" on it, and a semiauto version might be manufactured for the U.S. civilian market. In addition to these, a look-alike training air rifle is also manufactured.

All in all, the French seem to have developed a compact and lightweight rifle that can be adapted to left-handed shooters without special bolts or other equipment (there is a little risk involved in this design since the bolt can be put in with the extractor facing the wrong way).

Currently there are no other models or calibers of the rifle. The next logical step would seem to be to create a systems weapon or to adapt the FAMAS to perform duties other than its intended rifle/submachine gun role. At the time of this writing, a semiauto model is being developed for the police and civilian market.

FAMAS Specifications

Barrel length . . . . 19.2 in.
Caliber . . . . .223 (or .222) Remington
Cyclic rate (approx.) . . . . 950 rpm
Length . . . . 29.8 in.
Magazine (standard) 25-round
Muzzle velocity (approx.) . . . . 3150 fps
Rifling . . . . . 4 grooves, 1-in-12 in., right-hand twist
Weight unloaded (approx.) . . . . 7.5 lbs.

FG42

The German FG42 (*Fallschirmjager Gewehr*, "Paratrooper Rifle") ran into the same problems later

encountered by the FN LAR and the M14. It was an attempt to create a lightweight, selective-fire weapon chambering full-power rifle ammunition. Like the FN LAR and M14, the results created a good rifle, although the FG isn't as well balanced, thanks to its side-mounted magazine. But the weapon failed to replace the machine gun because of heat buildup and, most importantly, excessive recoil.

Early FG42s had a stamped steel stock, while later ones had a wooden stock and pistol grip. Only 5,000 to 7,000 of the rifles were made. The United States tested several of the rifles in other chamberings and later incorporated elements of the FG42's trigger mechanism in the T44 machine gun. The T44 later led to the development of the M60 machine gun, which also incorporated the belt feed of another German weapon, the MG42. The FG42 also greatly influenced the design of the experimental LMR which was developed by TRW as a possible replacement for the M16.

FG42 Specifications

Barrel length . . . . 20 in.
Caliber . . . . 7.92mm Mauser
Length . . . . 37 in.
Magazine (standard) 20-round
Muzzle velocity (approx.) . . . . 2500 fps
Rifling . . . . 4 grooves, right-hand twist
Weight unloaded (approx.) . . . . 9.9 lbs.

FN FAL, OR FN LAR

The *Fabrique Nationale d'Armes de Guerre* (National

Factory for Arms of War) in Belgium has been famous for nearly a century as a manufacturer of fine firearms. Their FAL (*Fusil Automatique Leger* or, in English, LAR—Light Automatic Rifle) dates back to the Model 49 (also known as the Saive, SAFN, or ABL). This rifle was designed by Dieudonne J. Saive during World War II while Belgium was occupied by Germany. Following the war, Fabrique Nationale offered the rifle in three versions, a selective-fire rifle, an automatic-only weapon, and a sniper rifle. It sold well in the post-World War II market in a wide variety of calibers, including .30-06, 7×57mm, and 7.92mm.

Money from Model 49 sales was channeled into research and development of the LAR, which was marketed in 1950 in .308 Winchester (experimental versions have been made in other calibers, including the German 7.92mm short and the British .280 experimental round). The rifle had a number of features that made it ahead of its time, including a pistol grip, 20-round magazine, and selective fire. Early rifles differed very little from modern versions except that wood furniture was often used and the carrying handle was missing.

A heavy-barreled version of the rifle is nearly identical to the standard model but has a bipod and heavier barrel. Though designed to fill the SAW role, these rifles are generally hard to control in automatic fire due to their light weight and the power of the .308 NATO round. Some of the HB versions have trouble sustaining automatic fire as well, with failure to feed taking place after 2- or 3-round bursts. Because of these problems, many countries order LARs which are capable of semiauto fire only.

A number of nations have used the FN LAR, including Argentina, Austria, Belgium, Canada, Chile, Ecuador, England, India, Ireland, Israel, Libya, the Netherlands, and South Africa. A large number of variations of the LAR exist; the most common differences being among the handguards (both in shape and materials, which include wood, metal, and plastic), pistol grips, flash suppressors (or lack thereof), grenade-launching rings, barrel lengths, and various types of folding and fixed stocks. The standard FN bipod is designed to fit into grooves on the handguard when folded. Like many other assault rifles with a separate stock and handguard, the point of impact may change several inches when a bipod is used. LAR bayonets have a wide spike blade and tubular handles that fit over the flash suppressor.

The charging handle is on the left side of the receiver, as is the selector, which is conveniently located above the pistol grip. A downward pull brings it from "safe" to "fire." Travel is long and somewhat awkward; this is said to be the case so that the user can tell the selector setting in the dark. The bolt carrier locks open after the last shot on most LARs. To reload, the user places a full magazine in the well, then either pulls down the release lever on the bottom left side of the receiver or retracts the charging handle. The magazine release is located opposite the bolt release on the right side of the receiver behind the magazine well.

The LAR's gas regulator is located just ahead of the gas tube and can be adjusted with a screwdriver. It is possible to set the regulator so that gas will not operate the bolt for grenade launching with ballistic cartridges or to create a single-shot training or sniping rifle. With judicious use, the regulator will enable the shooter—and especially the handloader—to fire a wide range of ammunition. But if too low a setting is used with powerful ammunition, it could damage the rifle. The reverse situation could cause the rifle to fail to cycle.

Most LARs have a carrying handle mounted at the barrel/receiver balancing point. This handle can be folded down and out of the way when not in use. The chamber and barrel are chrome-lined, like most modern combat rifles.

The front sight is adjustable for elevation and the rear sight for windage. The rear sight is also adjustable in the field for elevation by sliding the aperture along a ramp with detents for 200 to 600 meters. Fabrique Nationale also markets a four-power scope and mount for the LAR rifles.

Currently in the United States, Springfield Armory (a privately owned firm) is importing FN LAR parts and assembling them on their own receivers. These rifles are offered in several styles under the trade name of SAR-48. While most are semiauto, Springfield also offers a selective-fire version to qualified buyers. The SAR-48, made from all new parts, offers a nice savings over assembled imported rifles. The large number of accessories and spare parts available are frosting on the cake.

FAL, SAR-48, FN LAR Specifications

Barrel length	21 in.
Caliber	7.62mm NATO
Cyclic rate (approx.)	675 rpm
Length	43.5 in.
Magazine (standard)	20-round
Muzzle velocity (approx.)	2800 fps
Rifling	4 grooves, 1-in-12 in., right-hand twist
Weight unloaded (approx.)	9.4 lbs.

FN LARs with folding stocks are generally known as PARA models. There are currently two models in pro-

Springfield Armory's FN LAR rifles are being offered in several styles under the trade name SAR-48. The FN LAR is considered by many to be the best .30 caliber rifle ever made. Photo courtesy of Springfield Armory.

duction: the 50.63 and the 50.64. The 50.63 has a fixed battle sight set at 300 meters, a folding charging handle, no bolt stop, no carrying handle, and a shorter flash hider. The 50.63 also enjoys slightly lighter weight. The 50.64 is similar to the standard LAR except for the folding stock and a rear flip sight with positions for 150 and 250 meters.

FN LAR PARA 50.63 Specifications
Barrel length . . . . 18 in.
Caliber . . . . 7.62mm NATO
Cyclic rate (approx.) . . . . 675 rpm
Length . . . . 40 in.
Length (stock folded) . . . . 33.25 in.
Magazine (standard) 20-round
Muzzle velocity (approx.) . . . . 2800 fps
Rifling . . . . . 4 grooves, 1-in-12 in., right-hand twist
Weight unloaded (approx.) . . . . 8.6 lbs.

FN LAR PARA 50.64 Specifications
Barrel length . . . . 21 in.
Caliber . . . . 7.62mm NATO
Cyclic rate (approx.) . . . . 675 rpm

Length . . . . 43 in.
Length (stock folded) . . . . 33.25 in.
Magazine (standard) 20-round
Muzzle velocity (approx.) . . . . 2800 fps
Rifling . . . . . 4 grooves, 1-in-12 in., right-hand twist
Weight unloaded (approx.) . . . . 8.6 lbs.

There are two heavy-barreled models of the FN LAR used as sniper weapons or SAWs; these generally are equipped with a wooden handguard and bipod. The carrying handle is reversed to give better balance with the heavier barrel/bipod arrangement. The HB models are nearly identical internally to the LAR. The 50.41 HB has a synthetic stock, while the 50.42 has a wooden stock with folding shoulder rest and a catch plunger. The sights on the two models are identical to those of the standard LAR. For maximum accuracy, the LAR should be head-spaced to the minimum dimension. The head-space can be reduced by replacing the locking shoulder.

FN LAR HB 50.41 Specifications
Barrel length . . . . 21 in.

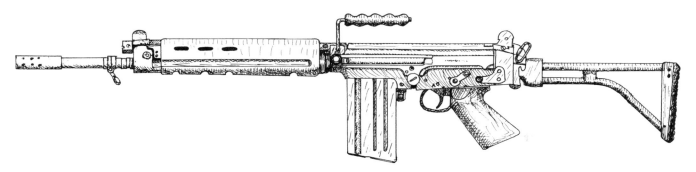

FN LARs with the folding stock are generally known as PARA models. There are currently two models of the PARA rifle in production: the 50.63 (shown) and the 50.64. The 50.63 has a single, fixed battle sight, folding charging handle, no bolt stop or carrying handle, and a shorter flash-hider. The 50.63 also enjoys a slightly lighter weight.

Caliber .... 7.62mm NATO
Cyclic rate (approx.) .... 675 rpm
Length .... 45 in.
Magazine (standard) 20-round
Muzzle velocity (approx.) .... 2800 fps
Rifling ..... 4 grooves, 1-in-12 in., right-hand twist
Weight unloaded (approx.) .... 11.25 lbs.

FN LAR HB 50.42 Specifications
Barrel length .... 21 in.
Caliber .... 7.62mm NATO
Cyclic rate (approx.) .... 675 rpm
Length .... 45 in.
Magazine (standard) 20-round
Muzzle velocity (approx.) .... 2800 fps
Rifling ..... 4 grooves, 1-in-12 in., right-hand twist
Weight unloaded (approx.) .... 13.25 lbs.

Field-stripping procedures for all LAR models are basically the same. The following procedure is used after removing the magazine and cycling the rifle to be sure it is empty:

1. Depress the catch at the left rear of the receiver and pivot the receiver open so that the trigger assembly is exposed.

2. Withdraw the bolt/bolt carrier and gas assembly through the rear of the receiver.

3. Slide off the receiver cover.

4. To disassemble the bolt/bolt carrier, lift up the bolt while pulling it forward and lift it out of the carrier.

5. To free the firing pin, push out the retaining pin. Hold the rear of the firing pin to avoid losing it and its spring.

6. To free the extractor, insert a small tool under it and pull out and upward to release it.

7. The front of the gas plug can be unscrewed and removed. This will allow the piston and spring to be removed so that the inside of the tube can be cleaned. This area should not be lubricated.

8. The handguards do not normally need to be removed. They are held in place with a screw near the front sight.

Reassembly is basically the reverse of the above procedure.

With the trend toward the smaller .223/5.56 NATO round, the LAR rifle probably has passed its peak demand. Nevertheless, it is a good rifle used by many shooters, police marksmen, survivalists, etc. Because many LARs are being placed on the military surplus market, it will probably be in use for a long time.

FN CAL AND FNC

With the introduction of the .223 Remington round, Fabrique Nationale developed a rifle chambered for the new ammunition. Work began in 1963, but the scaled-down LAR rifles proved expensive to manufacture and less reliable than might be hoped, so a new design was created. When the CAL (*Carabine Automatique Legere*—Light Automatic Carbine) was introduced in 1966, although it appeared to be a scaled-down version of the LAR, in fact, many internal parts were quite different.

The CAL has a 3-round burst capability in addition to semiauto and full auto. The four-position selector is located in the same position used by the LAR. The reciprocating charging handle is located on the upper right side of the top receiver above the ejection port. A PARA model was available in addition to the fixed-stock version.

Despite many good features, the rifle was expensive to produce, hard to field-strip, and had a short life under combat conditions. The rifle never enjoyed any large sales and was therefore replaced by the FNC in 1975.

FN CAL Specifications
Barrel length .... 18.5 in.
Caliber .... .223 Remington
Cyclic rate (approx.) .... 850 rpm
Length .... 38.5 in.
Magazine (standard) 20-round
Muzzle velocity (approx.) .... 3200 fps
Rifling .... 6 grooves, right-hand twist
Weight unloaded (approx.) .... 6.5 lbs.

In development for four years, the FNC finally went into production in 1979 after a short period of testing with NATO, during which it was withdrawn by Fabrique Nationale for further improvement. This early model, the FNC 76, differs outwardly from the current models principally in its magazine, which was straight rather than curved, and handguard/gas piston cover, which has round ventilation holes rather than slots. The new model was introduced in 1980 and designated the FNC 80.

Because of European fears that the .223 with a 1-in-12 twist is "inhumane," the rifle's development has been coupled with work on the SS109 round, also designed by Fabrique Nationale, which has been accepted as the new 5.56mm NATO round. In order to maintain accuracy with the SS109, the FNC has a fast 1-in-7 twist. This twist creates a more stable bullet rather than one that tumbles on impact. As noted elsewhere, the effort to develop a more humane round actually appears to

The folding stock FNC PARA has a plastic sleeve on its stock to protect the user's cheek from the metal in cold temperatures. The handguard and butt plate are made of plastic.

have created one that inflicts even larger wounds. In a final irony, the FNC is also offered with a 1-in-12 twist.

The FNC 80 uses the same magazines as the AR-15/M16, and the magazine release is nearly identical. The release button is located on the right side of the receiver, just ahead of and above the trigger guard. Unlike the LAR, the FNC's charging handle is on the right side of the receiver and reciprocates with the bolt carrier. A special spring-loaded cover located at the rear of the charging handle slot closes following each cycling of the action so that dirt cannot easily enter.

The upper receiver is stamped from sheet metal. The bolt locks into a barrel extension so that the FNC can be light without sacrificing safety. The bolt carrier/gas system/recoil spring system is very similar to that of the AK-47.

The selector is located on the left side of the receiver just above the pistol grip. It has four positions: "S" (safe), "1" (semiauto), "3" (3-round burst), and "A" (full automatic). A gas regulator similar to that of the LAR allows the shooter to compensate somewhat for underpowered rounds or dirty operating conditions.

The rear sight is the flip type with apertures for 0 to 250 and 250 to 400 meters. Windage is adjusted via a tool at the rear sight, while elevation is adjusted with the front sight. A special scope is available whose mount locks into lugs on the top of the receiver. The military models of the FNC have a flip-up grenade sight behind the front sight.

Two styles of stock are available. With the folding stock, the FNC gains the PARA designation. The standard model has a plastic stock with classic LAR lines, complete with the hump near the butt end. Unfortunately, the PARA stock covers the magazine release when folded. While this is not much of a problem, it can be a bit unhandy at times. The FNC PARA stock has a sling stud on its top near the butt end rather than a swivel next to the receiver as does the LAR; coupled

with the rotating front swivel, this makes it very practical to use the assault carry with a sling. The top of the folding stock has a plastic sleeve to protect the user's cheek in cold temperatures. The handguard and butt plate are made of plastic. Unlike the LAR, the FNC does not have a carrying handle.

Several models of the FNC are available, including short-barreled and semiauto versions. Both the 1-in-7 and 1-in-12 barrels are available with each model. Barrel, chamber, gas port block, and piston are all chromed.

Field-stripping is quite simple. After removing the magazine and cycling the weapon to be sure it is empty, the following procedure should be used:

1. Push the rear push pin from the left to the right. Pivot the receiver halves open.

2. Pull the charging handle to the rear past the channel cover; pull it out to the right.

3. Withdraw the bolt/bolt carrier and recoil spring through the rear of the upper receiver.

4. To disassemble the bolt/bolt carrier, press the rear plate of the action spring and rotate the plate 90 degrees in either direction. This will free the spring and guide rod to be removed to the rear.

5. Rotate the bolt and pull it out the front of the carrier using extreme care not to lose the firing pin and its spring. Further disassembly of the bolt is not recommended in field-stripping.

6. The handguard halves are removed by sliding the front retaining clip forward out of its notch.

7. To remove the gas cylinder, set the gas regulator past its left position so that it is at 90 degrees from the receiver block.

8. Pull the gas cylinder to the rear and lift it up and away from the barrel.

Reassembly is basically the reverse of the above procedure. Military models should be reassembled with the grenade sight in its "up" position. Care should also be taken to line up the locking lugs of the bolt and bolt carrier with the receiver rails.

The FNC is produced with computerized equipment which keeps its cost down and makes it a strong contender in the military market.

At the time of this writing, Argentina is testing a group of 5.56mm NATO rifles based somewhat on a scaled-down LAR system, though the gas system, bolt, and bolt carrier are more similar to the AK-47. Work began on this rifle, the FAA Modelo 81, in 1976. The firearm has the same layout as the LAR but has a sheet-metal stamped receiver and a plastic folding stock with the basic lock mechanism of the LAR PARA rifles.

FN FNC 80 Specifications

Barrel length . . . . 17.7 in.
Caliber . . . . 5.56mm NATO
Cyclic rate (approx.) . . . . 670 rpm
Length . . . . 39 in.
Magazine (standard) 30-round
Muzzle velocity (approx.) . . . . 2890 fps
Rifling . . . . 6 grooves, 1-in-7 in. (1-in-12 in.),
right-hand twist
Weight unloaded (approx.) . . . . 8.4 lbs.

FN FNC 80 PARA Specifications

Barrel length . . . . 17.7 in.
Caliber . . . . 5.56mm NATO
Cyclic rate (approx.) . . . . 670 rpm
Length . . . . 39 in.
Length (stock folded) . . . . 30 in.
Magazine (standard) 30-round
Muzzle velocity (approx.) . . . . 2890 fps
Rifling . . . . 6 grooves, 1-in-7 in. (1-in-12 in.),
right-hand twist
Weight unloaded (approx.) . . . . 8.4 lbs.

Argentine FAA 81 Specifications

Barrel length . . . . 17.3 in.
Caliber . . . . 5.56mm NATO
Cyclic rate (approx.) . . . . 670 rpm
Length . . . . 38.6 in.
Length (stock folded) . . . . 29.6 in.
Magazine (standard) 30-round
Muzzle velocity (approx.) . . . . 3100 fps
Rifling . . . . 6 grooves, right-hand twist
Weight unloaded (approx.) . . . . 8.6 lbs.

HAC-7

The HAC-7 is often referred to as the "American FN LAR" because its lines are very similar to the European weapon. In fact, the rifle is very different from the FN LAR rifles though it does incorporate a number of its features.

The HAC-7 was created by Robert Holloway who, on the basis of combat experience in Vietnam and Rhodesia, decided that the .308 was a better combat round than the .223. Holloway has built a weapon which takes advantage of modern manufacturing techniques and has a sound design.

The HAC-7 has a milled aluminum receiver manufactured on computer-controlled equipment rather than by expensive handwork. This creates an inexpensive, strong, and light receiver that looks more appealing than the usual stamped steel. The front sight is similar to the AR-15 sight and is adjustable for elevation. The rear sight is also of AR-15 heritage with a two-position aperture adjustable for windage with a bullet tip. A scope base is epoxy-bonded and screwed to the upper receiver of newer models.

The gas system closely resembles that of the AK-47. The front of the tube has a gas regulator which allows the rifle to function with a wide range of ammunition. A separate gas cutoff valve allows the weapon to be used in a "bolt action" mode or with rifle grenades. The bolt has only two locking lugs to reduce friction during cycling.

The charging handle is located on the upper left side of the receiver, high enough to be easily reached by either hand. The magazine release is directly behind the magazine well to the front of the trigger guard. The selector and bolt release are reversible with the selector located just above the pistol grip. Left-handed models of the HAC-7 are available which eject empty brass to the left. The muzzle brake/flash suppressor is also adjustable for left- or right-handed use. Care should be taken to mount the flash suppressor tightly, however, or it can shake loose during sustained fire. The two notches in the end of the flash suppressor aren't for tightening the unit; they are placed there to allow a soldier to place the muzzle against barbed wire and fire the rifle to cut the wire.

Three models are available: the standard rifle, HAC-7; the carbine, HAC-7C; and a heavy bull-barrel/sniper rifle based on the standard rifle. The buyer has the option of selective fire or semiauto only. Other calibers may be offered in the future, including .243, 5.56mm NATO, .358 Winchester, 7mm-08, and possibly even 12-gauge.

Field-stripping the rifle is very simple and similar to that of the AR-15. Unfortunately, the Holloway firearms have been plagued with the usual new rifle bugs, com-

The HAC-7 is often called the American FN LAR because its lines are very similar to those of the European weapon of that name. It is, in fact, very different from the FN LAR rifle, though it does incorporate a number of good features found in the FN LAR (as well as other rifles).

pounded by the use of surplus AR-10 magazines and quality-control problems with the early rifles. The Holloway Company may have some rough times ahead until it establishes its reputation. Overall, however, the HAC-7 is a modern, lightweight, and well-designed rifle which should—with the bugs worked out and better magazines—find a niche in U.S., if not international, markets.

HAC-7 Specifications

Barrel length . . . . 20 in.
Caliber . . . . (see above)
Cyclic rate (approx.) . . . . 675 rpm
Length . . . . 43 in.
Length (stock folded) . . . . 33 in.
Magazine (standard) 20-round
Muzzle velocity (approx.) . . . . 2800 fps
Rifling . . . . . 6 grooves, 1-in-10 in., right-hand twist
Weight unloaded (approx.) . . . . 8.8 lbs.

HAC-7C Specifications

Barrel length . . . . 16 in.
Caliber . . . . (see above)
Cyclic rate (approx.) . . . . 675 rpm

Length . . . . 39 in.
Length (stock folded) . . . . 29 in.
Magazine (standard) 20-round
Muzzle velocity (approx.) . . . . 2800 fps
Rifling . . . . . 6 grooves, 1-in-10 in., right-hand twist
Weight unloaded (approx.) . . . . 8.5 lbs.

HECKLER & KOCH SYSTEMS RIFLES

The Heckler & Koch family of combat rifles has a long and convoluted history. The internal locking system and basic configuration of many of the rifles are derived directly from the Mauser Assault Rifle StG44 designed in Germany during World War II.

At the Mauser Werke, a new model of the StG44 was being developed at the close of World War II. The experimental rifle never saw combat and only one model, designated the StG45, was known to have been assembled. The three engineers involved with designing the rifle, Edmund Heckler, Theodor Koch, and Alexis Seidel, founded a firm in Spain to manufacture precision machinery. The company won the contract to design a battle rifle for the Spanish army, which led to the development of the CETME rifle, whose design was

Germany's Heckler & Koch G3 rifle is very tough and reliable. A number of countries have purchased the rifle for military use. A semiauto version of the G3A4 rifle, created for the civilian and police markets, is sold in the United States as the HK-91.

based in large part on the StG45.

West Germany adopted the CETME, designated the G1. Later, the German military switched to the FN FAL, which became the G2. The FN FAL wasn't satisfactory, and in 1954 the Germans purchased a license to manufacture the CETME in Germany; this modified rifle became the G3.

The G3 proved to be very tough and reliable. A number of countries purchased the rifle for military use and Heckler & Koch developed a weapons system based on it. The major variations in their weapons family are created by different chamberings, barrel lengths, a retractable stock, a bipod, an HK-69 detachable grenade launcher, and a belt-feed system. The main rifles in the .308 Winchester/7.62mm NATO group are the G3A3 selective-fire rifle, G3A4 selective-fire rifle with telescoping stock, G3K short-barreled automatic rifle with telescoping stock, G3SG/1 or PSG/1 sniper rifles, H&K11 LMG, and the belt-fed HK-21A1 Machine Gun. In addition to bipods, a column mount for vehicles and a tripod are available for the machine guns. A semiauto version of the G3A4 rifle was also created for the civilian/police market; in the United States, this is sold as the HK-91 and, with a retractable stock, as the HK-91A3.

Due to the success of the G3 family as well as an aggressive effort to capture more of the world market, a smaller family based around the Soviet 7.62×39mm round was also created as were others for 9mm Luger and .223 Remington. The 7.62×39mm family includes two selective-fire rifles, the HK-32A2 and HK-32KA3 (the latter having a retractable stock), a short-barreled HK-32KA1 rifle with retractable stock, the HK-12 LMG, and a belt-fed HK-21A1 machine gun. No sniper rifle

is available with this group, and the grenade launcher is also generally omitted. The .223 family has the largest selection of rifles: the HK-33A2 standard rifle; the HK-33A3 retractable stock rifle; the HK-33K short-barrel, retractable stock rifle; two versions of the HK-53 with an extra short barrel and shortened handguard and charging lever (one has no stock and is designed as a port-firing rifle); with a retractable stock, it can be used as a submachine gun; the HK-21A1 machine gun (a lightweight version is designated the HK-23); the HK-13 LMG; and the HK-33SG1 sniper rifle. The HK-69 grenade launcher can be mounted on all the rifles except the HK-53. A semiauto version, the HK-93, is also available with a regular or retractable stock (HK-93A3).

With the adoption of the SS-109 round by NATO, the H&K family will undergo some modification including a cosmetic change to the handguard, changing the magazine well/latch to accept the AR-15/M16 magazine, and modifying barrels to a faster 1-in-7 twist. Though the new rifles will be nearly identical to the old models, the designation of the basic rifle will be changed from HK-33 to HK-41.

Heckler & Koch's 9mm submachine gun uses the same roller locking system as the other rifles which allows the submachine guns to fire from a closed bolt and gives greater accuracy. Although "cook off" can be a problem with closed bolts in automatic fire, this is not too great a problem in the close-range fighting in which a submachine gun is normally used. The submachine gun was introduced in 1966 in a variety of models thanks to its ability to use stocks designed for the HK-93 rifle, as well as a special foregrip and a very good sound suppressor. The basic submachine gun is the MP5A2. The addition of the suppressor creates the MP5SD2 (standard stock), MP5SD3 (retractable stock), or MP5SD1 (stockless). The short-barreled, nonsuppressed, stockless version with a foregrip is the MP5K and it's small enough to be easily concealed in a briefcase or under a heavy jacket. A new version of the MP5A2 and A3, designated the HK-54, is currently used by some West German police units. A special adapter mount with a vision port is also marketed by Heckler & Koch to adapt the MP5 for use in an APC.

There is also a 16-inch barrel semiauto carbine for civilian use, designated the HK-94. Like the semiauto versions of other Heckler & Koch firearms, the HK-94's magazine release is on the right side of the receiver. The barrel on the HK-94 is longer to conform to U.S. regulations for stocked firearms. In an effort to spice up the longer barrel, a ventilated barrel shroud with an "assault grip" is also offered. The shroud goes on and off the barrel in a few seconds; it is held in place by tightening the grip. Most accessories available for the MP5 are interchangeable with the HK-94, including stocks, magazines, scope mounts, etc. The rear sights of the MP5 submachine gun do not change elevation; the different settings give the user a choice of aperture sizes. Original parts for the MP5 are available in the United States from Pars International; standard parts are available from the H&K plant in the United States.

Each of these four groups of weapons have interchangeable stocks (except between the .308 versions and the other calibers) and can use many of the same accessories. The controls and positions of the selector,

charging lever, etc., are nearly identical from one weapon to the next. All of this creates a workable "weapons system" in a wide array of calibers, allowing a short training period to familiarize shooters with all types of weapons and simplifying repair, maintenance, and stocking since many of the internal parts are interchangeable. Since accessories also are generally interchangeable, it is possible to customize weapons for special use very easily. All in all, Heckler & Koch offers an extremely flexible off-the-shelf weapons system.

A wide array of accessories is available for the Heckler & Koch weapons. The Heckler & Koch sling allows the rifle to be carried at port arms without using either hand to hold it; to shoulder the rifle, it need only be pulled into position. The sling takes up or gives out the slack. It is also possible to sling the rifle around to the wearer's back from the port arms or shouldered position. The sling can be used as a carrying "handle" or to carry the rifle over one shoulder. One has to wonder why this simple but flexible sling arrangement isn't found on combat rifles other than those of Heckler & Koch.

The trigger group of Heckler & Koch rifles is easily removed and replaced and, in effect, can be treated as an accessory. This makes it possible to modify rifles for semiauto-fire-only or add a three-round burst capability to automatic weapons.

Cleaning kits, ejection port buffers, .22 LR adapters for practice and training, bipods, scope mounts, bayonet mounts, carrying handles, scopes, magazine loading tools, etc., are all available from Heckler & Koch as are

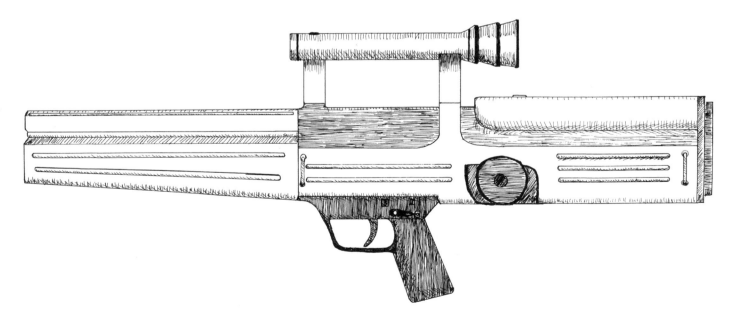

The H&K G11 rifle is a radical departure from current arms technology. Outwardly, the rifle has a bullpup appearance; inwardly, it's vastly different from other firearms, since it uses a caseless round.

the foregrip or stockless butt mount. This company probably has the largest accessory catalog in the military marketplace. The only criticism of the Heckler & Koch accessories is the high prices. They are well-made, however, and consistently effective.

Heckler & Koch rifles have a good reputation for reliability and seem to have minimal parts breakage. They are also simpler than many other rifles since the roller locking system does away with the gas tube, gas pistons, etc. The locking system also allows a wide range of ammunition to be used with the rifle without failure to cycle. Heckler & Koch weapons have the reputation of being able to digest anything.

Besides the roller system, the chamber of the rifles is fluted. This causes the brass to float on a gas jet and makes for positive extraction. For reloaders, the Heckler & Koch rifles don't damage the brass; the markings left by the fluting are cosmetic only. The rifles do hurl the empty brass some distance, however, so reloaders would do well to purchase Heckler & Koch's ejection port buffer.

One weakness of the Heckler & Koch rifles is their human engineering. The selector lever on the left side of the receiver is a little awkward to reach, although it does have an indicator on its right side which shows its setting, a nice plus, and the magazine release on the semiauto versions (HK-91, HK-93, HK-94) is impossible to reach without removing the hand from the pistol grip. The bolt can be tricky to put back together, especially if it is locked while disassembled. Trigger pull is a little heavy for most, usually around eight pounds and sometimes as high as 10 to 12 pounds. Three other problems are the charging handle, which is hard to operate when the action is locked on an empty chamber; the lack of a bolt hold-open device; and a hump in the stock that seems to be right at nose level for tall, large-nosed shooters like the author.

It should be stressed, however, that these problems are quite minor, and most shooters are willing to put up with them from a strong, reliable, reasonably priced rifle. Aftermarket products can alleviate most of the problems.

The trigger is designed to meet NATO requirements. It has a heavy pull for stressful combat conditions when it is too easy to twitch off a shot accidentally with a light trigger pull. Under some conditions, though, it would be useful to have a lighter trigger pull, especially if the rifle is used with a scope. The mechanism defies normal gunsmith "tuning" since cutting of springs or grinding the sear will render these rifles unsafe. One answer to the problem is the Williams modification and/or set trigger.

The Williams modification consists of hand-fitting the trigger group parts without altering the springs or sear and eliminating the over-travel of the trigger with an internal trigger stop. This work is called the "Grade I" treatment and will lower the pull to five or six pounds. Grade II is the Grade I work plus a stainless-steel trigger that gives the user better leverage. Grade III consists of the previous grades' work plus a set trigger mode which is adjusted with a new selector notch that is added to the safety. The trigger can be used with its regular pull or set to a two-pound pull with the selector lever. The work is done by Williams Trigger Specialties, Inc.; prices are $65 for Grade I, $100 for Grade II, and $150 for Grade III.

The magazine latch problem on semiauto rifles (HK-91, HK-93, HK-94 and their variants) can be overcome with the Tac-Latch III, a machined steel lever that can be user-installed with a drift punch and a small hammer. The Tac-Latch III lever sits behind the magazine and allows the user to hold the magazine and toggle the lever to the right to release it.

Length of pull with the stock can be adjusted with an adjustable stock extension available from E & L Manufacturing. The butt plate adds from half an inch to one-and-a-half inches to the pull and enables the shooter to use the hollow stock as a storage compartment.

The lack of a bolt hold-open device can be partially overcome with the addition of a bolt catch to the magazine follower. This will hold the bolt open after the last shot. The shooter can then latch the bolt open with the charging lever, remove and replace the empty magazine, then release the bolt to chamber a round. Most shooters find this much quicker and easier than having to fight the charging lever after it has closed on an empty chamber. The devices are available for $3.50 each from A.R.M.S.

Another solution is to load a tracer round in the magazine in the next-to-last position. When the tracer is fired, the shooter knows that it's time to switch magazines.

The rear sight on the various rifles (but not the submachine guns) is an offset drum that allows the shooter to use an open battle sight or select apertures for 200, 300, or 400 meters. The sighting-in and elevation adjustment is done with a special sight-adjustment tool after loosening the lock screw. To use a scope with the Heckler & Koch rifles, there are several options. The easiest is to purchase the Heckler & Koch scope and mount designed for the rifle, but this is also rather expensive. Another route is to purchase the Heckler & Koch scope claw mount and add an A.R.M.S. adapter bracket. This universal bracket is machined from steel and allows the shooter to mount any scope with Weaver rings as well as NATO standard scopes and night-vision equipment.

Field-stripping of the Hecker & Koch rifles and carbines is nearly identical for all models and quite easy:

1. Remove the magazine and set the selector to the "safe" position. Check to be sure the chamber is empty and then allow the action to slam shut.

2. Remove the stock pins and place them in the storage rivets in the fixed stock or replace them in the stock after removing it.

3. Slide the stock and its plate off the receiver.

4. Remove the grip/trigger group by pushing them downward.

5. Pull back the charging handle to remove the bolt carrier. The bolt head can be removed by rotating it 90 degrees to the right.

6. If the locking piece is rotated half a turn, the firing pin, firing-pin spring, and locking piece can all be removed. This will allow most of the major moving parts to be cleaned and lubricated.

Reassembly is basically the reverse of this procedure. If the bolt rollers are locked in their "out" position, you'll discover it is impossible to reassemble the rifle. After assembling the bolt head, move it forward away from the carrier slightly until the rollers unlock. This will allow the carrier to slip into the receiver. Another sticky spot is getting the bolt head into the carrier if you've stripped the carrier that far. Lifting the "beak" of the check lever so that it will slip into the track on the bolt is the secret.

The Heckler & Koch rifles have become popular enough for customized rifles to appear in the United States. One interesting modification is done by Fleming Firearms. The work consists of cutting the barrel of a standard .308 Heckler & Koch rifle to a little under nine inches. The front sight is moved back, the charging lever shortened, the barrel rethreaded for a flash suppressor, and a short MP handguard is placed on the rifle. While the muzzle flash with this ultra-compact .308 rifle is excessive, the recoil is greatly reduced. Such a weapon has limited usefulness but allows the use of .308 ammunition in a "submachine gun." Fleming Firearms has dubbed the rifle the "Model 51." Fleming also converts semiauto Heckler & Koch firearms to selective fire and will do custom work on other models of Heckler & Koch firearms, including the HK-93 and HK-94.

Another alteration that was an attempt to create a bullpup configuration was the S*A*T*S kit from Tomark Industries. This consisted of a handguard and trigger group which simply replaced those of the standard rifle. Though this quickly created a bullpup, it was awkward and lacked a sighting system, since the rear sight was too far back for normal use while the charging handle's position made it hard to mount a scope. The user ended up with a powerful cartridge suitable for long-range shooting coupled with a weapon capable of only short-range accuracy. Additionally, the magazine was too large to hold like a pistol grip. With a price tag of $234, the S*A*T*S system was too limited to gain much acceptance.

A number of other aftermarket accessories are available for the Heckler & Koch rifles. Some of the better ones are the Choate Machine and Tool folding stock, Defense Moulding Enterprises' plastic magazines, and the Cherokee cheek pad if you use a scope.

G3 (HK-91) Specifications

Barrel length . . . . 17.7 in.
Caliber . . . . .308 Winchester (7.62mm NATO)
Cyclic rate (approx.) . . . . 550 rpm
Length . . . . 40.2 in.
Length (stock retracted, A3 version) . . . . . . 31.9 in.
Magazine (standard) 20-round
Muzzle velocity (approx.) . . . . 2620 fps
Rifling . . . . . 4 grooves, 1-in-12 in., right-hand twist
Weight unloaded (approx.) . . . . 10.3 lbs.

HK-33A2 (HK-93) Specifications

Barrel length . . . . 15.4 in.
Caliber . . . . .223 Remington
Cyclic rate (approx.) . . . . 600 rpm
Length . . . . 36.1 in.
Length (stock retracted, A3 version) . . . . . . 28.7 in.
Magazine (standard) 30-round
Muzzle velocity (approx.) . . . . 3180 fps
Rifling . . . . . 6 grooves, 1-in-12 in., right-hand twist
Weight unloaded (approx.) . . . . 7.8 lbs.

HK-41 Specifications

Barrel length . . . . 18.9 in.
Caliber . . . . 5.56mm NATO
Cyclic rate (approx.) . . . . 850 rpm
Length . . . . 39.3 in.
Length (stock retracted, A3 version) . . . . 31 in.
Magazine (standard, M16) 30-round
Muzzle velocity (approx.) . . . . 3250 fps
Rifling . . . . . . 6 grooves, 1-in-7 in., right-hand twist
Weight unloaded (approx.) . . . . 7.9 lbs.

HK-53 Specifications

Barrel length . . . . 8.9 in.

Caliber .... 5.56mm NATO
Cyclic rate (approx.) .... 600 rpm
Length .... 30.1 in.
Length (stock retracted, A3 version) .... 22 in.
Magazine (standard, M16) 40-round
Muzzle velocity (approx.) .... 2460 fps
Rifling ..... 4 grooves, 1-in-12 in., right-hand twist
Weight unloaded (approx.) .... 7.4 lbs.

HK MP5A2(A3)/HK-54 Specifications
Barrel length .... 8.9 in.
Caliber .... 9mm Luger
Cyclic rate (approx.) .... 650 rpm
Length .... 26.5 in.
Length (stock retracted, A3 version) ...... 19.3 in.
Magazine (standard) .... 15- or 30-round
Muzzle velocity (approx.) .... 1312 fps
Rifling .... 6 grooves, right-hand twist
Weight unloaded (approx.) .... 5.5 lbs.

HK MP5K Specifications
Barrel length .... 4.5 in.
Caliber .... 9mm Luger
Cyclic rate (approx.) .... 840 rpm
Length .... 12.8 in.
Magazine (standard) .... 15- or 30-round
Muzzle velocity (approx.) .... 1312 fps
Rifling .... 6 grooves, right-hand twist
Weight unloaded (approx.) .... 4.4 lbs.

Heckler & Koch is currently engaged in a number of experimental projects which might affect furture small-arms development. One of these projects is the HK-36 assault rifle. The HK-36 is chambered for the 4.6mm Loffelspitz (spoon-point) round. The round would conform to the conventions of war which require FMJ bullets while greatly increasing the round's wounding potential. The bullet has an asymetrical ogive with one side scooped out like the inside of a spoon. This shape increases the bullet's yaw in flight and causes it to cut a large curved channel upon impact.

The G11 rifle is a radical departure from current arms technology. Tilo Moller, Gunter Kastner, Dieter Ketterer, and Ernst Wossner are the design engineers, and Dynamit Nobel has been working on the caseless ammunition. The West German military may adopt this weapon for infantry use and bypass the .223/5.56mm NATO round.

Outwardly, the rifle has a "bullpup" appearance. Inwardly, it's vastly different from other firearms since it uses a caseless bullet with a rectangular chunk of propellant molded around it with a primer encased in its base and a center core of explosive to powder the propellant at the instant of firing. The 4.7mm bullets travel at high velocity and can be fired in semiauto, three-round bursts, or full auto. Because the weapon cycles quickly, the three-round burst won't climb and the recoil will feel like a single push. Disposable 50-round magazines are inserted into the top of the rifle parallel to the barrel. The rounds feed off the magazine at right angles to the barrel; a special feed mechanism rotates the round 90 degrees for loading. Because the ammunition is caseless, there is no ejection port, though provision is made for removing rounds which fail to fire.

The G11 has plastic cheek rest, handguard, and pistol grip with a stamped-steel receiver which seals the inner parts almost completely from dirt. The trigger is sealed with a flexible membrane, as is the magazine release button. The circular charger is located on the side of the rifle (early models had a Plexiglas cocking lever below the handguard); to load the rifle, the nonreciprocating charger is rotated to strip a cartridge from the magazine and place it in the firing position.

A small port located on the bottom of the receiver

The Heckler & Koch submachine gun was introduced in 1966 and has a variety of models. The short-barreled, nonsuppressed, stockless version with a foregrip is the MP5K. It's small enough to be easily concealed in a briefcase or under a heavy jacket.

allows gas to escape during action cycling. The port opens only for a fraction of a second, making it hard for dirt to enter. The muzzle is the only opening on the entire firearm when the magazine is in place.

The integral one-power scope doubles as a carrying handle. Because the scope doesn't magnify the target, the shooter can use it with both eyes open. The scope also has a battery-operated illuminated reticle for low-light conditions.

The rifle is designed to give the shot dispersal needed to maximize the chance of hitting a fleeting target in combat. The firearm has also been engineered to minimize infrared signature and make it easy to decontaminate on a chemical/biological/nuclear battlefield. The human engineering seems well thought out. The pistol grip allows one-hand operation, and operating controls are conveniently located.

Only time will tell whether or not the G11 is a harbinger or an interesting oddity in weapons development.

G11 Specifications

Barrel length . . . . 21.3 in.
Caliber . . . . 4.7×21mm OH*
Cyclic rate (approx., automatic) . . . . 600 rpm
Cyclic rate (approx., three-round burst) . . 2000 rpm
Length . . . . 29.5 in.
Magazine (standard) 50-round
Muzzle velocity (approx.) . . . . 3051 fps
Rifling . . . . polygonal "rifling," 1-in-12 in.,
                                               right-hand twist
Weight unloaded (approx.) . . . . 7.9 lbs.
*Ohne Hulse. German term meaning caseless.

Another Heckler & Koch experimental project is being done in conjunction with Winchester; they are both working on prototype weapons for the U.S. military's CAWS (Close Assault Weapons System) program. The CAWS prototypes are basically souped-up selective-fire bullpup shotguns. The aiming system will probably be a telescopic "handle" similar to the G11. The greatest challenge is to create a flechette or pellet load which is lethal at 150 yards (let alone the 300-yard maximum normal combat range). There are other drawbacks: the firearm has to be nearly two to three pounds heavier than current assault rifles in order to reduce felt recoil; only ten rounds are available per magazine (though a number of projectiles are fired with each shot); and the ammunition is bulky (about the size of commercial 12-gauge ammunition).

The multiple-projectile idea seems sound, based on the SALVO Project's findings. But, it would seem that it could occasionally become essential to engage an enemy at the extreme combat ranges of 300 yards or

to deliver very precise single shots rather than a volley of projectiles. Neither option will be open with the CAWS as currently designed. Finally, a change of tactics by soldiers with longer-ranged weapons might work greatly to the disadvantage of CAWS-equipped troops.

Because of the bulkiness of the CAWS and its ammunition and limited range, many feel that the concept will prove to be a dead end. Again, only time will tell.

HK CAWS (Prototype) Specifications

Barrel length . . . . 18.1 in.
Caliber . . . . Modified 12 gauge
Cyclic rate (approx., automatic) . . . . 240 rpm
Length . . . . 33.9 in.
Magazine (standard) 10-round
Rifling . . . . None
Weight unloaded (approx.) . . . . 9.9 lbs.

KALASHNIKOV RIFLES

In 1947, the USSR fielded a rifle designed by Mikhail T. Kalashnikov, known as the AK-47 (*Avtomat Kalashnikova*, Model 1947). The original model had a receiver that was part machined steel and part stampings; rivets held the whole thing together—for a while; then the rifle had a tendency to come apart. Around 1950 a new model of the rifle was fielded with a machined receiver.

In 1959 another model of the AK was introduced which used riveted steel stampings. This model is designated the AKM (*Avtomat Kalashnikova Modernizirovannyi*), and most Soviet rifles are now built around this style of receiver. The AKM has a slightly altered stock design, a reduced weight, and, on later versions, a flange-like muzzle compensator. The AKM also has an internal safety device in the trigger group which is sometimes mistakenly called a rate reducer.

The AK-47 and AKM are chambered for the M43 7.62×39mm cartridge originally developed for the SKS carbine. A new model of the AKM, the AK-74, first appeared with Soviet forces in Afghanistan. The AK-74 is basically an AKM chambered for the Soviet 5.45×39mm cartridge. It is believed that the Soviet military will be switching from the AKM to the AK-74, though existing AKMs will undoubtedly be in service for some time.

The AKM receiver and other parts form the basis of a weapons system which includes a folding stock version of the rifle, the AKMS; the RPK LMG; the PK general-purpose machine gun with bipod; the PKS medium machine gun with tripod mount; the PKT tank machine gun; and the PKB for armored personnel carriers. The RPK, which fires the M43 round, is basically a standard AKM with a longer barrel. It uses 30- or 40-round box magazines or a 75-round snail magazine. The belt-fed PK versions fire the larger Mosin Nagent 7.62×54mm (rimmed) cartridge and have quick change barrels. An improved version of the PK is designated the PKM (*Pulemyot Kalashnikova Modernizironvannyi*). In order to accommodate the belt-feed, the PK models have inverted gas piston/barrel installations; the same technique was used by Fabrique Nationale with their MAG design and by Stoner with his 63 Systems machine guns.

The AK-74 weapons family includes the folding stock RPKS74 LMG, which has an AR-15-style flash suppressor; the folding-stock AKS-74 rifle which seems to be more common than the wood-stocked model; and a short carbine (the AKR Krinkov) with a folding stock and greatly abbreviated barrel and gas piston assembly.

In addition to its excessive weight, the basic AK design has some minor faults: the rear sight placement gives the rifle a very short sighting radius; the rear tangent sight is a rather crude open "V" that makes long-range accuracy hard (even though the tangents are marked from 100 meters to an optimistic 1,000 meters on the AK-74!); there is no bolt hold-open device, and the safety/selector is located rather inconveniently on the right side to help keep dirt out of the rifle, and, worse yet, makes a distinctive "clack" when moved. (This can be minimized by bending the selector slightly away from the receiver and placing a small piece of plastic tape on its underside.)

The charging handle is located on the right side of the receiver and the magazine release lever behind the magazine well. The AKM has a muzzle brake which angles out and down to help keep the point of aim steady during automatic fire. The AK-74's newly designed muzzle brake actually reduces recoil somewhat at the cost of increased noise and muzzle flash; the muzzle brake is threaded onto the barrel and held in place with a spring-loaded lug. The AK-74 is easily distinguished from the AKM by its less sharply curved plastic magazine, muzzle brake, and a small horizontal groove cut into the stock. Both models have chrome-lined barrels which give good accuracy with decent ammunition, but retain the AK-47's poor sights. A three-position safety/selector is used on nearly all variations of the AK. The upward position is "safe," the second position is full auto, and the lowest position is semiauto.

The folding stocks on the AKS-47 and AKMS have a large release button located just above the pistol grip on the left side of the receiver. When the stock is released, it folds under the rifle. These stocks were not very rigid, and a new style was created for the AKS-74. The AKS-74 stock's release button is on the left side of the rear of the receiver. This stock folds to the left and is held in place by a spring-loaded hook on the receiver.

Field-stripping an AK weapon is quite simple and requires no tools:

1. Remove the magazine and cycle the action to be sure it is empty.

2. Push in the retaining lever on the rear receiver cover to release it. Rotate the rear of the receiver cover up and remove it.

3. Remove the action spring and retaining rod by pushing them forward to release, then lifting them up and back.

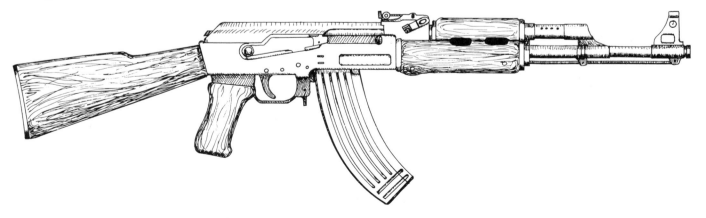

In 1947, the USSR started to field a new rifle designed by Mikhail T. Kalashnikov. The rifle became known as the AK-47 (Avtomat Kalashnikova, Model 1947). The original model had a receiver that was part machined steel and part steel stampings; around 1950 a new model of the rifle with a machined receiver was fielded.

4. Remove the bolt and bolt carrier with its permanently attached gas piston by pulling them back and out.

5. Remove the bolt by twisting it counterclockwise and pulling it out of the front of the carrier.

6. Remove the gas cylinder by pulling it backward and then lifting it out.

Reassembly is the reverse of the above procedure.

It is believed that from 36 million to over 70 million AK-style rifles have been produced. A number of Eastern Bloc and nonaligned countries, as well as China and North Korea, manufacture their own models of the AK weapons. Additionally, a number of spin-offs of the rifle are made by Israel, Finland, Egypt, and others. Though the AK is heavy and often poorly made, it functions well in battlefield conditions, stands up to considerable abuse, and is cheap to manufacture—important features in an assault rifle.

USSR AK-47 Specifications
Barrel length . . . . 16.34 in.
Caliber . . . . 7.62×39mm Soviet (M43)
Cyclic rate (approx.) . . . . 600 rpm
Length . . . . 34.25 in.
Magazine (standard) 30-round
Muzzle velocity (approx.) . . . . 2330 fps
Rifling . . . . 4 grooves, right-hand twist
Weight unloaded (approx.) . . . . 9.8 lbs.

USSR AKM Specifications
Barrel length . . . . 16.34 in.
Caliber . . . . 7.62×39mm Soviet (M43)
Cyclic rate (approx.) . . . . 600 rpm
Length . . . . 34.25 in.
Magazine (standard) 30-round
Muzzle velocity (approx.) . . . . 2330 fps
Rifling . . . . 4 grooves, right-hand twist
Weight unloaded (approx.) . . . . 8.9 lbs.

USSR AK-74 Specifications
Barrel length . . . . 15.8 in.
Caliber . . . . 5.45×39mm Soviet
Cyclic rate (approx.) . . . . 650 rpm
Length . . . . 36.6 in.
AKS length (stock folded) . . . . 27 in.
Magazine (standard) 30-round
Muzzle velocity (approx.) . . . . 2950 fps
Rifling . . . . 4 grooves, 1-in-5.8 in., right-hand twist
Weight unloaded (approx.) . . . . 7.9 lbs.

Bulgaria
Bulgarian AK-47s and AKMs are identical to the Soviet models and use the same model designations.

Most rifles are manufactured in Bulgaria, though other countries, especially Poland, have manufactured rifles for Bulgaria in the past.

People's Republic of China
The Chinese adopted a version of the AK-47, designated the Model 56, which is almost identical to the Soviet weapon except for a permanently mounted folding spike bayonet. The Type 56 has the usual tangent-notch rear sight adjustable from 100 to 1,000 meters. A folding stock version, the Type 56-1, usually lacks the bayonet, as do rifles manufactured for export. Barrels are normally chrome-lined.

Semiauto versions of the Type 56 and 56-1 are imported into the United States by a number of companies, including Clayco Sports, Ltd., Pacific International (which offers the most competitive price at the time of this writing), and SILE. Unfortunately, the rifles are marketed as "AKS" rifles whether or not they have folding stocks; the USSR "AKS" designation is only used with folding stocks. The rifles do not come with the standard integral Chinese spike bayonets but have an optional detachable knife bayonet available. Spare parts for AK-47s are available in the United States from Pars International.

In the United States, a number of modifications can be made to the Chinese AKs, the most innovative perhaps being those of Fleming Firearms. Their "Mini-47" is a semiauto folding stock "AKS" modified to selective fire with the barrel shortened to 12 inches. The gas tube, cleaning rod, and piston are modified accordingly. Weighing 7.7 pounds, its overall length is 22.6 inches with the stock folded. The cyclic rate is reduced to 500 rpm, and the modified firearm is quite reliable and similar in concept to the Soviet AKR Krinkov.

Rather than adopt the AKM, the Chinese designed their own rifle, the Type 68, which looks outwardly like the Soviet SKS though internally it is a modified AK design. The Type 68 rifle is selective fire with a one-piece wooden stock and a folding spike bayonet. Standard AK magazines fit into the Type 68 only if the bolt stop is ground off. The gas regulator is adjustable and has two settings. There are no known grenade-launching capabilities.

A "Type 73" rifle (the official designation is unknown at this time) is also being developed. It is believed that this is based on the Type 68, though outwardly it looks like an AK. The rifle will also probably have the usual folding spike bayonet.

A Chinese-manufactured AKM is finding its way into the arsenals of Afghan rebels. The rifle has no bayonet or bayonet lug, no muzzle brake or flash suppressor, and red-brown plastic furniture, including a distinctively shaped pistol grip. Whether this weapon is produced only for export, is a new rifle produced for the Chinese arsenal, or is actually the Type 73 is unknown at this time.

Chinese Type 56 Specifications

Barrel length . . . . 16.34 in.
Caliber . . . . 7.62×39mm Soviet (M43)
Cyclic rate (approx.) . . . . 600 rpm
Length . . . . 34.25 in.
Magazine (standard) 30-round
Muzzle velocity (approx.) . . . . 2330 fps
Rifling . . . . 4 grooves, right-hand twist
Weight unloaded (approx.) . . . . 9.8 lbs.

Chinese Type 68 Specifications

Barrel length . . . . 20.5 in.
Caliber . . . . 7.62×39mm Soviet (M43)
Cyclic rate (approx.) . . . . 750 rpm
Length . . . . 40.5 in.
Magazine (standard) 15-round
Muzzle velocity (approx.) . . . . 2400 fps
Rifling . . . . 4 grooves, right-hand twist
Weight unloaded (approx.) . . . . 7.7 lbs.

Czechoslovakia

The Czech Vz58, patterned after the AK-47, is seen in two versions; the Vz58P with standard stock and the Vz58V with metal single-strut folding stock. Early models have wooden furniture while newer ones use wood fiber/plastic or all plastic. These selective-fire rifles are chambered for the 7.62×45mm Czech copy of the Soviet M43 round.

Internally, the rifle is somewhat different from the standard AK-47. The bolt tilts to lock in place and has a simplified trigger mechanism. Though the rifle is only slightly smaller than its Soviet counterpart, it has an empty weight 2½ pounds below the AK-47. An optional bipod attaches below the front sight.

Czechoslovakian Vz58P (Vz58V) Specifications

Barrel length . . . . 15.8 in.
Caliber . . . . 7.62×39mm Soviet (M43)
Cyclic rate (approx.) . . . . 620 rpm
Length . . . . 33.2 in.
Vz58V length (stock folded) . . . . 23.2 in.
Magazine (standard) 30-round
Muzzle velocity (approx.) . . . . 2330 fps
Rifling . . . . 4 grooves, right-hand twist
Weight unloaded (approx.) . . . . 6.9 lbs.

East Germany

East German AK-47s and AKMs are nearly identical to those of the USSR. Nomenclature is slightly different, however. The German designations include the weapon type, followed by the first letter of the designer's name, followed by a letter to designate variations. Thus, the AKM becomes the MPiKM (*Maschinenpistole Kalashnikova Modern*) and the folding stock version, the MPiKMS.

Among the AK rifles in East German use are the AK-47, AK-47 with folding stock, AKM, RPK (German designation: LMGK), RPD, and a 12.7mm armor machine gun. One distinctive version is the MPiKS 72, an AKM with a heavy wire stock that folds to the right of the receiver rather than the usual left or bottom. A small .22 rimfire model of the AK is also used in East Germany for training.

Egypt

While the Soviets were in Egypt's good graces, a plant was set up in Egypt to produce AKMs. When the Soviet advisors were kicked out for trying to overthrow the government, the Egyptians continued to produce the AKMs and have even exported some. The Egyptian AKM has a laminated wood stock and a checkered plastic pistol grip. Starting in 1982, a semiautomatic version was imported to the United States by Gun South. Unfortunately, the price of the Egyptian rifle is a bit too high to compete with the Chinese models.

Egyptian AKM Specifications

Barrel length . . . . 16.3 in.
Caliber . . . . 7.62×39mm Soviet (M43)
Cyclic rate (approx.) . . . . 650 rpm
Length . . . . 34.6 in.
Magazine (standard) 30-round
Muzzle velocity (approx.) . . . . 2300 fps
Rifling . . . . 4 grooves, right-hand twist
Weight unloaded (approx.) . . . . 6.7 lbs.

Finland

After World War II, the Allies required Finland to dismantle its arms factories, a ban which continued until the late 1950s. At that time, the Finns were allowed to produce a modified AK rifle and light machine gun. The principal development work was carried out by Valmet, a government-owned combine.

From 1958 to 1960 a number of rifles were created and tested, based on the AK design. In 1960, two versions were fielded for trials, differing only in the inclusion or omission of various types of winter triggers, flash suppressors, trigger guards, bayonet mounts, etc. In 1962,

From 1958 to 1960, a number of rifles were created around the AK design and tested by the Finns. By 1962, a version designated the M62 was adopted for military use.

a version was adopted for military use, designated the M62. There were two models, one with a standard stock and the M62T with a folding stock. (The "T" suffix for folding-stock versions is used for later models except for those made for export.) Full-scale production by Valmet started in 1965, with the Finnish SAKO plant handling extra capacity.

The basic model was modified in 1969 with flip-up luminous dot night sights; these in turn were replaced with tritium night sights in 1972. Other variations include changes in the pistol grip, strengthening of the stock, etc. The distinctive Finnish flash suppressor has open "fingers" and a bayonet lug on its lower side.

In 1976, the M62-76 was fielded. This rifle has a stamped-steel receiver and is similar to the Soviet AKM. Three models are currently made: the M62-76P with wooden stock, the M62-76M with plastic stock, and the M62-76T with a folding metal tubular stock.

Several variations of the M62-76 are made for export and are designated the M71 series. They have sheet-metal receivers and slightly altered furniture. They are offered in both .223 Remington and 7.62×39mm. Strangely enough, most of these rifles have the sights placed in Soviet positions (at the front of the barrel and the receiver) rather than the usual Valmet positions. A semiauto version of the M71 developed for civilian sales in the United States is designated the M71S.

In 1976, the M76 family of rifles was created for the export market in .223 Remington, 7.62×39mm, and .308 Winchester/7.62mm NATO; in 1978, an LMG was added to the group; and in 1982, a forward-looking bullpup design was created. (In a concession to English-speaking countries, the "T" in an M76 rifle's designation stands for "tubular stock" in the M76 group; "F" for "folding stock"; "W" for "wood stock"; and "P" for

"plastic stock.") The following rifles are offered in either .223 or 7.62×39mm: the M82 Bullpup rifle; the M76F, T, W, and P rifles; the M78/83S sniper rifle with scope mount and plastic stock; and the M78 Light Machine Gun. The M78 LMG and M78/83S are also offered in the .308 Winchester/7.62mm NATO chambering. Semiauto versions of these rifles are available for the civilian market. Excellent automatic conversion work on these rifles, as well as the shortening of their barrels to 11 inches and other custom work, is done by Fleming Firearms.

The M82 may well be the next stage of development of the AK rifles. This rifle is little larger than many submachine guns without the hassle of a folding stock. The one-piece plastic stock is enlarged on the left side for the shooter's cheek and the sights are canted to the left as well. (The rifle cannot be used with a left-handed hold since the reciprocating bolt would be dangerous in that position.)

Internally, the Finnish rifles are nearly identical to their AK counterparts; operation and field-stripping are the same. The rifles are every bit as reliable as others in the AK family, and the finish is much better than that of rifles made in most communist nations.

Finnish M62 Specifications

Barrel length	16.5 in.
Caliber	7.62×39mm Soviet (M43)
Cyclic rate (approx.)	650 rpm
Length	36 in.
Magazine (standard)	30-round
Muzzle velocity (approx.)	2400 fps
Rifling	4 grooves, right-hand twist
Weight unloaded (approx.)	10.2 lbs.

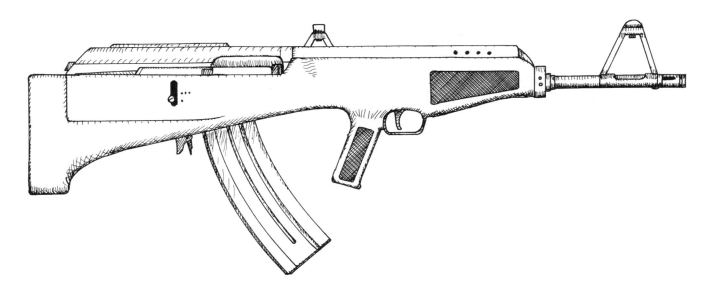

In 1982, Valmet released a bullpup version of its AK rifles. The M82 is available chambered in either .223 or 7.62 x 39mm.

Finnish M76 Specifications

Barrel length . . . . 16.6 in.
Caliber . . . . .223 Remington
Length . . . . 36.6 in.
Magazine (standard) 30-round
Muzzle velocity (approx.) . . . . 2900 fps
Weight unloaded (approx.) . . . . 8.2 lbs.

Finnish M82 Specifications

Barrel length . . . . 17 in.
Caliber . . . . .223 Remington
Length . . . . 27 in.
Magazine (standard) 30-round
Muzzle velocity (approx.) . . . . 2900 fps
Weight unloaded (approx.) . . . . 7.5 lbs.

Hungary

Hungary uses several types of AKMs, which differ from the Soviet models mainly in their furniture. The Hungarian model has a plastic stock (often a light blue or dark green), a plastic pistol grip, a forward pistol grip, and a ventilated metal handguard to protect the hands when carrying the rifle. There is no top cover over the gas piston rod, and the exposed gas tube and metal handguard get excessively hot during extended firing. Interestingly, the forward grip has the reverse shape of the rear pistol grip.

A short version of the AKM, designated the AMD, is also manufactured in Hungary. It has a single strut folding stock which folds to the right of the receiver and allows operation of the weapon when folded. The

barrel and gas rod/piston tube have also been shortened to give the rifle a handy overall length, and a special muzzle brake is mounted. The muzzle blast and flash are rather excessive with the AMD, as is its weight. While it does fill the submachine gun role well with a potent round, it is far from without its drawbacks.

Hungarian AKM Specifications

Barrel length . . . . 16.3 in.
Caliber . . . . 7.62×39mm Soviet (M43)
Cyclic rate (approx.) . . . . 600 rpm
Length . . . . 34.3 in.
Magazine (standard) 30-round
Muzzle velocity (approx.) . . . . 2330 fps
Rifling . . . . 4 grooves, right-hand twist
Weight unloaded (approx.) . . . . 10.7 lbs.

Hungarian AMD Specifications

Barrel length . . . . 12.6 in.
Caliber . . . . 7.62×39mm Soviet (M43)
Cyclic rate (approx.) . . . . 650 rpm
Length . . . . 33.5 in.
Length (stock folded) . . . . 25.5 in.
Magazine (standard) 30-round
Muzzle velocity (approx.) . . . . 2200 fps
Rifling . . . . 4 grooves, right-hand twist
Weight unloaded (approx.) . . . . 7.9 lbs.

Israel

Following the Six Day War, the Israelis, who had been disappointed with the performance of their FN LAR

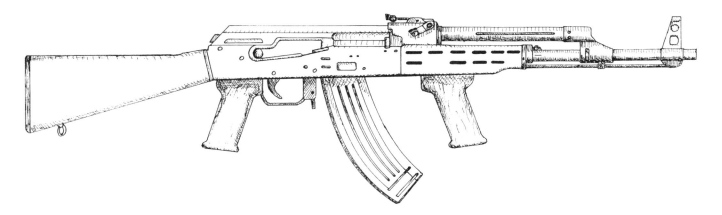

Hungarian AKMs differ from the Soviet models mainly in the furniture of the rifles. The Hungarian model has a plastic stock, plastic pistol grip, forward pistol grip, and ventilated metal handguard. There is no top cover over the gas piston rod, and so the exposed gas tube and metal handguard get excessively hot (read "hand searing") during extended firing.

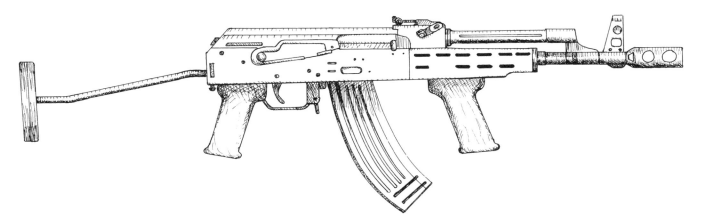

The Hungarian AMD has a single-strut folding stock. Despite a special muzzle brake, muzzle blast and nighttime flash are excessive.

rifles, tested and evaluated a number of captured AKs. Following an endurance contest between a number of rifles including the AKs, the decision was made to adopt a new rifle based on a test weapon created from an AK with a Stoner 63 magazine and barrel. After making a number of modifications, Israel Military Industries (IMI) started producing the much modified AK in 1973 as the standard Israeli infantry rifle.

The weapon is known as the Galil, after Israel Galil, the principal designer. (Though the Galil is the official Israeli arm, the M16 is often seen in the hands of Israeli troops a decade after the Galil was fielded, because large numbers of the Galil have been exported.)

South Africa, the Netherlands, and Sweden have been licensed to build Galil rifles. The South African versions have been accepted as issue weapons; Sweden has designated its version the FFV-890C, and the Netherlands, the MN1.

Among the modifications made to the AK to create the Galil were the adoption of the .223 Remington/ 5.56mm chambering. Other modifications include an improved selector switch which has been moved to the left side of the receiver (a bar on the right side of the receiver is also available); a charging handle, bent upward for easy left-hand use; a pivoting carrying handle; a bipod/wire cutter; a standard-issue folding metal stock (patterned after the FAL); a ribbed wooden handguard (lined with "Dural" to withstand heat) which covers only the barrel, leaving the top of the gas cylinder exposed; and even a bottle opener in the underside of the handguard (to keep troops from using magazines for that task and, in the process, destroying the magazine lips). Export weapons offer the option of a plastic or wood stock and handguard.

Israel's modified AK is the Galil. Among the changes made in its design were the adoption of the more potent .223 Remington/5.56mm NATO chambering, an improved selector, a handier charging handle, and improved sights. Photo courtesy of Magnum Research.

A semiauto Galil ARM chambered for the .308 Winchester/7.62mm NATO is available on the export market. Photo courtesy of Magnum Research.

The sights are placed on the gas cylinder and the rear of the receiver cover. The rear sight is an AR-15 flip type with settings for 300 and 500 meters. Windage and elevation adjustments are made on the hooded front sight; a screwdriver can adjust windage, but a special tool is needed to change elevation. Night sights with radioactive glow-in-the-dark markings flip up for easy use on all models, and sniper scopes are also available. The bayonet lug is on the upper side of the barrel just in front of the front sight.

A gas cutoff valve is located below the front sight for grenade launching with ballistic cartridge. The AR-15-style flash suppressor accommodates this function. Strangely, no grenade sights are available.

The standard rifle is the ARM (Assault Rifle/Light Machine Gun); because of the rifle's dual role, the barrel is quite heavy. A short-barreled SAR (Short Assault Rifle) lacks the bipod and carrying handle. Two semiauto ARM models are available on the export market, chambered for .223 or .308 Winchester/7.62mm NATO.

There are two standard magazines, 35- and 50-round, and a 12-round ballistic cartridge magazine (the .308 rifle has a 25-round magazine). An adapter for using AR-15/M16 magazines is also available.

Field-stripping is the same as for other AK weapons.

Users of the Galil may find fault with a few features: the trigger has a tendency to pinch the shooter's finger; the 50-round magazine is too long for use with the bipod; the selector on the left of the receiver is convenient but operates opposite from what most users find natural (safe is forward, firing modes are to the rear); the selector still makes the AK clacking noise; the rifle's weight may seem excessive to shooters used to the AR-15; and finally, the Galil flings its brass quite a distance and often puts a large dent in it as well (the optional brass catcher and ejection port buffer are two accessories that reloaders should consider purchasing).

These are minor drawbacks, however. The weight of the rifle makes it very strong and controllable in the automatic mode, and the weapon has the same reliability of other AKs. The Galil is capable of excellent accuracy thanks to good sights, readily available scopes and the general high quality of the .223 round.

Israeli Galil ARM Specifications

Barrel length . . . . 18.1 in.
Caliber . . . . .223 Remington (5.56mm)
Cyclic rate (approx.) . . . . 650 rpm
Length . . . . 38.6 in.
Length (stock folded) . . . . 29.8 in.
Magazine (standard) . . . . 35- or 50-round
Muzzle velocity (approx.) . . . . 3110 fps
Rifling . . . . . 6 grooves, 1-in-12 in., right-hand twist
Weight unloaded (approx.) . . . . 8.5 lbs.

Israeli Galil SAR Specifications

Barrel length . . . . 13 in.
Caliber . . . . .223 Remington (5.56mm)
Cyclic rate (approx.) . . . . 650 rpm
Length . . . . 32.3 in.
Length (stock folded) . . . . 23.6 in.
Magazine (standard) . . . . 35- or 50-round
Muzzle velocity (approx.) . . . . 3010 fps
Rifling . . . . . 6 grooves, 1-in-12 in., right-hand twist
Weight unloaded (approx.) . . . . 7.7 lbs.

Galil ARM (.308/7.62mm NATO) Specifications

Barrel length . . . . 21 in.
Caliber . . . . .308 Winchester (7.62mm NATO)
Length . . . . 41.3 in.

Length (stock folded) . . . . 31.9 in.
Magazine (standard) 25-round
Muzzle velocity (approx.) . . . . 2820 fps
Rifling . . . . . 4 grooves, 1-in-12 in., right-hand twist
Weight unloaded (approx.) . . . . 8.7 lbs.

North Korea

The North Korean Type 58 rifle is virtually identical to the AK-47. The Type 68 is nearly identical to the AKM except that the front grip is similar to that of the AK-47 rather than the thicker AKM, and the internal safety device (often mistakenly called a "rate reducer") is missing. Folding stock versions are similar to the Soviet design except that they have large perforations in the stock struts to reduce the rifle's weight.

Poland

AK-47s identical to the Soviet model were made in Poland and are designated the kbkAK. A variation of the AK-47 produced by Poland, designated the kbkPMK-DGN, could launch rifle grenades. Modifications included a removable barrel adapter/launcher, a detachable recoil stock boot, a 10-round magazine with a block to prevent anything other than ballistic rounds being loaded into it, special grenade sights, and a cutoff switch on the gas tube.

Since the early 1960s, the Polish-manufactured AKM is virtually identical to the Soviet AKM except that it has a flange-type muzzle compensator. The model PMK-DGN is also known as the KbKg Model 1960.

Romania

The Romanian AKM-based weapons family has been manufactured since the early Sixties. The weapons, designated "AIM," are basically identical to Soviet models, with minor changes including a laminated wood pistol grip on the lower side of the handguard.

A folding stock AKMS and a sniper rifle chambered for the old M1891 Mosin cartridge have also been recently added to the Romanian arsenal. The sniper rifle, the FPK, is equipped with a 10-round magazine and a special muzzle brake. The rifle is based on the RPK mechanism.

South Africa

Before 1977, South Africa imported most of its small arms from Great Britain and Belgium, but in 1977 the United Nations imposed an arms embargo against South Africa. Since the South Africans were faced with a guerrilla movement supplied from the USSR and China, they had little choice but to produce their own weapons. Thus, the South African state arms agency,

ARMSCOR, was created.

Rather than produce the heavy LAR (R1) rifle, the South Africans obtained a license to manufacture a slightly modified version of the Israeli Galil. The South African versions of the Galil are now standard issue; the ARM is designated the R4 rifle and the SAR, the R5. The weapons have a carbon fiber-reinforced composite stock which is cooler in the hot sun. The stock is also slightly lengthened to accommodate the larger size of the average Afrikaner. Barrel twist rate has been increased very slightly, and the overall weight of the rifle is greater.

A second-generation passive night scope, the Kentron Eloptro MNV, is also available for the rifle, and runs on two AA batteries. A semiauto version of the rifle is produced for civilian use, designated the LM-4.

South African R4 Specifications

Barrel length . . . . 18.1 in.
Caliber . . . . .223 Remington (5.56mm)
Cyclic rate (approx.) . . . . 650 rpm
Length . . . . 39.2 in.
Length (stock folded) . . . . 29.1 in.
Magazine (standard) 35-round
Muzzle velocity (approx.) . . . . 3220 fps
Rifling . . . . 6 grooves, 1-in-11.8 in., right-hand twist
Weight unloaded (approx.) . . . . 11.7 lbs.

South African R5 Specifications

Barrel length . . . . 13 in.
Caliber . . . . .223 Remington (5.56mm)
Cyclic rate (approx.) . . . . 650 rpm
Length . . . . 33.3 in.
Length (stock folded) . . . . 23.6 in.
Magazine (standard) 35-round
Muzzle velocity (approx.) . . . . 3010 fps
Rifling . . 6 grooves, 1-in-11.8 inch, right-hand twist
Weight unloaded (approx.) . . . . 9.5 lbs.

Yugoslavia

Yugoslav AKs are part of the FAZ weapons family, similar to that of the Soviets. Included are two LMGs, Models 65A and 65B, and rifles capable of firing grenades. The 65A and 65B are modified AK-47s rather than copies of the RPK. The Yugoslav rifles have slightly longer barrels and also feature a much needed bolt hold-open device; the unfortunate trade-off is that Soviet magazines won't work in the rifles.

The Model 64 uses a 20-round magazine and has a grenade-launcher sight attached to the gas tube (a launching device must be substituted for the flash suppressor to launch grenades). Model 64A is similar but

has a shorter barrel and a 30-round magazine; the 64B is like the 64A except that it has a folding steel stock. Model 70 is similar to 64A but has a few different components and a longer barrel, and lacks finger serrations on the pistol grip; Model 70A is the folding-stock version of Model 70. A semiauto Model 77/82 in 7.62mm NATO was manufactured for export to the United States for a short time.

Yugoslav Model 64 Specifications

Barrel length . . . . 19.7 in.
Caliber . . . . 7.62×39mm Soviet (M43)
Cyclic rate (approx.) . . . . 600 rpm
Length . . . . 40.9 in.
Magazine (standard) 20-round
Muzzle velocity (approx.) . . . . 2395 fps
Rifling . . . . 4 grooves, right-hand twist
Weight unloaded (approx.) . . . . 8.6 lbs.

Yugoslav Model 64A (64B) Specifications

Barrel length . . . . 14.7 in.
Caliber . . . . 7.62×39mm Soviet (M43)
Cyclic rate (approx.) . . . . 600 rpm
Length . . . . 36.1 in.
Length (stock folded, 64B) . . . . 25.6 in.
Magazine (standard) 30-round
Muzzle velocity (approx.) . . . . 2280 fps
Rifling . . . . 4 grooves, right-hand twist
Weight unloaded (approx.) . . . . 8.3 lbs.

Yugoslav Model 70 (70A) Specifications

Barrel length . . . . 16.3 in.
Caliber . . . . 7.62×39mm Soviet (M43)
Cyclic rate (approx.) . . . . 620 rpm
Length . . . . 37.7 in.
Length (stock folded, 70A) . . . . 27.2 in.
Magazine (standard) 30-round
Muzzle velocity (approx.) . . . . 2297 fps
Rifling . . . . 4 grooves, right-hand twist
Weight unloaded (approx.) . . . . 8.3 lbs.

LEADER RIFLE

The Leader rifle is manufactured by Leader Dynamics of Smithfield, New South Wales, Australia, and is designed by Charles George. The Leader is a close copy of the AR-18 rifle, the only notable changes being decreasing the number of bolt lugs from eight to three, placing the charging handle above and to the left of the handguard, and welding a carrying handle to the top receiver which doubles as a scope mount. Like the

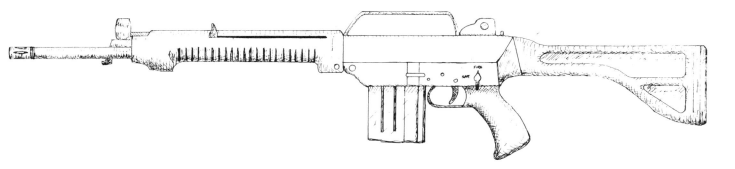

Inwardly, the Leader rifle is pretty much a copy of the AR-18 rifle. While it has the potential to be a good assault rifle, thus far the Leader hasn't made the grade due to the "new gun bugs."

AR-18, the upper and lower receiver are steel stampings carrying the rear sight assembly. The Leader has plastic furniture that makes it appear different than its AR-18 parent. The rifle is available in several models; their main differences are in barrel length and the selective-fire or semiauto-only options. Hardwood furniture is also available with semiauto models. The rifle uses AR-15/M16 magazines.

The Leader rifles have a bad reputation in the United States where they were imported by the World Public Safety Corporation. Despite an overall good design, many of the rifles were imported with a fake flash suppressor with no gas porting slots (a few had small holes drilled in a line around the suppressor). Chambers were undersized in some rifles, causing chambering problems after a little use. Additionally, it was possible to push a magazine up into the bolt area when the bolt was held back. Finally, the rifle seems to have frequent feeding problems; whether this is a quality control problem or another design defect remains to be seen. All in all, shooters were not impressed with the Leader rifles and they became casualties of "new gun bugs" in the United States at least.

The rear sight is adjustable for windage and elevation. Some shooters may find that the carrying handle interferes with the sight picture, though generally this problem "goes away" with continued use. The front sight is adjustable for elevation. Unfortunately, it is a blade rather than a post and must be turned at least 180 degrees when making adjustments; this is not a great problem, however, since elevation slack can be taken up with rear sight adjustment.

Field-stripping the Leader is similar to the AR-18. A spring-loaded catch at the rear of the receiver is depressed. This allows the upper receiver to be rotated on the pivot pin at the front of the two receiver halves. The exposed bolt carrier and recoil springs can then

be removed from the rear of the upper receiver.

The Leader rifle has the potential to be a good assault rifle but thus far hasn't made the grade.

Leader T2-MK5 Specifications
Barrel length . . . . 16.2 in.
Caliber . . . . .223 Remington
Cyclic rate (approx.) . . . . 600 rpm
Length (stock extended) . . . . 35.9 in.
Magazine (standard) 30-round
Muzzle velocity (approx.) . . . . 3040 fps
Rifling . . . . . 4 grooves, 1-in-12 in., right-hand twist
Weight unloaded (approx.) . . . . 7.7 lbs.

M1 .30 CARBINE/M2/M3

The .30 Carbine is one of many weapons that were put to completely different uses than military thinkers originally planned. In 1940 the call went out for a lightweight weapon to replace the .45 ACP pistol and the Thompson submachine gun. The pistol was not capable of long-range engagements and the Thompson was too heavy and expensive. The thinking was that a new weapon would be used by NCOs, cooks, mortar men, clerks, etc., while infantry troops continued to use their standard rifles.

Tests of 11 different rifles (including one designed by John Garand) began in mid-1941. The winner was the creation of David M. "Carbine" Williams, a genius just this side of the law who designed the carbine while serving time for moonshining. Unfortunately, the well-designed rifle was saddled with an anemic cartridge, as it was hurried into production with little testing and few modifications. The .30 Carbine cartridge developed by Winchester was little more than a revamped version of the .32 Winchester round, which had itself fallen into disfavor because of lack of power and inaccuracy, both of which were problems with the .30 Carbine round.

Despite a lack of power and accuracy, the .30 Carbine became very popular with U.S. troops because of its handy size and light weight, and it saw much more use than anyone had imagined. Meanwhile, the .45 Auto continued to be used and the M3 grease gun replaced the Thompson.

Three models of the .30-caliber carbine were made: the M1, which had a few minor variants with cosmetic differences in the top of the receiver, etc.; a somewhat flimsy, folding-stock version designated the M1A1; a selective-fire M2; and the M3 (also occasionally referred to as the T3) which was an M2 with a cone flash-hider bolted on and a scope-mount groove milled into its receiver for use with night-vision equipment. Interestingly, the automatic mode was originally specified for the M1 model but automatic fire proved so erratic that the function was dropped until popular demand brought it back on the M2. The M2 was somewhat unreliable in the automatic mode, especially with a 30-round magazine.

Despite its shortcomings in accuracy and stopping power, the .30 Carbine was a smashing success, and soon a number of different companies including Underwood, Quality Hardware, IBM, and Winchester were making the rifles by the hundreds of thousands. By the end of the Korean War, over six million of the rifles had been made, more than any other small arm the United States has used.

Following the decommission of the weapon in 1956, huge numbers of carbines were sent to U.S. allies in the Far East and sold to U.S. citizens via the NRA marksmanship program. Since then, the M1 Carbine has seen combat use worldwide and will probably be seen for some time to come. Not all carbines in use are military surplus. Several companies that manufactured the rifle for the government continued to do so for the civilian and law-enforcement markets as well as overseas military markets.

Perhaps the development that might make the greatest difference in the .30 Carbine's combat potential is the development of new chamberings. One of these rounds is the 5.7mm Johnson, also called the .22 Spitfire. This round was the brainchild of Melvin M. Johnson, who also invented the Johnson rifle which saw limited use in World War II. The round is made by necking down .30 Carbine brass to accept a 40-, 50-, or 55-grain .224 bullet. The bullet has a high muzzle velocity of 2800 to 3000 fps necessary for successful combat rifle cartridges. The round can be fed through standard .30 Carbine magazines; all that needs to be altered on the rifle is the barrel and a few other parts. One has to wonder what would have happened if the .30 Carbine had been chambered for this round in the first place. Currently, the 5.7mm Johnson chambering is offered for M1 Carbines manufactured by Iver Johnson.

Another chambering with a lot to offer is the .256 Winchester Magnum. This round was developed in 1960 as a handgun cartridge but the handgun, the Ruger Hawkeye, never appeared. Marlin made a lever-action rifle for the round and Thompson-Center a Contender barrel for their pistol. Little heralded at the time, Universal also developed an M1 Carbine for the round called the "Ferret." By the early Eighties, only the Contender remained available for the .256 Winchester Magnum, but in 1985, Universal reintroduced the Ferret rifle; it will be interesting to see if it catches on, with present interest in combat and survival weapons.

The .256 Winchester Magnum is a rimmed cartridge which is basically a necked-down .357 Magnum case. The factory round has a 60-grain bullet with a muzzle velocity of 2760 fps, well within the high-velocity range of a combat weapon. Though the velocity drops off a little quickly for extreme combat ranges, it is certainly more potent than the .30 Carbine cartridge.

The Ferret is different internally from other M1 Carbines and many parts are not interchangeable between the two firearms, and special magazines are needed for the weapon. It might be ideal for a reloader

Despite the shortcomings of the round in the accuracy/stopping department, the U.S. .30 Carbine was a smashing success as far as troops were concerned. By the end of the Korean War, over 6 million of the rifles had been made, more than any other small arm the United States has ever used.

who uses a .357 Magnum pistol.

Along with Iver Johnson and Universal, Springfield Armory also currently makes copies of the M1. These manufacturers may face stiff competition as new federal laws allow the importation of military-surplus carbines in late 1985.

Iver Johnson has been very aggressive in seeking out the civilian market and also offers a 9mm Luger version of the carbine as well as plastic pistol-grip and folding-stock models. Universal has a .22 LR lookalike and several folding-stock variations of its own. As with the Mini-14/XGI family of rifles, the .30 Carbine has become a small family of weapons as more chamberings are developed.

Another variation of the rifle sold by both Iver Johnson and Universal is the "Enforcer Pistol," which saw limited use in Vietnam among Special Forces and Intelligence groups. The Enforcer is basically a chopped M1 with the barrel cut to nine to ten inches and the stock replaced with a pistol grip. The weapons are awkward to aim but incorporate the power of the .30 Carbine round, which is greater than most pistol ammunition, into a package nearly as small as a pistol. Occasionally a similar firearm with a 16-inch barrel and a wire stock is also seen. The rear sights and inner parts of the Enforcer are identical to the standard rifle and magazines and many accessories are interchangable. Because the Enforcer is manufactured as a pistol, it is legal in the United States. The same is not true of do-it-yourself "Enforcers" created by cutting off the barrel and stock of an M1; these are illegal modifications if made without first getting government permission and paying the $200 tax to the BATF.

The rear sight of the .30 Carbine is adjustable for windage with a knob on its right side; elevation is adjustable from 100 to 300 yards by sliding the rear aperture forward or backward on its ramp. The front sight has protective dog ears with holes to aid in lighting the sight. The charging handle is located on the right side of the receiver and the selector switch is just ahead of the trigger guard; the magazine release button is just ahead of it.

Field-stripping is as follows:
1. Remove the magazine and cycle the weapon to be sure it is empty.
2. Loosen the front barrel/stock band (the screw is designed to be loosened with a cartridge rim if a screwdriver is not available). Slide the band onto the barrel by pressing the front end of the latch spring on the right side of the stock toward the rear to release it.
3. Slide the top half of the handguard forward and pivot it off the barrel. This will allow the trigger group/barrel/receiver assembly to be lifted up at the front and pulled out and up from the front of the stock.
4. Place the barrel/receiver/trigger group upside down on a flat surface. Pull back on the recoil spring and its guide slightly to free them, and then lift them out of the assembly (be careful; these are under spring tension). Separate the guide from the spring; the guide will be used as a tool for further disassembly.
5. Push out the cross pin at the front of the trigger housing with the guide. Push the housing forward to release it and remove the trigger assembly.
6. Turn the receiver right side up and pull the charging lever toward the rear until it lines up with the disassembly notch in the barrel groove; remove it from the receiver.
7. Push the bolt assembly to the rear until its front is behind the locking shoulder in the receiver. Rotate it so its locking lug points upward and to the right, and remove it from the receiver.

Normal maintenance and lubrication can be accomplished with this much disassembly. Reassembly is basically the reverse of the above procedure. To reassemble the charging lever, place the bolt toward the rear of the receiver.

Because of the huge numbers of military and civilian .30 Carbines that have been made, a wide variety of surplus and aftermarket accessories are available. Accessories include 10-, 20-, and 30-round magazines, bayonets, various folding stocks, pistol grip plastic stocks, and web gear and slings.

The best plastic stocks for the .30 Carbine are made by Choate Machine and Tool Company (which also makes the stocks for the Iver Johnson .30-caliber "Survival" Carbines). Choate's tough Zytel, glass-imbedded stocks are impervious to the elements and improve the handling qualities and accuracy of the rifle. There are two models of the Choate stock: one is a solid plastic stock with pistol grip; the other is a folding metal stock with a plastic pistol grip and handguard, which is a much better choice than the flimsy M1A1-style stock. The Choate folding stock sells for about $67, while the fixed stock runs around $45.

The 15-round magazine is much more reliable than most 30-round ones, which often work best with 28 rounds. Two sources of these magazines are Parellex Corporation and Sherwood International.

Though burdened with a poor cartridge, the .30 Carbine has proven to be one of the most popular rifles ever produced for the U.S. military and continues to see combat action worldwide, thanks to the large numbers that were manufactured.

M1/M2/M3 Carbine Specifications
Barrel length . . . . 18 in.
Caliber . . . . .30 Carbine
Cyclic rate (approx., M2/M3) . . . . 750 rpm
Length (approx.) . . . . 35.5 in.
Magazine (standard) . . . . 15- or 30-round
Muzzle velocity (approx.) . . . . 1960 fps
Rifling . . . . 4 grooves, right-hand twist
Weight unloaded (approx.) . . . . 5.5 lbs.

M1A1 Carbine Specifications
Barrel length . . . . 18 in.
Caliber . . . . .30 Carbine
Length (approx.) . . . . 35.5 in.
Length (stock folded) . . . . 25.4 in.
Magazine (standard) . . . . 15- or 30-round
Muzzle velocity (approx.) . . . . 1960 fps
Rifling . . . . 4 grooves, right-hand twist
Weight unloaded (approx.) . . . . 6.2 lbs.

5.7mm Johnson Carbine Specifications
Barrel length . . . . 18 in.
Caliber . . . . 5.7mm Johnson
Length (approx.) . . . . 35.5 in.
Magazine (standard) . . . . 15- or 30-round
Muzzle velocity (approx.) . . . . 3000 fps
Rifling . . . . 4 grooves, right-hand twist
Weight unloaded (approx.) . . . . 5.5 lbs.

Enforcer "Pistol" Specifications
Barrel length . . . . 9.5 in.
Caliber . . . . .30 Carbine
Length (approx.) . . . . 17 in.
Magazine (standard) . . . . 15- or 30-round
Muzzle velocity (approx.) . . . . 1800 fps
Rifling . . . . 4 grooves, right-hand twist
Weight unloaded (approx.) . . . . 4 lbs.

M14/M1A RIFLE

The M14 was originally developed by Army personnel as a replacement for the Garand, the .30 Carbine, the M3 grease gun, and the Browning Automatic Rifle. Specifications for the rifle called for it to fire in both semi- and full automatic. The original "Army Ground Forces Equipment Review Board Preliminary Board Study" called for a seven-pound weapon and a .30-caliber round. This weight/caliber combination might have been practical with a low-powered round like that of the M1 Carbine but was impossible with a full-powered rifle round.

In developing the cartridge for the rifle, the Army ignored all the military studies which showed that the battle rifles used in World War I and through the Korean War had too much power for their job. The U.S. Army created the T65 cartridge, a shortened version of the .30-06 round. The new round was not bad for a rifle but was too powerful for a lightweight automatic weapon—one of the prime requirements set up by the Army board. Despite the fact that the round was overly powerful, the NATO countries adopted the T65 as the standard 7.62mm NATO round.

While a number of other NATO countries adopted the FN LAR, the United States developed the T44 rifle for the new chambering. During tests of the T44, FN LAR, and the experimental T25 rifle, the FN LAR outperformed the T44, but the U.S. military gambled that the T44 could be modified into a superior weapon and continued its development.

The T44 was a modified M1 Garand rifle. Shortly after World War II, Lloyd Corbett, working at the U.S. Springfield Armory, altered the M1 into the T44 configuration. After a series of tests and improvements, the U.S. Army adopted two versions of the T44 rifles in 1957. One was a standard rifle, the T44E4, which became the M14 rifle; the other, the T44E5, was a heavy-barreled version which became the M15 rifle. The M15 was never produced in any numbers; while more satisfactory than the M14 in regard to muzzle climb and overheating, it didn't have the quick-change barrel necessary for heavy automatic fire and was thus obsolete before it was deployed.

The T44 used a 20-round magazine rather than the eight-round clip, which had a tendency to tell an enemy when it was empty by springing out of the rifle, had more inherent accuracy than the old Garand thanks to moving the gas port back eight inches, and had a less abrupt recoil. But it had problems. The T44 rifle was too light for good control during automatic fire and was hard to manufacture because of extremely close tolerances in the gas system and mechanism.

To make the rifle look good, tests against other contenders were often all but rigged. When the M14 was fielded, the explosion of several rifles during training exercises pretty well negated any of its good points. The new rifle was supposed to be a lightweight replacement for the Browning Automatic Rifle. The M14 was neither lightweight nor easily controllable in the automatic mode thanks to the recoil of the 7.62mm round, and large quantities of the rifle were finally issued without the automatic-fire selector.

Military designers created a new stock with a pistol grip and straight back design and a muzzle brake which fitted over the standard flash suppressor; under the

The M14 was modified slightly with an E2 stock in an effort to make it more controllable in automatic fire. The new stock was too little, too late as far as the U.S. military was concerned. Currently, the stock is available on Springfield Armory's M1A rifle. Photo courtesy of Springfield Armory.

The M14 is actually a modified M1 Garand rifle. After a series of tests and improvements, the U.S. Army adopted two versions of the rifle in 1957, one of which was a standard rifle which became the M14 rifle. Photo courtesy of Springfield Armory.

handguard, a folding grip was available to steady the weapon. A bipod, fastened to the gas regulator, rounded out the modifications. The new rifle was first designated the M14E2 and later accepted as the M14A1 in 1962.

While these modifications made the 12.8-pound M14A1 somewhat controllable in automatic fire, most shooters still couldn't control the rifle in the automatic mode and the barrel still tended to overheat during sustained fire. The 7.62 cartridge was just too much in the auto mode, and very few of the modified rifles were ever issued.

Internal changes were made in the weapon so that it gradually became easier to manufacture, and greater design tolerances made the gas piston less apt to lock up and bend if it became fouled. By the time production stopped, most of the bugs had been worked out of the design. Those who used the rifle usually thought highly of it, even though it was excessively heavy compared to the AR-15/M16.

In the end, the Army ended up with a good combat rifle, though it was not capable of replacing the submachine gun or light machine gun, but the changes came too late and many were convinced that the Army had chosen too large a caliber. The M14 turned out to be harder and more costly to mass-produce than had been expected while its competitor, the AR-15, was much cheaper to manufacture even in limited quantities.

The Army Materiel Command conducted rigged tests of the two rifles and "found" that the M14 was superior to the AR-15. Since glowing reports about the AR-15 were coming back from Vietnam, the Secretary of the Army had the Army's Inspector General look into the tests. The Inspector General found that the Army Materiel Command had rigged the tests by testing hand-picked target-grade M14s against AR-15s chosen at random. The group had then conducted a dry run to see how the two rifles performed; this was followed by an "official test" which did not include the parts of the dry-

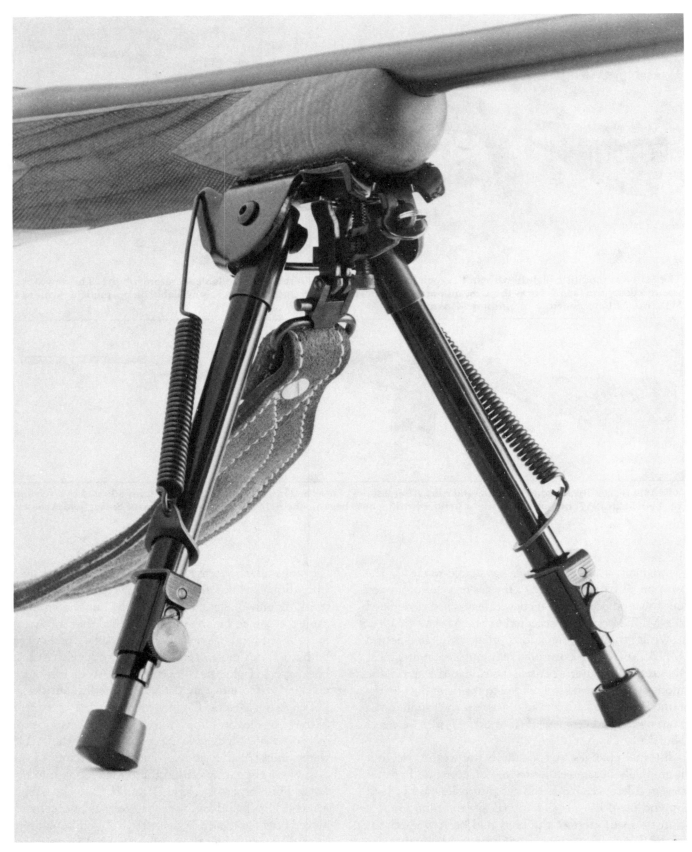

Probably the best bipod available for use on a "serious" sniping rifle is the Harris bipod. For accurate shooting, this unit is a "must have." Photo courtesy of Harris Engineering.

run test in which the AR-15 had outperformed the M14s. The results of the test backfired against those who were trying to keep the M14 in use when the Inspector General uncovered the truth.

Even after the AR-15/M16 was adopted, the M14 continued to be used as the M21 sniper weapon. In this mode, it is generally rebuilt, the barrel often glass-bedded, and a Leatherwood auto-ranging scope mounted on it. A few other types of stocks made for the sniper rifle during testing were often used in Vietnam, including stocks with heavy recoil pads, pistol grips, and raised combs for use with the telescopic sight. A somewhat similar rifle was developed for the National Matches by the U.S. military. It, too, was reworked for accuracy with a glass-bedded barrel. It was not used with a scope, however, so the rear sight was modified somewhat for finer calibration and the aperture was hooded.

Other variations include the M14M, the Type III, and the Type IV. The M14M was a rifle with the selector welded to prevent full-auto use; it was to have been used at NRA-sponsored shooting events but political considerations kept most of the rifles from being issued. The Type III and Type IV had folding stocks which proved to be unsatisfactory for combat use.

The M14 was produced by Harrington and Richardson, Springfield Armory, Thompson Products (TRW), and Winchester-Western (Olin). Government production of the rifle ceased in 1964, although several companies continue to manufacture the rifles for the civilian market. Probably the most notable of these "civilian" companies is the Springfield Armory. The company makes its own parts and receivers and actually produces a rifle better than the U.S. Army model. Among the Springfield Armory offerings are the fully automatic M14, the semiauto M1A, the short-barreled M1A-A1 available with a folding stock, and the M14 or M1A decked out with an E2 stock. (Shooters with smaller hands will find the E2 stock more comfortable than the standard M14 stock.) The Springfield Armory rifles are manufactured with a 1-in-10 twist for lighter .308 bullets and with a 1-in-12 twist for heavier bullets. In addition to the standard 20-round magazines, the company offers 5- and 10-round magazines for hunting use. Magazines can be filled a round at a time, off a stripper clip and guide, or with a stripper clip and the guide machined in the receiver's top.

Like the M1 Garand, the rear sight of the M14 is finger-adjustable for both windage (right knob) and elevation (left knob). The safety is located inside the trigger guard (pushing it forward places it in the "fire" position) and the magazine is just behind the magazine well, both convenient locations for left-handed use. The reciprocating charging handle is located on the right of the receiver. On rifles which fire in the automatic mode, the selector is located on the right side of the receiver above the trigger at the stock/receiver line. The "A" on the selector must be toward the rear for full-auto fire. Only very short bursts of two or three rounds should be used.

The M14 can fire grenades with a special barrel-mounted launcher tube. A special sight is available which mounts on the left side of the stock over the magazine well. A gas shut-off valve is located just ahead of the stock on the gas tube/barrel area; it can be turned with a cartridge rim. The slot of the valve is placed parallel to the barrel to shut off the gas for use with ballistic cartridges. Winter triggers and safeties are also available.

Field-stripping is nearly identical to the M1 Garand:

1. Remove the magazine and cycle the weapon to be sure it is empty.

2. Grasp the rear of the trigger guard and pull it forward and away from the rifle. This will allow the trigger group to be removed and free the barrel/receiver assembly.

3. If the stock doesn't readily separate from the barrel and receiver, push the receiver forward while pulling up slightly. This should free it.

4. On weapons with automatic-fire capabilities, it is necessary to remove the trip lever/connector assembly on the right side of the receiver, just below the charging lever. This is done with the bolt closed by pushing the connector forward until it can be rotated clockwise until the elongated hole in the connector assembly is aligned with the elongated stud on the sear release. By lowering the front end of the connector, the rear end can be lifted off the sear-release stud.

5. Place the barrel/receiver group upside down on a flat surface. Pull back on the recoil spring guide and the recoil spring slightly to free them, and then lift them out of the assembly (be careful: they are under a lot of spring tension).

6. Turn the receiver right side up and pull the charging lever toward the rear of the receiver until it lines up with the disassembly notch on the right side of the receiver. Rotate the charging lever assembly down and outward to free it; pull it to the rear to disengage it from the receiver.

7. Push the bolt assembly forward and pivot it out toward the ejection port to remove it.

Normal maintenance and lubrication can be accomplished with this much disassembly.

The M14 and M1A were designed for military

Springfield Armory created a rifle similar to the Italian BM-59 by clipping the M14's barrel and adding a folding stock. Photo courtesy of Springfield Armory.

ammunition; rifles on the civilian market are sometimes a little finicky about commercial ammunition. There are several cautions in using the mechanism itself: the M14 should not be dry-fired nor should the trigger be pulled when the bolt is not locked. Though it is unlikely to happen if only done occasionally, either of these actions could damage the sear.

A wide variety of accessories are available for the M14, and a number of companies manufacture equipment for the civilian versions of the rifle as well. Probably the widest selection is available from Springfield Armory. Notable equipment includes bayonets, night-vision devices, scopes, various training aids, special muzzle brakes, and even sound suppressors. A must-have accessory is the M14 combination tool, which fits into the butt trap. It can be used to take down the weapon's gas cylinder, has a rear-sight screwdriver, is a cleaning rod, and can be used to load the magazines. In addition to military metal magazines, a 30-round plastic magazine is produced by Tobias Guns.

Besides the military E2 stock and M1A1 folding stock, fiberglass and composite stocks are available from Fiberpro. Included in its line is the M1A folding stock (similar to the Beretta M59 but having a composite rather than wood stock) and the M1AE2 stock, available in either fiberglass or plastic composite. The cost for the fiberglass stocks is $120, while the composite costs $140. Both offer lighter weight and better accuracy than wooden stocks.

The M14 is a very potent weapon that will probably see limited use for some time thanks to military surplus, a wide range of accessories, and newly manufactured weapons.

M14 Specifications

Barrel length . . . . 22 in.
Caliber . . . . .308 Winchester (7.62mm NATO)
Cyclic rate (approx.) . . . . 750 rpm
Length (approx.) . . . . 44 in.
Magazine (standard) 20-round
Muzzle velocity (approx.) . . . . 2800 fps
Rifling . . . . 4 grooves, right-hand twist
Weight unloaded (approx.) . . . . 9.6 lbs.

M14/M1A Specifications

Barrel length . . . . 22 in.
Caliber . . . . .308 Winchester (7.62mm NATO)
Cyclic rate (approx.) . . . . 750 rpm
Length (approx.) . . . . 44 in.
Magazine (standard) 20-round
Muzzle velocity (approx.) . . . . 2800 fps
Rifling . . . . 4 grooves, right-hand twist
Weight unloaded (approx.) . . . . 12.8 lbs.

M1 OFFSPRING: BM-59

While the United States was experimenting with a variation of the Garand that later became the M14, Beretta of Italy was developing its own modified rifle. The Beretta plant had been manufacturing Garand rifles since the early 1950s, and it was only a matter of time before the innovative company started altering the basic—and somewhat outdated—design.

The major work was done by Domenico Salza and Vittorio Valle. In 1959, a number of their prototype rifles were tested by the Italian army. The weapon selected for production was quite similar to the M14 with its 7.62mm NATO chambering, selective-fire ability, stripper clip guide in the upper receiver, butt trap door, and 20-round detachable box magazine. (And it would still accept the Garand bayonet and some other accessories.) Like the Garand, the Beretta bolt stays open after the magazine is empty.

The rifle was slightly modified to become the BM-59 Mark I, and a rifle outfitted with bipod and flash suppressor/grenade launcher became the BM-59 Mark

Beretta developed its own modified rifle based on the Garand rifle. Later, Springfield Armory purchased the inventory of parts from Beretta and now offers semiauto versions of the rifle to buyers in the United States. Among the models available are the standard BM-59 (top), the BM-59 Alpine rifle (center), and the Nigerian Mark IV version (bottom). Photo courtesy of Springfield Armory.

IA (or BM-59D). The special flash suppressor/muzzle brake/grenade-launching attachment is often referred to as a "tri-compensator" since it has three different functions. Other versions included the Mark II, which had a pistol grip, winter trigger, and attached bipod; the Mark III PARA with folding stock for use by Alpine and Airborne divisions; and a heavy-barreled Mark IV with hinged butt plate, pistol grip, and a beefed-up bipod for use as a squad automatic weapon. The Mark III used by Alpine troops became the "Alpini" after its barrel was shortened and a permanent tri-compensator mounted, while the Airborne version with a detachable flash suppressor became the "Paracudisti." Nigeria purchased a BM-59 rifle nearly identical to the Mark I except for a plastic pistol-grip on the wooden stock which has an FN LAR cut to it.

In 1979, the Italian military adopted the .223-caliber AR70 rifle. In an effort to sell its remaining inventory of BM-59 parts, Beretta developed a lightened version of the Mark II for the American civilian market. This rifle was designated the BM-62 and is without flash suppressor, winter trigger, or bipod. Only about 2,000 BM-62s were made. Springfield Armory purchased the rest of Beretta's inventory of BM-59 parts and is currently building semiauto versions of the rifle. The Springfield Armory versions offer a wide variety of stocks and options. Interestingly, demand for the Alpine stock was so great that the company has started manufacturing its own version and has modified it for its M1A rifle.

As with the M14 and Garand, the rear sight of the BM-59 can be adjusted for windage (right knob) and elevation (left knob). The elevation is adjustable to a rather fanciful 1200 meters. The feed ramp of the BM-59 is wider than that of many other military rifles, so that it chambers hollow-point or other blunt-nosed ammunition more reliably. The safety is located inside the trigger guard (pushing it forward places it in the "fire" position) and the magazine is just behind the magazine well; both of these make the rifle ambidextrous, except that the charging handle is on the right side of the rifle which still isn't much of a problem for lefties.

Field-stripping is basically identical to that of the M14:
1. Remove the magazine and cycle the weapon to be sure it is empty.
2. Grasp the rear of the trigger guard and pull it forward and away from the rifle. This will allow the trigger group to be removed and free the barrel/receiver assembly.
3. If the stock does not readily separate from the barrel and receiver, push the receiver forward while pulling up slightly. This should free it.
4. On weapons with automatic-fire capabilities, it is necessary to remove the trip lever/connector assembly on the right side of the receiver, just below the charging lever. This is done with the bolt closed; push the connector forward until it can be rotated clockwise and the elongated hole in the connector assembly is aligned with the elongated stud on the sear release. By lowering the front end of the connector, the rear end can be lifted off the sear-release stud.
5. Place the barrel/receiver group upside down on a flat surface. Pull back on the recoil-spring guide and the recoil spring slightly to free them, and lift them out of the assembly (be careful: these are under a lot of spring tension).
6. Turn the receiver right side up and pull the charging lever toward the rear until it lines up with the disassembly notch on the right side of the receiver. Rotate the charging lever assembly down and outward to free it, then pull it to the rear to disengage it from the receiver.
7. Push the bolt assembly forward; pivot it out toward the ejection port to remove it.

Normal maintenance and lubrication can be accomplished with this much disassembly.

The BM-59 rifles are well made. Unfortunately, they soon became obsolete because of ammunition changes needed on the modern battlefield. Nevertheless, many of these weapons will continue to be used for hunting, self-defense, survival, law enforcement, etc., where the extreme power of the .308 chambering may be more important than the logistical advantages of the lightweight .223 ammunition.

BM-59 Specifications

Barrel length . . . . 19.3 in.
Caliber . . . . .308 Winchester (7.62mm NATO)
Cyclic rate (approx.) . . . . 800 rpm
Length (approx.) . . . . 43 in.
Magazine (standard) 20-round
Muzzle velocity (approx.) . . . . 2700 fps
Rifling . . . . . 4 grooves, 1-in-12 in., right-hand twist
Weight unloaded (approx.) . . . . 9.6 lbs.

BM-59 Alpini Specifications

Barrel length . . . . 19.3 in.
Caliber . . . . .308 Winchester (7.62mm NATO)
Cyclic rate (approx.) . . . . 800 rpm
Length (approx.) . . . . 43.7 in.
Length (stock folded) . . . . 33.7 in.
Magazine (standard) 20-round
Muzzle velocity (approx.) . . . . 2700 fps

Rifling . . . . . 4 grooves, 1-in-12 in., right-hand twist
Weight unloaded (approx.) . . . . 9.9 lbs.

BM-59 Paracudisti Specifications
Barrel length . . . . 18.4 in.
Caliber . . . . .308 Winchester (7.62mm NATO)
Cyclic rate (approx.) . . . . 810 rpm
Length (approx.) . . . . 43.7 in.
Length (stock folded) . . . . 28.5 in.
Magazine (standard) 20-round
Muzzle velocity (approx.) . . . . 2630 fps
Rifling . . . . . 4 grooves, 1-in-12 in., right-hand twist
Weight unloaded (approx.) . . . . 10 lbs.

BM-59 Mark IV Specifications
Barrel length . . . . 21 in.
Caliber . . . . .308 Winchester (7.62mm NATO)
Cyclic rate (approx.) . . . . 750 rpm
Length (approx.) . . . . 43 in.
Magazine (standard) 20-round
Muzzle velocity (approx.) . . . . 2730 fps
Rifling . . . . . 4 grooves, 1-in-12 in., right-hand twist
Weight unloaded (approx.) . . . . 12 lbs.

MINI-14 RIFLE

As one might expect, the Mini-14 is a scaled down version of the M14 rifle, which ironically comes closer to satisfying the original "Army Ground Forces Equipment Review Board Preliminary Board Study" than the M14 itself. Its only failure to comply is that, unlike the M14, the Mini-14 is chambered for the .223 Remington rather than the too-powerful .308 Winchester. The Mini-14 is capable of controllable auto fire and is under the seven-pound specifications required by the Review Board. One has to wonder what might have happened if a rifle like the Mini-14 had been fielded rather than the M14.

The Mini-14 is not just a scaled-down M14; it's also an improved version. The gas port has been moved back inside the stock, and parts of the receiver and trigger group have been refined and strengthened. The rifle borrows heavily, but is greatly improved. The Mini-14 was designed by Bill Ruger, who launched his designing career in 1949 with a successful .22 auto pistol and an improved Western-style revolver that took advantage of the fast-draw craze of the 1950s. Ruger's Mini-14, which was aimed at (and for a time, sold only to) the law-enforcement and military markets, was introduced in 1972. Because demand was great in the civilian market, the "sporterized" semiauto version with a 5-round magazine was introduced in 1976. Though no large military sales ever were secured, the rifle was very competitively priced. The public and police markets have made it a commercial success, so much so that Ruger had to build a special facility devoted just to building the Mini-14.

In addition to the price, which is often only half that commanded by many military-style rifles on the market, the Mini-14 has a traditional design with a wooden stock and blued metal. Those who abhor the plastic furniture and parkerized metal on most assault rifles often feel more at home with the hunting-rifle look of the Mini-14.

There are several series of the Mini-14. Early production models, which have a slightly different design and specifications from later models, were in the 180 series (denoted by the "180" in the serial number). The 181 series is the improved version and the 182 series includes all stainless-steel Mini-14 rifles; the 187 serial-number prefix is used for the new "Rancher" sporting version of the Mini-14.

Currently three models of the Mini-14 are available: a semiauto sporting version, the Mini-14/5; the police/military Mini-14/20GB with bayonet lug and flash suppressor; and the AC-556 selective-fire version, which is nearly identical to the GB but has a 3-round burst capability as well as semiauto and full-auto fire. Because the rifles are capable of being modified almost endlessly by both the factory and by gunsmiths, a wide range of options and models are found. Generally, the Ruger Company offers the following options to buyers of small numbers of weapons: stainless steel parts (denoted by a "K" prefix), folding stocks ("F" prefix), 5-round magazines ("5" suffix), 20-round magazines ("20" suffix), flash suppressor/grenade launcher/bayonet lug ("GB" suffix), and dovetail mounts milled into the top of the receiver for scope rings ("R" suffix).

With the three models and these options, the following groups of rifles are readily available from Ruger:

• Mini-14/5: semiauto, blued rifle with standard 5-round magazine.
• Mini-14/5R: semiauto, blued rifle with standard 5-round magazine and scope mount (special Ruger rings are also furnished with the purchase of the rifle).
• Mini-14/5-F: semiauto, blued rifle with standard 5-round magazine and folding stock.
• K Mini-14/5: semiauto, stainless-steel rifle with standard 5-round magazine.
• K Mini-14/5-F: semiauto, stainless-steel rifle with standard 5-round magazine and folding stock.
• Mini-14/20GB: semiauto, blued rifle with bayonet lug, flash suppressor, and 20-round magazine.

The Mini-14/5R "Rancher" has integral dovetails to allow the use of a scope. The rifle is different internally from earlier models and has a flip-up rear sight for use without a scope. Photo courtesy of Sturm, Ruger.

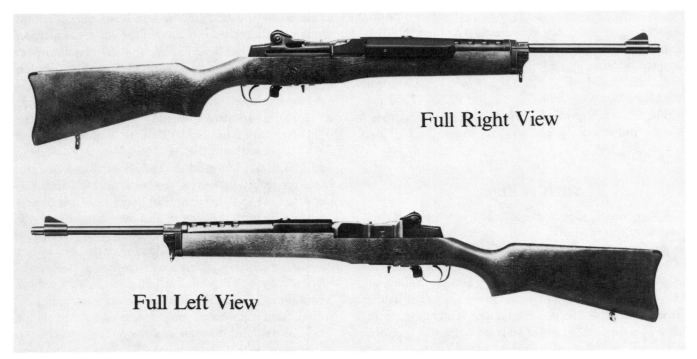

Full Right View

Full Left View

The Mini-14 is a scaled-down version of the U.S. M14 rifle (which in turn was a spin-off of the M1 Garand rifle). Ironically, the Mini-14 comes closer to satisfying the requirements of the original Army Ground Forces Equipment Review Board Study that led to the development of the M14 than the M14 itself does! Photo courtesy of Sturm, Ruger.

• Mini-14/20GB-F: semiauto, blued rifle with bayonet lug, flash suppressor, 20-round magazine, and folding stock.

• K Mini-14/20GB: semiauto, stainless-steel rifle with bayonet lug, 20-round magazine and flash suppressor.

• K Mini-14/20GB-F: semiauto, stainless-steel rifle with bayonet lug, flash suppressor, 20-round magazine, and folding stock.

• AC-556: blued, selective-fire rifle with 18-inch barrel, flash suppressor, and bayonet lug.

• AC-556 F: blued, selective-fire rifle with folding stock and usually a 13-inch barrel with flash suppressor but without bayonet lug.

• K AC-556: stainless-steel, selective-fire rifle with 18-inch barrel, bayonet lug, and flash suppressor.

• K AC-556 F: stainless-steel, selective-fire rifle with folding stock and usually a 13-inch barrel with flash suppressor.

The stainless-steel models are highly resistant to corrosion, making them ideal for environments which might quickly wreck steel weapons. Stainless steel does have one drawback, however; it retains more heat than regular steel. Because of this, the stainless-steel barrels are apt to overheat with excessive firing, especially in

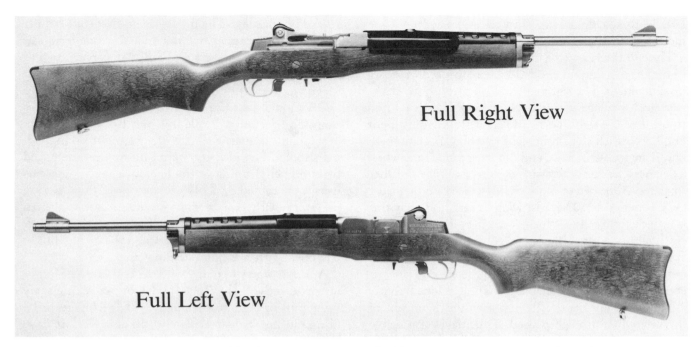

Full Right View

Full Left View

Stainless-steel models of the Mini-14—like this K Mini-14/5—are highly resistant to corrosion, making them ideal for use in environments detrimental to standard steel weapons. Photo courtesy of Sturm, Ruger.

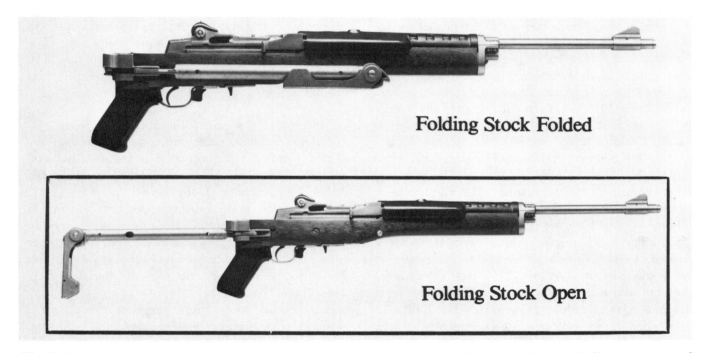

Folding Stock Folded

Folding Stock Open

The K Mini-14/5-F combines the handiness of a folding stock with the durability of stainless steel. Photo courtesy of Sturm, Ruger.

the automatic mode. This may or may not be a consideration for some users.

Early models of the Mini-14 had a wooden upper handguard; newer handguards have a ventilated fiberglass upper half with an aluminum heat shield. The "R" rifles, sometimes referred to as the "Rancher" models, also have a slightly different buffer, and the spring-loaded ejector of the standard rifle is replaced by a stationary ejector similar to that used in many .22 rifles (the Rancher's ejector is part of the bolt hold-open assembly).

Both of these changes prevent wear and tear on a scope mounted on the rifle.

Though the rear sight of the Mini-14 appears similar to that of the Garand and M14s, close inspection shows up differences. The sight assembly controls both elevation and windage with wheels: elevation with a knob in front of the sight, and windage with an adjustment knob on the left side of the sight assembly. Both of these knobs are locked in place and can be adjusted only when a detent is pressed down with the tip of a bullet or other small tool. One detent move changes the point of impact by 1.5 inches at 100 yards. Many users find that this is an advantage since the zero can't be thrown off accidentally, as is often the case in combat. The front sight appears fragile since it lacks the protective dog ears of most military rifles; in fact, it is quite strong, since it is nonadjustable, and is able to handle a lot of abuse.

The rear sight on the "R" models flips down out of the way when a scope is used. This makes it possible to use a much lower scope mount; the drawback is that the rear sight is rather fragile in the up position. Windage is adjusted on the Rancher model with a small hex wrench, while the elevation is adjusted (somewhat awkwardly) by loosening two small screws on either side of the peep hole. It should also be noted that when aftermarket stocks which are longer than the Ruger stock are mounted on the Rancher, proper mounting is hard to achieve because of the Ruger ring mount system.

Unlike the M14, the Ruger rifles do not have a stripper clip guide at the top of the receiver. The safety is located inside the trigger guard (pushing it forward places it in the "fire" position); the rifle can be put on "safe" before cycling the bolt—a good safety feature. The magazine release is just behind the magazine well, both convenient locations for left-handed use. The reciprocating charging handle is located on the right side of the receiver.

On rifles which fire full automatic, the selector is located on the right side of the receiver above the trigger at the stock/receiver line. The Ruger rifles feature both full auto and the more practical 3-round burst. As in semiauto fire, the firing pin is retracted until the bolt is locked; it is impossible to ignite a primer prematurely. A bolt hold-open device locks the action open following the last shot. The action can be closed on a new magazine by pulling back slightly on the charging lever and releasing it.

The trigger of the Mini-14 is lighter than that of many military rifles; it is set at the factory to pull at 4½ pounds. An additional plus is that, unlike many other combat rifles, it can also be lightened by a good gunsmith.

The Ruger rifles are not quite as robust as some military rifles; the plus side to this is that they weigh several pounds less. The minus side is that they require extra care and proper maintenance for long-term service. Many civilian users and police departments find that the extra care is more than offset by the rifle's light weight and low price.

Occasionally, a Mini-14 seems to be plagued with less than ideal accuracy. While this may not be much of a problem in combat, it can be aggravating to an individual shooter. Provided the barrel hasn't been damaged by improper cleaning or the like, inaccuracy problems usually are caused by a poor stock-to-barrel fit. Replacing the stock with one of the new plastic models often reduces the shot grouping by half. Some of the best offhand shooting I've ever seen was done by a Mini-14 equipped with a Choate folding stock.

Another worry to many who depend on the Mini-14 for self-defense is the Ruger policy of not selling spare firing pins or bolts to the public. What happens if the firing pin breaks in a crisis and the user doesn't have any way to replace it?

The reason Ruger doesn't sell these parts is that they need to be carefully fitted for reasons of safety. The solution to this quandary is quite simple: the owner of the rifle removes the bolt and firing pin from the rifle and sends the firearm to Ruger for replacement parts. The new parts fit, and the owner has spare parts that fit as well. Because of the low price of the Mini-14, this extra trouble still gives the user quite a savings.

Field-stripping is nearly identical to the M14:

1. Remove the magazine and cycle the weapon to be sure it is empty. The safety must be put into the "safe" position inside the trigger guard and the hammer cocked before field-stripping can be carried out.

2. Grasp the rear of the trigger guard and pull it forward and away from the rifle (a small punch or other tool can be placed in the hole at the rear of the trigger guard to aid in this task). This will allow the trigger group to be removed and free the barrel/receiver assembly.

3. If the stock does not readily separate from the barrel and receiver, push the receiver forward while pulling up slightly. This should free it. Though not necessary for field-stripping, the upper handguard half can be removed by pulling the rear end of the handguard away from the barrel to release its clip fastener. The rear of the handguard is lifted up and back for removal.

4. On weapons with automatic-fire capabilities, it is necessary to remove the trip lever/connector assembly on the right side of the receiver just below the charging lever. This is done with the bolt closed by pushing the connector forward until it can be rotated clockwise

and the elongated hole in the connector assembly is aligned with the elongated stud on the sear release. By lowering the front end of the connector, the rear end can be lifted off the sear-release stud.

5. Place the barrel/receiver group upside down on a flat surface. Push forward on the recoil-spring guide and the recoil spring slightly to free them and then lift them out of the assembly (be careful: these parts are under a lot of spring tension).

6. Turn the receiver right side up and pull the charging lever toward the rear of the receiver until the locking projections on the slide line up with the disassembly notch on the right side of the receiver. Rotate the charging lever assembly down and outward to free it, then pull it to the rear to disengage it from the receiver.

7. Push the bolt assembly forward and pivot it out toward the ejection port to remove it.

Normal maintenance and lubrication can be accomplished with this much disassembly. Reassembly is basically the reverse of the above procedure. The safety must be engaged and the hammer cocked before the trigger assembly can be replaced in the rifle.

With Rancher (Mini-14/5R) models, it is necessary to remove the bolt hold-open device before the bolt can be installed. To do this, lightly tap at the top of the cover plate on the left of the receiver. When the plate is removed, depress the plunger and pull the bolt stop out to the left of the receiver through the opening created by the removal of the plate. This will allow the bolt to be replaced in the receiver. Once this is done, replace the hold-open assembly.

The Mini-14 was designed for both sporting and military ammunition and is capable of digesting a wide variety of loads. The only round which might create problems with older models of the rifle is the new 5.56mm NATO round; its long bullet could create excessive pressure by being wedged against the rifling of the barrel when chambered.

Because of the number of military rifles chambered for the .223, a wide variety of surplus and aftermarket accessories are available for the Mini-14, including 20-, 30-, and 40-round magazines, bayonet lugs, folding and pistol-grip plastic stocks, flash suppressors, and a wealth of other products; a few in particular are worth noting.

One of the major companies that produces accessories for the Mini-14 is Choate Machine and Tool. Especially notable are its Zytel (glass-imbedded nylon) stocks. These often improve the accuracy of the Mini-14 as well as giving the user the popular pistol-grip configuration. There are two pistol-grip Choate stocks: one is a solid stock and the other is a folder. Many users prefer the Choate folding stock over the Ruger-style folding stock since

the butt plate doesn't have to be locked separately. The folding stock retails around $67, while the fixed stock runs around $45. In an effort to capture the "low range" of the stock market, Choate also manufactures a folder made of ABS; while not as tough as its Zytel stocks, it is far from fragile and the price is only $49. All three can be ordered directly from Choate or from dealers who carry Choate products.

More traditional plastic stocks are available for those who like the idea of a weather- and humidity-proof stock but dislike the spacey look of the pistol grips. One is manufactured by Mitchell Arms, Inc., for $70; the stock is actually stronger and lighter than the wooden stock but black and a bit longer with its recoil pad. Choate also makes a traditional-style Zytel stock for $47. The owner can install either of these without having to hire a gunsmith.

Choate also markets flash suppressors which improve sight picture and target lead since they replace the front sight with a dog ears sight. Three types are available: an AR-15 "birdcage," a long "M14" style, and a suppressor designed for nighttime use (it works well but creates a louder retort). The Choate flash suppressors do not have openings in the lower side; this cuts down on muzzle climb. Cost is around $30 each. For larger shooters, Choate offers an extended butt pad that adds one inch to the length of pull for $15. The company also offers a ventilated fiberglass handguard.

Another company making useful Mini-14 accessories is Ram-Line, Inc. They offer an excellent walnut/metal folding stock that is the spitting image of the Ruger model, which, until recently, wasn't available to civilian users. The company also makes a number of flash suppressors that slip around the front sight, a plastic upper handguard (again, nearly identical in design to the Ruger), as well as the best lightweight "clothespin" bipod available.

One of the most interesting innovations from Ram-Line is the Combo Mag. This is a tough 30-round plastic magazine which not only fits the Mini-14 but all assault rifles that use AR-15 magazines. While anyone who has pondered the differences between the Ruger and Armalite rifles may doubt that this is possible, the magazines work well. Interestingly, they are also transparent (but nonglare) and marked to show approximately how many rounds are left in the magazine. These retail for around $21 each and make a lot of sense for people or groups with several types of combat rifles.

A .22 LR conversion unit is available from Jonathan Arthur Ciener, Inc., for $140. It fits all but the 180 series and is easily installed. With its 30-round magazine and low recoil, the .22 conversion is perfect for training or

Ram-Line's excellent walnut/metal folding stock is the spitting image of the Ruger model.

One of the most interesting innovations from Ram-Line is the ''Combo Mag.'' This tough 30-round plastic magazine fits the Mini-14 as well as the AR-15/M16, AR-180/18, and all the new assault rifles that use AR-15 magazines. Photo courtesy of Ram-Line.

plinking. In addition to standard .22 LR ammunition, CCI's Long CB Caps can be used in the adapter for nearly silent practice; the rounds don't cycle the action, so that the Mini-14 becomes a bolt-action rifle—a definite plus in teaching beginners.

The Mini-14's inexpensive price has made it the "poor man's" assault rifle in many ways. With new bullpup kits offered by several companies, the Mini-14 may well become the "poor man's bullpup" as well. Leading the pack is the K-3 Bullpup Kit offered by Westminister Arms. The stock covers the rifle's factory trigger/safety assembly, and double rods connect the pistol grip trigger to the enclosed trigger. A new safety is mounted behind the new trigger; while this is not as safe as the Ruger safety, it is, in theory at least, as safe as many other combat rifles. A cheek pad is mounted in the old rear-sight assembly, and a rear sight/carrying handle which looks like the one found on the AR-15 and can use AR-15 scope mounts replaces the upper half of the handguard. A raised AR-15-style front sight clamps onto the barrel. This creates a very handy weapon but cannot be safely used by left-handed shooters since the reciprocating charging handle would make a left-hand hold dangerous.

Unfortunately, early Westminister K-3 bullpup stocks weren't very strong and fitted poorly. Currently, Westminister is correcting these problems and at the time of this writing is planning on marketing a "military grade" stock. The cost is $190.

Other aftermarket accessories that most Mini-14 users find of use are 20- and 30-round magazines. Two good sources of these are Parallex Corporation and Sherwood International.

The Mini-14 is a handy, affordable rifle that is capable of being modified for combat or used as a sporter.

Mini-14/5 Specifications

Barrel length	18.5 in.
Caliber	.223 Remington
Cyclic rate (approx.)	750 rpm
Length (approx.)	37.3 in.
Magazine (standard)	5-round

Muzzle velocity (approx.) .... 3300 fps
Rifling ..... 6 grooves, 1-in-10 in., right-hand twist
Weight (approx.) .... 6.4 lbs.

Mini-14/20GB Specifications
Barrel length .... 18.5 in.
Caliber .... .223 Remington
Cyclic rate (approx.) .... 750 rpm
Length (approx.) .... 37.3 in.
Magazine (standard) 20-round
Muzzle velocity (approx.) .... 3300 fps
Rifling ..... 6 grooves, 1-in-10 in., right-hand twist
Weight (approx.) .... 6.4 lbs.

AC-556 F Specifications
Barrel length .... 13 in.
Caliber .... .223 Remington
Cyclic rate (approx.) .... 750 rpm
Length (approx.) .... 33.5 in.
Length (stock folded) .... 23.8 in.
Magazine (standard) 20-round
Muzzle velocity (approx.) .... 3000 fps
Rifling ..... 6 grooves, 1-in-10 in., right-hand twist
Weight (approx.) .... 7.9 lbs.

XGI

Because of the success of the Mini-14 rifle, Ruger introduced an up-scaled model chambered for larger rounds in 1985. Since the M14 rifle had been retired from the U.S. military, the Ruger rifle's designation is a play on the words "Ex-Government Issue" or "XGI." Many of the dimensions of the new rifle are identical to those of the M14; the XGI in .308 will even accept the M14 magazine.

Except for a rubber recoil pad and a metal lining in the fiberglass upper handguard, the rifle is basically a large version of the Mini-14/5R right down to its flip-up rear sight and integral scope mount. The initial XGI to reach the market was chambered for .308 Winchester with a .243 Winchester being released about a half year later. More chamberings may be offered if the rifle meets with success.

Location of the safety, magazine release, etc., are identical to the Mini-14, making this an ideal weapon for someone who may switch from one caliber to another. In effect, the XGI in a choice of several calibers and the Mini-14—especially with a .22 conversion unit—is yet another "commercial" systems weapon. Strangely enough, while the HK, Stoner, AR-10 and AR-15 systems

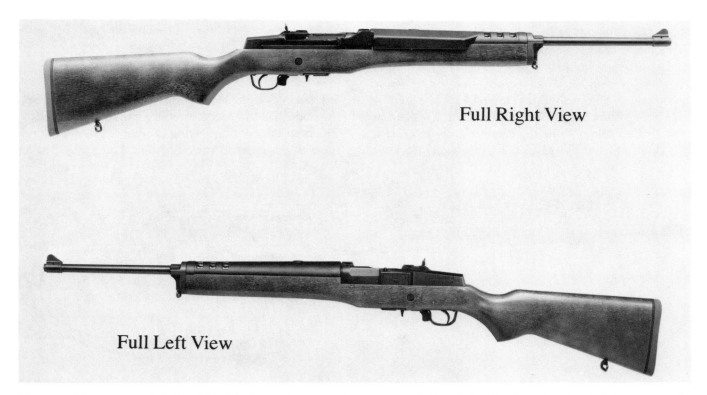

Full Right View

Full Left View

Because of the success of the Mini-14 rifle, Ruger introduced a new, up-scaled model of the rifle chambered for larger rounds in 1985. The M14 rifle had been retired from the U.S. military, and the Ruger rifle's designation is a play on the words ''Ex-Government Issue,'' or ''XGI.'' Photo courtesy of Sturm, Ruger.

families have failed to catch on, the Mini-14/XGI family may be a success.

While the XGI seems to have come full circle, back to the M14 which inspired the Mini-14, it should be noted that the relatively lightweight XGI rifle bears more resemblance to the Mini-14 than the heavy M14. The gas port is still encased in the stock, the bolt is much heavier than that of the M14, and the trigger mechanism is strengthened. Additionally, the rifle flings its empty brass to the side to prevent scope damage, and there are no plans to repeat the mistake of the M14 by making a full-automatic model.

It will be interesting to see what develops in the future as Ruger continues to market this family of rifles.

XGI Specifications

Barrel length . . . . 20 in.
Caliber . . . . .308 Winchester (7.62mm NATO)
or .243 Winchester
Length (approx.) . . . . 39.9 in.
Magazine (standard) 5-round
Muzzle velocity (approx.) . . . . 2800 fps
Rifling . . . . . 6 grooves, 1-in-10 in., right-hand twist
Weight (approx.) . . . . 8 lbs.

MKS AND MKR

Interdynamic AB of Stockholm has created two experimental rifles which may (or may not) be introduced to the international marketplace. The MKS is a fairly standard 5.56mm NATO rifle except that the magazine has become the pistol grip. Coupled with the folding stock, this feature has made a very compact, if somewhat awkward, weapon. While the idea certainly has merit, it is doubtful that the MKS will enjoy much success.

The MKR series of experimental weapons is of the bullpup pattern. The charging handles are located on top of the handguard, selector above the pistol grip, and the 5.56mm NATO version uses standard AR-15/M16 magazines. Of greater interest is the experimental 4.7×26mm rimfire, high-velocity cartridge developed for one version of the MKR. Equipped with a plastic circular 50-round magazine, the rifle would be quite controllable in the automatic mode while having the firepower needed for modern combat. This rifle/caliber combination will bear watching.

MKS Specifications

Barrel length . . . . 18.4 in.
Caliber . . . . 5.56mm NATO
Length (approx.) . . . . 34.2 in.
Length (stock folded, approx.) . . . . 24 in.
Magazine (standard) 30-round
Muzzle velocity (approx.) . . . . 3200 fps
Weight unloaded (approx.) . . . . 6 lbs.

MKR Specifications

Barrel length . . . . 23.6 in.
Caliber . . . . . 5.56mm NATO or 4.7×26mm rimfire
Length (approx.) . . . . 33 in.
Magazine (standard) . . . 30-round (5.56mm NATO)
or 50-round (4.7×26mm)
Muzzle velocity (approx., 4.7×26mm RF) . . . 3350 fps
Weight unloaded (approx.) . . . . 6.6 lbs.

RPS-001

Thailand's Rung Paisal Industries was created during the mid-1970s in order to produce military weapons for Thailand rather than having to import them. Among the weapons currently being produced are an M79-style

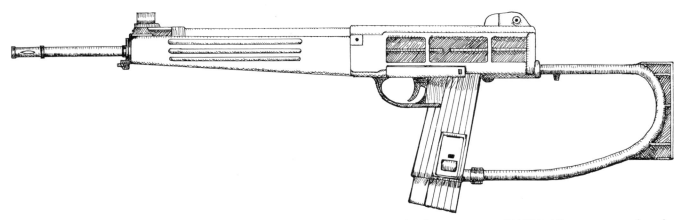

The Interdynamic AB of Stockholm experimental MKS is fairly standard as far as 5.56mm NATO rifles go, except that the magazine has become the pistol grip for the rifle. Coupled with the folding stock, it is a compact, if somewhat awkward, weapon.

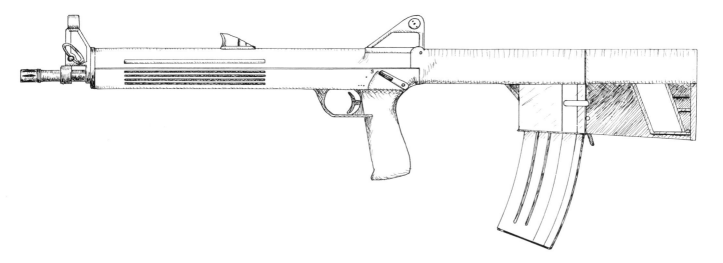

The Interdynamic AB of Stockholm experimental MKR bullpup rifles are currently chambered either for 5.56mm NATO (shown) or an experimental 4.7x26mm rimfire, high-velocity cartridge developed for the rifle.

grenade launcher, and RPG-2 and RPG-7 look-alikes.

Also introduced by Rung Paisal is a hybrid rifle, the RPS-001, which was produced by a team headed by Krairach Manadamrongtham. The rifle, basically an AK-47, has a machined steel receiver and uses a gas-operated piston. The selector is located on the right side of the receiver, and the magazine release is behind the magazine well. The front sight is hooded, and the rear sight is a notch similar to that of the AK.

The plastic furniture departs from the "straight-line" look of most modern assault rifles, thereby allowing the user to keep a low profile when aiming it. To compensate for the barrel climb created by this design as well as the rifle's light weight, a very efficient muzzle brake has been created.

Although the rifle offers little that is new, the features borrowed from other rifles have been put together very well to create a reliable and easy-to-use rifle. Currently, two models are available: the standard RPS-001 and a short carbine version, the RPS-001S. It is possible that a semiauto version will be produced as well.

RPS-001 Specifications

Barrel length . . . . 19.5 in.
Caliber . . . . 5.56mm NATO
Length . . . . 40.5 in.
Magazine (standard) 20-round
Muzzle velocity (approx.) . . . . 3200 fps
Cyclic rate . . . . 625 rpm
Weight unloaded (approx.) . . . . 7 lbs.

SAR 80

Armalite developed the AR-18 and licensed the

manufacturing rights first to the Japanese Howa Corporation; after revoking Howa's license in 1973, the rights were licensed to Sterling Arms of England in 1976. Sterling and Armalite did not work well together, so Armalite soon shifted AR-18 manufacture to the Philippines while Sterling started design work on a rifle of its own.

Meanwhile, CIS (Chartered Industries of Singapore), a Singapore government-chartered and owned enterprise, had been licensed by Colt to produce the M16A1. CIS went through endless frustrations trying to sell the rifles it manufactured (permission had to be obtained from the United States to sell the weapons) and finally decided to manufacture a rifle of its own design.

Sterling and CIS then combined their efforts on a new rifle loosely based on the AR-18. The designer in charge of this project was Frank Waters of the Sterling plant. By 1978 prototypes were being tested; a number were sent to the School of Infantry Weapons of the Singapore military. The Singapore government was interested in the design so CIS continued to work the bugs out.

By 1980, the weapon was functioning well and the rifle was designated the SAR 80 (Singapore Automatic Rifle 1980), although the rifle is sometimes referred to as the "Sterling Assault Rifle."

Like the AR-18, the SAR 80 has two recoil springs inside its receiver and uses a gas piston system. Upper and lower receivers are steel stampings; a minimum of high-tech tooling is used. Internally, the rifle has a few surprises: the trigger, disconnector, selector, hammer, etc., are forgings nearly identical to those of the AR-15. The front and rear sights are similar to those of the AR-15.

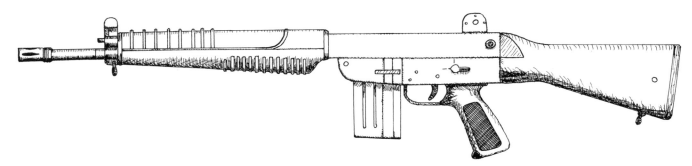

The SAR 80 (Singapore Automatic Rifle 1980) is occasionally referred to as the Sterling Assault Rifle, and is very similar to the AR-18. Early models of the SAR had wooden furniture; current product rifles sport plastic stocks, grips, and handguards.

Likewise, the flash suppressor, magazines, bayonet, etc., of the AR-15 fit the SAR 80. This allows CIS to have a wide range of accessories automatically available for its rifle; it also allows a country to switch from the AR-15 to the SAR 80 with a minimum of fuss.

The reciprocating charging handle is located on the right side of the rifle. The selector is on the right above the pistol grip. A gas regulator is located at the front of the gas port just ahead of the front sight. Early models of the SAR had wooden furniture; current product rifles sport plastic stocks, grips, and handguards.

Field-stripping is nearly identical to that of similar rifles and requires no special tools other than a blunt punch or cartridge tip. After removing the magazine and cycling the weapon to be sure it's empty, set the selector to the safe position, and continue as follows:

1. Push out the release pins at the front and rear of the lower receiver (be careful as they come all the way out).

2. Depress the recoil-spring detent in, and slowly let the recoil springs and their guides out of the rear of the upper receiver. Once spring tension is released, pull the springs out of the rear of the receiver.

3. Pull the charging handle all the way to the rear of its track and pull it out to the right.

4. Turn the receiver so that the bolt carrier/bolt slides out its rear end.

5. Push the spring-loaded firing pin from its rear side so that the cross pin that retains it can be pulled out the left side of the bolt carrier. This will free the firing pin and its spring.

6. Remove the inertia rod and its retainer.

7. When the firing pin is removed, the cam pin can be pulled out to the left of the bolt carrier. This will free the bolt, which can be pulled from the front of the bolt carrier.

8. The upper handguard half is released when the recoil spring assembly is removed. Pull it up at its rear

end and pivot it up and off the barrel.

9. Move the piston rod toward the receiver, tilt it to one side, and remove the assembly to expose the gas tube.

This is all that normally needs to be done to clean and maintain the SAR 80. Reassembly is basically the reverse of the above procedure. When putting the bolt back into the carrier, be sure to point the extractor to the right and get the cam pin right side in so that the firing pin can go through it.

The SAR 80 has very little that is innovative; it does not have a folding stock or a three-round burst feature. While the overall design is sound, unless the SAR 80 can be offered at a very competitive price, it has little to recommend it over other assault rifles. While Singapore may purchase the rifle, whether or not it will do well on the international market remains to be seen.

SAR 80/Sterling Assault Rifle Specifications

Barrel length . . . . 18.1 in.
Caliber . . . . .223 Remington
Cyclic rate (approx.) . . . . 700 rpm
Length . . . . 38.2 in.
Magazine (standard) 20-round
Muzzle velocity (approx.) . . . . 3200 fps
Rifling . . . . . 6 grooves, 1-in-12 in., right-hand twist
Weight unloaded (approx.) . . . . 8 lbs.

SIG RIFLES: THE ROLLS ROYCE RIFLES

The Swiss citizen army was armed with a straight-pull, bolt-action rifle up until the early 1950s when the SIG Sturmgewehr 57 was adopted. Earlier, the manufacturer of the Sturmgewehr 57, SIG (Schweizerische Industrie-Gesellschaft), had tried to sell its Model 46 to the Swiss army, but had failed in its effort since money was tight following World War II. A number of rifles were produced in an effort to capture the Swiss market (since it would seem obvious that the Swiss would soon be needing a new rifle to replace their ancient rifles). The Direx and AM55 were two other notable failures.

In 1953, SIG again tried for the Swiss army market with the AK53, which had a stationary bolt and a barrel which cycled forward. This rifle had the conventional assault rifle layout but was not accepted by any major buyer. Finally SIG brought out the model SG57 (or StuG57). Thus, the Swiss jumped directly from a bolt-action to a modern assault rifle.

The SG57 is not chambered for an intermediate caliber. The Swiss landscape makes a long-range cartridge essential in combat. Thus, the Swiss retained the potent round used in their old straight-pull Schmidt-Rubin rifles. This round had been created with black powder in mind in 1889. In 1911, however, the round was upgraded for smokeless powder and a 174-grain spitzer bullet replaced the original round-nosed lead projectile. The 1911 round is very similar to the 7.62mm NATO. Dangerously similar, in fact. The NATO round will chamber in the SG57 but won't fire.

The SIG uses a lot of the technology developed for the CETME, including the twin roller-locked bolt and fluted cartridge chamber. These enable the rifle to use a wide range of ammunition and—coupled with the straight stock design and head-up sighting system—help to reduce felt recoil. Unlike the CETME, the SG57 fires from a closed bolt in the automatic mode.

All SG57s come equipped with a versatile telescoping bipod capable of rotating a full 360 degrees. The front and rear sights flip down for storage. The front sight is adjustable for windage and elevation, and the rear sight has a twist setting which allows a shooter to dial up any range from 100 to 650 meters.

The upper receiver has a carrying handle which flips up when needed. On the right side of the rifle, just below the edge of the magazine well, is a lever that can be pulled down and used for a winter trigger. The trigger system is the common two-stage military type with a heavy trigger pull. The charging lever is located on the right side of the receiver and has an upward bend to allow cocking with either hand.

The selector is located in a rather awkward position on the left of the rifle. "E" is the semiauto position, "M" is full auto, and "S" is safe. The magazine release is located at the forward end of the trigger guard.

The barrel is covered with a ventilated shroud, and a plastic handguard is located just ahead of the receiver. Plastic is also used for the pistol grip and stock. No folding stocks are available with the SG57 rifles. The barrel has a muzzle brake/flash suppressor which helps control recoil.

The SG57 is very simple to field-strip:
1. Remove the magazine and cycle the weapon to be sure it is empty.
2. Depress the catch and rotate the stock 90 degrees to the right.
3. Remove the stock and action spring.
4. Pull the operating handle to remove the bolt assembly.

Reassembly is basically the reverse of the above steps.

In addition to the selective-fire SG57, a semiauto version was also available, marketed as the "SIG 57." Prices for these rifles were extremely high and manufacture has recently been discontinued since the SIG 57s cannot compete against other less expensive weapons. Price considerations aside, the rifles are well made and every bit as reliable as one might hope.

SG57 Specifications
Barrel length . . . . 23 in.
Caliber . . . . 7.5mm Model 11
Cyclic rate (approx.) . . . . 475 rpm
Length (approx.) . . . . 43.4 in.
Magazine (standard) 24-round
Muzzle velocity (approx.) . . . . 2490 fps
Rifling . . . . 4 grooves, right-hand twist
Weight (approx.) . . . . 12.25 lbs.

Following the acceptance of the 7.62mm cartridge as NATO standard, SIG created a rifle aimed at this market. The rifle, the SIG510, is little more than an SG57 rechambered for the 7.62mm NATO round. Other models were created at the same time, including a lightweight version for the 7.62×39mm Soviet round. The commercial semiauto model of this rifle, available in the United States, was the SIG-AMT. The last of these models were produced in 1974 (a few are still available from Osborne Brothers).

The SG510-1 was the standard 510 rifle; the 510-2 was a lightened version; the 510-3 chambered for the Soviet cartridge; and the 510-4 was the standard military weapon chambered for the 7.62mm NATO round.

Among the changes made from the SG57 rifle were the addition of an optional bipod which folds up over the barrel, an indicator to show the amount of ammunition in the magazine, and a sniping scope mount. Many rifles have wooden stocks and handguards with a plastic pistol grip. Sights on the SG510 are also slightly different with the rear sight having an aperture mounted on a ramp; detents are used to elevate or lower it from 100 to 600 meters. Neither sight flips down. The barrel and chamber are chrome-lined.

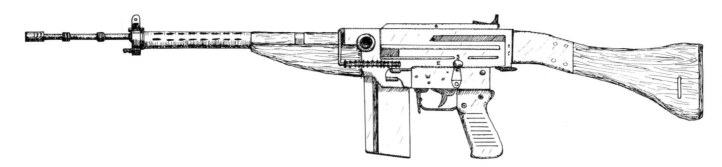

The SIG company created the SIG 510 to compete with other rifles in the military marketplace. It is little more than a revamped SG 57 rechambered for the 7.62mm NATO round. Other models of this rifle were created at the same time, including a lightweight version for the 7.62x39mm Soviet round and a commercial semiauto model known as the SIG-AMT.

The SG510 has a rotating adjustment for changing the head-space to suit the ammunition being used. Great care should be taken in making this adjustment, since it can quickly create a dangerous condition.

Unfortunately for SIG, its rifles came onto the market a little too late to capture much business and are too expensive for any but the richest buyers.

SG510-1, -4 Specifications

Barrel length . . . . 19.8 in.
Caliber . . . . 7.62mm NATO
Cyclic rate (approx.) . . . . 575 rpm
Length (approx.) . . . . 40 in.
Magazine (standard) 20-round
Muzzle velocity (approx.) . . . . 2640 fps
Rifling . . . . 4 grooves, right-hand twist
Weight (approx.) . . . . 9.4 lbs.

SG510-3 Specifications

Barrel length . . . . 16.5 in.
Caliber . . . . 7.62×39mm Soviet
Cyclic rate (approx.) . . . . 525 rpm
Length (approx.) . . . . 35 in.
Magazine (standard) 30-round
Muzzle velocity (approx.) . . . . 2300 fps
Rifling . . . . 4 grooves, right-hand twist
Weight (approx.) . . . . 8.25 lbs.

SIG's next Sturmgewehr was the SG530-1. This .223 design uses steel stampings and plastic furniture in an effort to hold down costs. Originally this rifle was to be a scaled-down SG510 but experimental models did not cycle reliably with the roller action. Thus, a gas tube and piston assembly were added to the system. A folding-stock version of the rifle was created as well.

The magazine catch is still located just ahead of the trigger guard, but the selector has been moved back to a more convenient location above the pistol grip on the

left side of the rifle. The "S" position is the safety, "1" is semiauto fire, and "30" is full auto (a three-round burst mode is optional). The charging lever has been moved to the top of the gas tube over the handguard. The system is roller-locked in the same way as is the SG510. The rifle has scope blocks welded to the receiver top and the birdcage flash suppressor doubles as a grenade launcher. The receiver halves pivot around a pin at their front.

To field-strip the SG530-1:

1. Remove the magazine and cycle the action to be sure the rifle is empty.

2. Depress the receiver catch at the rear of the top receiver and pivot the stock open.

3. Remove the operating spring.

4. Pull back on the charging handle and remove the bolt carrier and bolt.

Reassembly is the reverse of this procedure.

SG530-1 Specifications

Barrel length . . . . 15.5 in.
Caliber . . . . .223 Remington
Cyclic rate (approx.) . . . . 600 rpm
Length (approx.) . . . . 39.5 in.
Length, stock folded (approx.,
    folding stock only) . . . . 30.8 in.
Magazine (standard) 30-round
Muzzle velocity (approx.) . . . . 3150 fps
Rifling . . . . 4 grooves, right-hand twist
Weight, standard stock (approx.) . . . . 8.4 lbs.
Weight, folding stock (approx.) . . . . 8.5 lbs.

Two new models of SIG rifles have recently been added to the company's offerings. Though outwardly the rifles resemble the SG530-1, internally, they use rotating cams similar to those of the AK rifles to lock the bolt. The SG540 is chambered for the 5.56mm

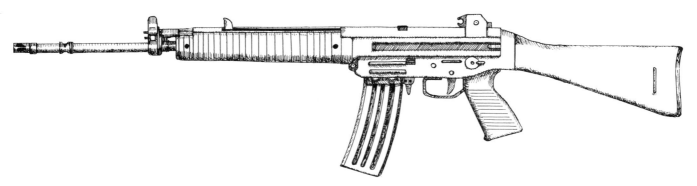

SIG's SG 530-1 design uses steel stampings and plastic furniture in an effort to hold down costs and is chambered for the .223 Remington. This rifle was originally to be a scaled-down SG 510, but experimental rifles did not have a reliable cycling action with the roller blocks alone. Thus, a gas tube and piston assembly were added to the system.

NATO round; the SG542 is chambered for the 7.62mm NATO. The rifles have an optional drop-in, three-round burst attachment that may be added without modification or special tools. The new rifles have ambidextrous safeties.

The SIG540 comes with the usual accessories including scopes, bipods, and bayonets. The flash suppressor allows grenade launching. A folding stock version is also available.

In 1983 the Swiss army adopted the SG540 as its battle rifle, joining the many countries using the .223 round. The modified version has been designated the SG541 by SIG and Stgw90 by the Swiss military. The military version has a folding plastic stock with a cutout area (its release is on the left side of the stock near the receiver). An integral bipod folds up under the handguard and the barrel is modified for grenade launching.

The new SIG rifles have a chance to compete with other manufacturers on the world market. SIG has managed to maintain high-quality workmanship while cutting costs—and prices—by using modern industrial techniques and steel stampings. Thus far, 17 countries have adopted the SG540.

SG540 Specifications

Barrel length . . . . 19.3 in.
Caliber . . . . 5.56mm NATO
Cyclic rate (approx.) . . . . 725 rpm
Length (approx.) . . . . 37.5 in.
Length, stock folded (approx.,
    folding stock only) . . . . 28.7 in.
Magazine (standard) 30-round
Muzzle velocity (approx.) . . . . 3220 fps
Rifling . . . . 4 grooves, right-hand twist
Weight, standard stock (approx.) . . . . 6.8 lbs.

SG541 Specifications

Barrel length . . . . 21 in.

Caliber . . . . 5.56mm NATO
Cyclic rate (approx.) . . . . 775 rpm
Length (approx.) . . . . 39.4 in.
Length, stock folded (approx.,
    folding stock only) . . . . 30.6 in.
Magazine (standard) 30-round
Muzzle velocity (approx.) . . . . 2950 fps
Rifling . . . . 4 grooves, right-hand twist
Weight, standard stock (approx.) . . . . 9.2 lbs.

SG542 Specifications

Barrel length . . . . 19.5 in.
Caliber . . . . 7.62mm NATO
Cyclic rate (approx.) . . . . 700 rpm
Length (approx.) . . . . 38.9 in.
Length, stock folded (approx.,
    folding stock only) . . . . 30.1 in.
Magazine (standard) 20-round
Muzzle velocity (approx.) . . . . 2690 fps
Rifling . . . . 4 grooves, right-hand twist
Weight, standard stock (approx.) . . . . 7.8 lbs.

STONER M63

After leaving Armalite, Eugene Stoner worked for Colt Firearms on design changes in the AR-15. Shortly after, he left Colt and started his own company under the direction of the Cadillac Gage Division of the Excello Corporation based in Warren, Michigan. He quickly hired the other two members of his old design team, Robert Fremont and James Sullivan. Their first system, the Stoner 62, was based on the .308 Winchester/7.62mm NATO round. When the .223 became popular, Stoner modified his weapon system to accommodate the smaller round. The weapons system was made up of the M63 rifle, M63 carbine, M63 LMG, etc. After extensive testing, the Stoner system was modified somewhat; the new models have the designation of M63A1.

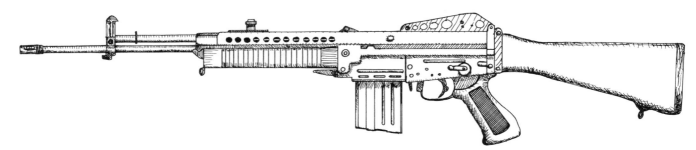

The Stoner M63A1 weapons system allowed a soldier with little training to fire any one of a family of weapons. This system simplifies repair and maintenance and does away with many supply and manufacturing procedures. Unfortunately, few military planners saw the logic of this, and the standard rifle was a bit heavy. Therefore, the system has not met any great success in sales.

Any weapons system always has one major advantage: if a soldier can fire one of the weapons, he can probably fire any of them with little further training. This simplifies training, repair, and maintenance, thereby doing away with many supply and manufacturing procedures. Unfortunately, few military planners see this logic and few weapons systems are seen in military inventories. This proved to be the case with the Stoner M63 family.

The Stoner 63 System is the do-it-yourselfer's weapons system if ever there was one. The basic weapons can easily be modified in the field to suit the soldier's needs. The two basic systems are a rifle and a short carbine with a 15.7-inch barrel, but by substituting a few parts and turning the barrel and gas tube over, it's possible to create weapons which fire from an open bolt. These variations include a belt-fed LMG; a magazine-fed LMG; a medium machine gun; and a solenoid-fired, vehicular machine gun. A folding stock which folds over the top of the rifle and fixed stock are available for most of the combinations, and a little tinkering could conjure up other variations. In all, there are 15 mix-and-match assemblies as well as a machine gun tripod and a light bipod in the M63 series.

In the 1960s, the U.S. Army tested the rifle (SM22), carbine (SM23), and belt-fed LMG(XM207). The U.S. Navy tried the LMG as the MK23 and adopted it for limited use by SEAL teams in Vietnam. A number of factors worked against the adoption of the Stoner 63 System, and the M16 had become well entrenched in the U.S. military system by the mid-Sixties.

The weight of the basic Stoner 63 rifle worked at cross-purposes to its most common use. Because its receiver had to be robust enough to handle its LMG role, the rifle was nearly a pound heavier than the M16. This may be the major reason the Stoner 63 System has gained almost no military acceptance. Ironically, the U.S. Army's new M16A2 is nearly as heavy as the M63 rifle while other modern rifles like the Galil, AR70, etc., are

as heavy or even heavier!

The upper handguard/barrel shroud is an extension of the sheet-metal upper receiver, which also contains the gas tube. The lower handguard is attached to the magazine well and forms an abbreviated lower receiver to which the stock fits. The whole rifle is assembled/disassembled with a group of push pins, and the barrel is quickly and easily removed—a definite plus in the weapon's LMG role.

In order to power a belt-fed mechanism, the gas piston of the M63 has a long power stroke. The gas piston is attached to the bolt carrier, and a recoil spring and guide fit inside the piston. The bolt is similar to that of the AR-18 and locks into a barrel extension in the same manner as the AR-18 and the AR-15 rifles.

The charging knob is located on the upper side of the handguard and the safety is on the left of the receiver above the pistol grip. The magazine release is located on the lower side of the receiver behind the magazine well.

Though a bit heavy, the Stoner M63 family is a fine, reliable weapons system. Unfortunately, though, the rifle didn't capture any market and production ceased in the mid-Seventies. The basic design was sound, however, and it is very possible that the last of the Stoner 63 has not been seen.

Stoner M63 (Rifle) Specifications

Barrel length . . . . 20 in.
Caliber . . . . .223 Remington
Cyclic rate (approx.) . . . . 700 rpm
Length . . . . 40.3 in.
Magazine (standard) 30-round
Muzzle velocity (approx.) . . . . 3250 fps
Rifling . . . . . 6 grooves, 1-in-12 in., right-hand twist
Weight unloaded (approx.) . . . . 7.8 lbs.

TRW SYSTEMS' LMR

The M16 (AR-15) rifle was having troubles in Viet-

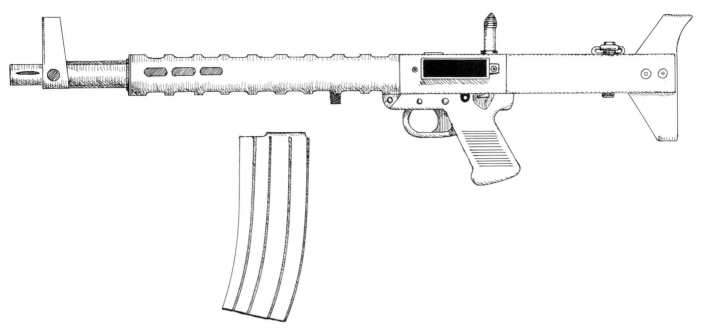

In an effort to cash in on the early problems with the M16 rifle in Vietnam, TRW developed the LMR (Low Maintenance Rifle). Corrosion-resistant materials were used wherever possible, as well as dry lubrication to minimize dirt buildup. The LMR also had a gas piston.

nam during the late 1960s. Though the problems were traced to fouling caused by improper ammunition and lack of maintenance, it looked for a time as if the problem might be with the design of the rifle itself.

In an effort to cash in on the M16's problems, TRW—which had been manufacturing the M14 rifle—developed the LMR (Low Maintenance Rifle) under project head Don Stoehr. The rifle used corrosion-resistant materials wherever possible, had a design that kept fragile parts protected, used "dry lubrication" to keep down dirt buildup, and had a gas piston rather than a gas tube as on the AR-15. The rifle used the trigger/pistol grip assembly from the M60 machine gun as well as the M16 magazine and accepted the M16 bayonet. The magazine well was at right angles to the

rifle on the left side of the receiver with its release on top of the magazine well while the gas piston extended down the right side of the barrel. The rifle had high front and rear sights, putting the stock directly in line with the barrel to improve automatic-fire control. The selector was located on the left of the trigger group above the pistol grip and the charging lever was just ahead of the ejection port on the right side of the receiver.

Unfortunately for TRW, the problems with the M16 were cleared up and the LMR was shelved.

LMR Specifications
Barrel length . . . . 20 in.
Caliber . . . . .223 Remington
Length . . . . 34.5 in.

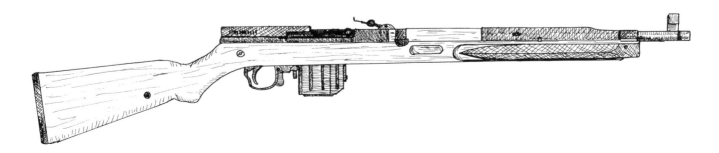

The Vz52 is an "assault rifle" that technically isn't an assault rifle. Though it has a detachable magazine, fires an intermediate cartridge, etc., it isn't selective fire. Early rifles were chambered for the Czech Vz52; in 1957, the rifles were modified slightly and chambered for the Soviet 7.62mm M43 cartridge. Such rifles were designated Vz52/57.

Magazine (standard) 30-round
Muzzle velocity (approx.) .... 3200 fps
Rifling .... 1-in-12 in., right-hand twist

Vz52

The Vz52 is an assault rifle that isn't an assault rifle. Though it has a detachable magazine, fires an intermediate cartridge, etc., it isn't selective fire. For all practical purposes, however, it's an assault rifle. The rifle is chambered for the Czech Vz52. In 1957, the rifles were modified for the Soviet 7.62mm M43 cartridge; these rifles were designated Vz52/57. Internally, the rifle unblushingly copies the M1 Garand's trigger group and uses a mechanically inefficient tilting bolt-locking system. Permanently mounted at its front is a somewhat flimsy

spear-point folding bayonet. The rifle's LMG counterpart, the Lehky Kulomet Vz52, proved to be too sensitive to dirt for reliable functioning on the battlefield. That, coupled with pressure to adopt an AK-47-style rifle, sealed the fate of the Vz52 rifle, which has been relegated to Home Guard use in Nicaragua.

Vz52 (52/57) Specifications

Barrel length .... 20.5 in.
Caliber .... Vz52 (Soviet 7.62mm M43)
Length .... 39.5 in.
Magazine (standard) 10-round
Muzzle velocity (approx.) .... 2440 fps
Rifling ..... 4 grooves, 1-in-12 in., right-hand twist
Weight unloaded (approx.) .... 9 lbs.

APPENDIX A: TROUBLESHOOTING

While sportsmen can put up with occasional firearm failures, a combat weapon must function when you need it. Failure can prove fatal to the weapon's owner. Combat weapons, after all, are expected to work for extended periods under conditions that would destroy a sporting weapon. Note the following suggestions to maintain a safe, effective, and reliable weapon.

- Be sure that you have a weapon that is rugged and designed for combat—not a modified sporting firearm.
- Be sure that the ammunition and magazines will get the best out of the weapon. A large percentage of weapons malfunctions can be directly traced to poor ammunition and magazines.
- Break in your weapon. Firearms come from the manufacturer with some rough edges that quickly wear down as the weapon is used. After several hundred rounds go through a firearm, it will custom fit its parts and function very reliably.
- Have a gunsmith smooth out the feed ramp and throat the barrel so that the weapon can digest a wide range of ammunition. You can never tell what you may be forced to use in a survival/battlefield situation. Having a firearm that will only work reliably with FMJ ammunition is a handicap that could prove disastrous.
- Keep the weapon clean and well maintained. While manufacturers and writers like to tell how a weapon can be filled with grime and still work, all weapons will eventually fail with dirt in their action and chambers. A clean weapon lasts longer and is less apt to fail than an identical—but dirty—firearm. Avoid over-lubricating a weapon; this attracts dirt. Replace parts when they show signs of excessive wear. A spare parts kit consisting of firing pin, extractor, and various springs and small parts is a good idea if you're interested in surviving combat.
- Take care of ammunition. Don't get oil, bore cleaner, etc., on it; such fluids deactivate primers. Don't let it get corroded or hot. Treat ammunition as well as you do your weapon and its magazines: your life may depend on them all.
- Don't try any do-it-yourself modifications unless you really know what you're doing. A gunsmith once confided to me that most of his business comes from kitchen-table gunsmiths. If it's not broken, don't fix it.
- When a weapon fails to fire, there are some quick steps that you should go through:
  1. Tap the magazine to be sure it's seated.
  2. Pull back on the charging knob again, and check that a case is ejected and a shell isn't jammed in the weapon.
  3. If the chamber is clear and your weapon fires from a closed bolt, release the charging handle to chamber a new round. Do not "ride" the bolt forward.
  4. Check the safety/selector to be sure it is on the proper setting.
  5. Try to fire again.
  6. Go through steps one through five one more time.
  7. If this fails to get the weapon to function, remove the magazine, cycle the weapon to be sure it's empty, and check out the inside of the ejection port while you pull back the bolt. This may reveal a problem.
  8. If you haven't found the fault, change magazines and try firing again.

Despite these steps and the care you take in keeping

your weapon clean and well maintained, your weapon will probably fail some of the time. Knowing what to look for to get it functioning quickly can mean the difference between life and death. Read and study the procedures below so you know what to do. There's no greater tragedy than the body of a brave fighter next to a firearm that failed him.

Some of the following procedures are dangerous. If you aren't in combat with your life on the line, don't attempt the actual measures with live ammunition. The best way to get a firearm fixed when it's not working right is to take it to a gunsmith! Let me repeat: the following procedures can be very dangerous and should only be attempted when not having a functioning firearm puts your life in jeopardy.

It should also be noted that since there is a wide difference in parts and operation among the various types, brands, and models of weapons, some of the following steps will not apply to your weapon.

FIREARM TROUBLESHOOTING PROCEDURES

PROBLEM	WHAT TO CHECK FOR	REPAIR PROCEDURE
1. Bolt does not hold open after the last round (if weapon has hold-open device).	Fouled/broken bolt latch.	Clean or replace.
	Bad magazine.	Discard magazine.
2. Bolt is hung up in the receiver.	Round jammed between bolt and charging handle.	*Stay clear of the muzzle.* Remove the magazine; hold the charging handle back, and slam the butt of the firearm against the ground. *Caution:* When round is freed, the bolt will remain under tension. While bolt is held back, push charging handle forward and let the round fall through the magazine well.
3. Bolt won't unlock.	Dirty or burred bolt.	Clean or replace.
4. Bolt won't lock.	Fouling in locking lugs.	Clean and lubricate lugs.
	Frozen extractor (in down position).	Remove and clean extractor.
	Buffer/spring not moving freely.	Remove, clean, and lubricate.
	Bolt/bolt carrier not moving freely.	Remove, clean, and lubricate.
	Gas tube/guide rod/piston bent.	Check to be sure key goes over gas tube/piston in rod; if not, straighten rod or tube as necessary.
	Inside of gas tube fouled.	Replace gas tube.
	Loose or damaged key or piston.	Tighten or replace.
5. Double feeding.	Defective magazine.	Replace.
6. Firearm won't cock; selector doesn't work properly.	Worn, broken, or missing parts.	Check parts and replace.

7. Firearm continues to fire after release of trigger.	Dirt in trigger/sear mechanism.	Clean.
	Broken sear/trigger.	Replace sear/trigger.
	Weak sear/trigger spring.	Replace spring.
	Weak ammunition (blow-back weapons only).	Replace ammunition.
8. Firearm won't fire.	Selector on "Safe".	Place in fire position.
	Firing pin is in the wrong position.	Reassemble so that retaining pin is between two shoulders of the firing pin.
	Too much oil or dirt in firing pin recess.	Wipe or clean.
	Poor ammo.	Remove or discard.
	Firing pin broken.	Remove or replace pin or bolt (on open-bolt weapons).
	Lower receiver parts defective, worn, or broken.	Remove, clean, or replace.
	Weak or broken hammer, striker, or sear spring.	Replace.
	Bolt isn't locking.	Clean dirty parts.
9. Round won't chamber.	Dirty or corroded ammo.	Clean ammo.
	Damaged ammo.	Replace.
	Fouling in chamber.	Clean with chamber brush.
10. Rounds won't eject.	Broken ejector.	Replace.
	Frozen ejector.	Clean and lubricate.
	Bad spring.	Replace.
11. Rounds won't extract.	Broken extractor.	Replace.
	Dirty/corroded ammo.	Remove (may have to be carefully pushed out with cleaning rod).
	Carbon or fouling in chamber or extractor lip	Clean chamber and lip.

	Broken extractor or bad spring.	Replace.
	Dirty or faulty recoil spring.	Clean or replace.
12. Rounds won't feed.	Dirty or corroded ammo.	Clean ammo.
	Low-powered ammo.	Use different ammo.
	Defective magazine.	Replace magazine.
	Dirt in magazine.	Clean and lubricate magazine.
	Too many rounds in magazine.	Remove several rounds.
	Poor buffer movement.	Remove buffer/spring and clean and lubricate them.
	Insufficient gas to cycle action fully.	Clean all gas passages, gas rods, etc.
	Magazine is not seated.	Magazine catch may need to be tightened. Push release button down, and tighten or loosen the catch by turning it.
	Broken magazine catch.	Repair or replace.
13. Selector lever binds.	Fouling/lack of lubrication.	Lubricate; if it still binds, disassemble and clean.
14. Short recoil (New rounds aren't fed into the chamber.)	Gaps in bolt rings.	Remove bolt and stagger rings.
	Fouling in carrier key/outside of gas tube/gas piston.	Clean key/tube end and lubricate.
	Carrier key damaged or defective.	Replace key.
	Missing or broken gas rings.	Replace rings.
	Broken or loose gas tube/piston rod.	Replace or resecure.

APPENDIX B: BALLISTICS TABLES FOR COMBAT ROUNDS

Nearly as important as the weapon a fighter carries is the ammunition he puts in it. Modern bullet design can give a fighter an advantage that cannot be gained even with a larger-caliber weapon loaded with inferior ammunition. Expanding bullets are especially effective. Their designs give fighters a greater edge in combat; don't limit yourself with poorly designed bullets.

Getting your bullet on target is often a major problem. Practice and proper weapon zeroing is essential for this, but careful study of these ballistic charts (as well as those in reloading manuals and other sources) will greatly aid you in getting your bullets to your target.

When looking at ammunition/ballistic tables, pay attention to the barrel length used in the tests; it can make a big difference. Take some time to see what your bullet can do and where it will be "out there." With commercial 9mm Luger, for example, a 16-inch barrel can enjoy 22-percent greater muzzle velocity than its 4-inch counterpart; this translates to about 200 fps (feet per second) with some loads. A good rule-of-thumb is that the difference between a 4-inch barrel and one up to 12 inches long can be figured at around 28 fps for each inch of difference. After 12 inches, the velocity gain varies from 4.5 to 17.5 fps for each inch of barrel. Beyond 16 inches of barrel length, increments of increase are small; with 20 inches or more, most ammunition will start to lose velocity.

Results can be just as dramatic with rifles: a 10-inch .223/5.56mm can have a muzzle velocity 250 fps less than a 20-inch barreled weapon. While these speeds may not make a great difference at close ranges, they will at extended ranges.

According to extensive U.S. military studies, most combat takes place within 150 yards with 300 yards being the extreme range. While many would-be fighters find

this hard to believe, in fact, terrain and human eyesight coupled with an evasive enemy make the 300-yard extreme range seem pretty generous.

When possible, try to use a "battle zero" which allows you to fire over your combat range without adjusting your weapon's sights. For rifle cartridge weapons, the 200- or 250-yard zero works well; with firearms chambered for pistol cartridges, a 100-yard zero works well in combat, though, with some weapons and in some conditions a 50-yard zero may make more sense.

With blow-back weapons, case wall thickness of the brass is important; thin-walled brass tends to cause such weapons to malfunction and may also be dangerous since parts of the case wall won't be supported during the bolt's initial recoil. New aluminum-cased ammunition (CCI Blaze and Winchester, for example) may not work well in some blow-back actions. Military rounds are designed to use with unlocked systems and Norma, Smith & Wesson, Federal, Remington, and Frontier all currently have thick-walled cases which work well in most blow-back weapons. Choose ammunition carefully and always try it out.

When studying a rifle round, the factor that determines its wounding ability is its speed. The cutoff point depends on altitude, atmospheric conditions, and other considerations, but a good rule-of-thumb speed is 2,000 fps. Above that speed, the bullet takes on added lethality. Below 2,000 fps, the damage is dependent on the caliber size and/or its ability to expand at the lowest speed.

As you look over these figures, remember that actual numbers for your gun and ammunition may vary greatly from those shown below. These tables should be used for reference only.

PISTOL CALIBERS

Foot pounds of energy (fpe) are useful for comparing the energy levels within a certain caliber but do not tell a lot about the wounding capability of different calibers. Factors such as bullet design, speed, etc., come into play, so that it is a mistake to assume that one caliber of bullet is more lethal than another simply because it has more foot pounds of energy at a given distance.

Multiple hits are best for quick stopping power with pistol caliber FMJ bullets. With diminutive calibers like the .32 ACP, .380 ACP, or even the .22 LR, automatic fire is essential. Expanding bullets or multiple-projectile rounds will be effective in 9mm Luger, and .45 ACP will generally be effective without automatic fire though hit probability may not be as great.

Speeds are given in feet per second (fps), and energy levels in foot pounds of energy (fpe). In general, a faster bullet which expands will be much more lethal than its heavier counterpart. Expanding bullets will be more lethal on all but armored targets.

Due to the differences in manufactured ammunition, velocities will produce different energy levels with identical bullets.

.22 LONG RIFLE (40-GRAIN)

	Muzzle	50 yds.	100 yds.
Velocity (fps)	1200	1069	1016
Energy (fpe)	128	102	92
Deviation (in.)	0	—	-4

.22 LONG RIFLE HIGH-VELOCITY (32-GRAIN)

	Muzzle	50 yds.	100 yds.
Velocity (fps)	1560	1282	1090
Energy (fpe)	173	117	84
Deviation (in.)	0	—	-3.8

.25 ACP/6.35mm (50-GRAIN)

	Muzzle	50 yds.	100 yds.
Velocity (fps)	760	707	659
Energy (fpe)	64	56	48
Deviation (in.)	0	-2	-8.7

.32 AUTO/7.65mm (71-GRAIN)

	Muzzle	50 yds.	100 yds.
Velocity (fps)	905	855	810
Energy (fpe)	129	115	97
Deviation (in.)	0	-1.4	-5.8

.32 AUTO/7.65mm (110-GRAIN)

	Muzzle	50 yds.	100 yds.
Velocity (fps)	1295	1094	975
Energy (fpe)	410	292	232
Deviation (in.)	0	-0.8	-3.5

.32 AUTO/7.65mm (125-GRAIN)

	Muzzle	50 yds.	100 yds.
Velocity (fps)	1450	1240	1090
Energy (fpe)	583	427	330
Deviation (in.)	0	-0.6	-2.8

.380 ACP/9mm BROWNING SHORT (88-GRAIN)

	Muzzle	50 yds.	100 yds.
Velocity (fps)	1000	921	860
Energy (fpe)	189	160	140
Deviation (in.)	-0.8	+4.5	0

.380 ACP/9mm BROWNING SHORT (90-GRAIN)

	Muzzle	50 yds.	100 yds.
Velocity (fps)	955	865	785
Energy (fpe)	190	160	130
Deviation (in.)	-0.8	0	-11.4

.380 ACP/9mm BROWNING SHORT (90-GRAIN)

	Muzzle	50 yds.	100 yds.
Velocity (fps)	1100	993	860
Energy (fpe)	242	197	140
Deviation (in.)	-0.8	+3.97	0

9mm LUGER (90-GRAIN)

	Muzzle	50 yds.	100 yds.
Velocity (fps)	1300	1119	1006
Energy (fpe)	338	250	202
Deviation (in.)	-0.8	+3.05	0

9mm LUGER (90-GRAIN)

	Muzzle	50 yds.	100 yds.
Velocity (fps)	1500	1234	1077
Energy (fpe)	450	304	232
Deviation (in.)	-0.8	+2.45	0

9mm LUGER (115-GRAIN)

	Muzzle	50 yds.	100 yds.
Velocity (fps)	1200	1086	1007
Energy (fpe)	368	301	259
Deviation (in.)	-0.8	+3.27	0

9mm LUGER (115-GRAIN)

	Muzzle	50 yds.	100 yds.
Velocity (fps)	1400	1221	1101
Energy (fpe)	500	381	310
Deviation (in.)	-0.8	+2.51	0

.45 AUTO (185-GRAIN)

	Muzzle	50 yds.	100 yds.
Velocity (fps)	1000	920	865
Energy (fpe)	411	348	307
Deviation (in.)	−0.8	+4.68	0

.45 AUTO (230-GRAIN)

	Muzzle	50 yds.	100 yds.
Velocity (fps)	800	769	741
Energy (fpe)	341	315	292
Deviation (in.)	−0.8	+6.89	0

.45 AUTO (185-GRAIN)

	Muzzle	50 yds.	100 yds.
Velocity (fps)	1200	1051	957
Energy (fpe)	591	453	376
Deviation (in.)	−0.8	+3.51	0

.45 AUTO (230-GRAIN)

	Muzzle	50 yds.	100 yds.
Velocity (fps)	900	861	826
Energy (fpe)	432	395	363
Deviation (in.)	−0.8	+5.45	0

RIFLE CALIBERS

Rifle bullets need to travel 2,000 to 2,500 fps to be lethal. Below this speed, the bullet loses a lot of its potential regardless of caliber. This drop can be created by distance or barrel length; remember barrel length when looking at ballistic tables. Most of the figures shown below were obtained using standard-length barrels; if your rifle has a short barrel, take that into account. One inch of barrel will make around a 20 fps velocity change with bullets which travel from 2,000 to 3,000 fps. That means a 10-inch barrel will have a muzzle velocity about 200 fps below its 20-inch counterpart. This can cut down the effective range of shorter-barreled carbines. Bullets which expand give the best combat performance. After that, bullets which shatter (as with the 1-in-7 twist with 5.56mm NATO) perform best, followed by bullets which tumble (like the .223 Remington with the 1-in-12 twist). FMJ bullets which fail to tumble perform poorly in battle, with the .308 caliber often doing poorer than its .223 counterpart.

5.57mm JOHNSON/.22 "SPITFIRE"
40-GRAIN (.224) WITH 250-YARD ZERO

	Muzzle	100 yds.	200 yds.	300 yds.	400 yds.	500 yds.	600 yds.
Dev. from 0 (in.)	−1.5	4.68	4.20	−8.08	—	—	—
Velocity (fps)	3000	2316	1738	1304	—	—	—
Energy (fpe)	799	476	268	151	—	—	—

.223 REMINGTON (5.56mm)
55-GRAIN (FMJ) .224 WITH 250-YARD ZERO

	Muzzle	100 yds.	200 yds.	300 yds.	400 yds.	500 yds.	600 yds.
Dev. from 0 (in.)	−1.5	1.5	2.5	−3	−17.8	−45	−90
Velocity (fps)	3100	2640	2226	1859	1544	1277	1093
Energy (fpe)	1174	852	605	422	291	199	146

.223 REMINGTON (5.56mm)
55-GRAIN (FMJ) .224 WITH 250-YARD ZERO (MAXIMUM LOAD)

	Muzzle	100 yds.	200 yds.	300 yds.	400 yds.	500 yds.	600 yds.
Dev. from 0 (in.)	−1.5	1	2.8	−4.1	−18.3	−41.6	−87
Velocity (fps)	3240	2877	2543	2232	1943	1679	1455
Energy (fpe)	1282	1011	790	608	461	344	259

.223 REMINGTON (5.56mm)
55-GRAIN (FMJ) .224 WITH 300-YARD ZERO

	Muzzle	100 yds.	200 yds.	300 yds.	400 yds.	500 yds.	600 yds.
Dev. from 0 (in.)	−1.5	4.8	6	0	−16.4	−47	−98
Velocity (fps)	3100	2640	2226	1859	1544	1277	1093
Energy (fpe)	1174	852	605	422	291	199	146

.223 REMINGTON (5.56mm)
55-GRAIN (FMJ) .224 WITH 300-YARD ZERO (MAXIMUM LOAD)

	Muzzle	100 yds.	200 yds.	300 yds.	400 yds.	500 yds.	600 yds.
Dev. from 0 (in.)	−1.5	4.4	5.6	0	−15.1	−43.8	−91.7
Velocity (fps)	3200	2732	2307	1931	1604	1324	1126
Energy (fpe)	1251	912	650	456	314	214	155

.223 REMINGTON (5.56mm)
60-GRAIN .224 WITH 250-YARD ZERO

	Muzzle	100 yds.	200 yds.	300 yds.	400 yds.	500 yds.	600 yds.
Dev. from 0 (in.)	−1.5	3.25	2.9	−4.3	−20	−48	−92.5
Velocity (fps)	3000	2633	2296	1991	1716	1467	1260
Energy (fpe)	1199	924	703	528	392	287	211

.223 REMINGTON (5.56mm)
60-GRAIN .224 WITH 250-YARD ZERO (MAXIMUM LOAD)

	Muzzle	100 yds.	200 yds.	300 yds.	400 yds.	500 yds.	600 yds.
Dev. from 0 (in.)	−1.5	1.9	2.9	−2	−14.8	−37.6	−74
Velocity (fps)	3200	2820	2467	2145	1854	1596	1365
Energy (fpe)	1365	1060	811	613	458	340	248

.223 REMINGTON (5.56mm)
69-GRAIN .224 WITH 250-YARD ZERO (MAXIMUM LOAD)

	Muzzle	100 yds.	200 yds.	300 yds.	400 yds.	500 yds.	600 yds.
Dev. from 0 (in.)	−1.5	2	3.5	−4	−12.4	−35	−71
Velocity (fps)	3000	2724	2462	2214	2004	1786	1555
Energy (fpe)	1379	1137	929	751	615	488	370

.256 WINCHESTER MAGNUM ("FERRET")
60-GRAIN WITH 250-YARD ZERO

	Muzzle	100 yds.	200 yds.	300 yds.	400 yds.	500 yds.	600 yds.
Dev. from 0 (in.)	−1.5	6.2	5.6	−10.6	—	—	—
Velocity (fps)	2800	2084	1505	1110	—	—	—
Energy (fpe)	1045	579	302	164	—	—	—

.256 WINCHESTER MAGNUM ("FERRET")
75-GRAIN WITH 250-YARD ZERO

	Muzzle	100 yds.	200 yds.	300 yds.	400 yds.	500 yds.	600 yds.
Dev. from 0 (in.)	−1.5	9.1	7.8	−14	—	—	—
Velocity (fps)	2400	1760	1264	996	—	—	—
Energy (fpe)	768	413	213	132	—	—	—

.30 CARBINE
110-GRAIN .308 WITH 100-YARD ZERO

	Muzzle	100 yds.	200 yds.	300 yds.	400 yds.	500 yds.	600 yds.
Dev. from 0 (in.)	0.5	0	−13.5	−49.9	−118.6	−228.2	—
Velocity (fps)	1990	1567	1236	1035	923	842	—
Energy (fpe)	967	600	373	262	208	173	—

7.62×39mm RUSSIAN
110-GRAIN .308 WITH 250-YARD ZERO

	Muzzle	100 yds.	200 yds.	300 yds.	400 yds.	500 yds.	600 yds.
Dev. from 0 (in.)	−1.5	6.9	6	−11	−46.7	—	—
Velocity (fps)	2500	1956	1500	1162	970	—	—
Energy (fpe)	1527	935	550	330	230	—	—

7.62×39mm RUSSIAN
150-GRAIN .308 WITH 300-YARD ZERO

	Muzzle	100 yds.	200 yds.	300 yds.	400 yds.	500 yds.	600 yds.
Dev. from 0 (in.)	−1.5	8.7	9.9	0	−23.6	−65	—
Velocity (fps)	2200	1980	1777	1592	1417	1266	—
Energy (fpe)	1612	1306	1051	844	669	534	—

.308 WINCHESTER (7.62mm NATO)
150-GRAIN .308 WITH 250-YARD ZERO

	Muzzle	100 yds.	200 yds.	300 yds.	400 yds.	500 yds.	600 yds.
Dev. from 0 (in.)	−1.5	3.5	3	−4.5	−20	−47	−90
Velocity (fps)	2820	2593	2396	2210	2035	1869	1714
Energy (fpe)	2648	2240	1913	1628	1379	1164	979

.308 WINCHESTER (7.62mm NATO)
165-GRAIN .308 WITH 300-YARD ZERO

	Muzzle	100 yds.	200 yds.	300 yds.	400 yds.	500 yds.	600 yds.
Dev. from 0 (in.)	−1.5	5.8	6.8	0	−15.8	−42.8	−82.8
Velocity (fps)	2600	2378	2169	1974	1791	1623	1462
Energy (fpe)	2477	2072	1724	1427	1175	966	783

.308 WINCHESTER (7.62mm NATO)
180-GRAIN .308 WITH 250-YARD ZERO

	Muzzle	100 yds.	200 yds.	300 yds.	400 yds.	500 yds.	600 yds.
Dev. from 0 (in.)	−1.5	4	3.25	−4.8	−21.75	−49.7	−90
Velocity (fps)	2600	2393	2198	2015	1842	1682	1535
Energy (fpe)	2703	2290	1932	1623	1357	1131	942

.30-06
150-GRAIN .308 WITH 300-YARD ZERO

	Muzzle	100 yds.	200 yds.	300 yds.	400 yds.	500 yds.	600 yds.
Dev. from 0 (in.)	−1.5	5.1	5.9	0	−14	−38	−73.4
Velocity (fps)	3000	2729	2473	2234	2012	1806	1618
Energy (fpe)	2998	2481	2038	1663	1349	1087	873

.30-06
180-GRAIN .308 WITH 300-YARD ZERO

	Muzzle	100 yds.	200 yds.	300 yds.	400 yds.	500 yds.	600 yds.
Dev. from 0 (in.)	−1.5	5.1	5.9	0	−14	−38	−73.4
Velocity (fps)	2700	2488	2287	2098	1921	1754	1602
Energy (fpe)	2914	2474	2091	1760	1475	1230	1025

APPENDIX C: FIREARMS AND ACCESSORIES MANUFACTURERS AND DISTRIBUTORS

Action Arms, Ltd.
P.O. Box 9573
Philadelphia, PA 19124
(Importer of semiauto Uzi weapons)

Armalite, Inc.
118 East 16th St.
Costa Mesa, CA 92627
(Owner of manufacturing rights to AR-18/180,
    AR-15, and AR-10 rifles)

Auto-Ordnance Corp.
Box ZG
West Hurley, NY 12491
(Manufacturer of Thompson submachine
    gun/carbine)

Beretta USA
17601 Indian Head Highway
Accokeek, MD 20607
(Manufacturer of AR-70 rifle; importer of Modello
    12 submachine gun)

Bushmaster Firearms, Inc.
803 Forest Ave.
Portland, ME 04103
(Manufacturer of Bushmaster rifle and pistol)

Cadillac Gage Company
Stoner 63 Marketing Division
P.O. Box 1027
Warren, MI 48090
(Hold rights to Stoner 62/63 Weapon Systems)

Clayco Sports, Ltd.
625 W. Crawford
Clay Center, KS 67432
(Importer of semiauto Chinese AK)

Colt Industries
Firearms Division
P.O. Box 1868
Hartford, CT 06101
(Manufacturers of AR-15A2, AR-15 Carbine, and
    military M-16)

Commando Arms, Inc.
Box 10214
Knoxville, TN 37919
(Manufacturers of Mark 45 and Mark 9 Carbines)

D.B. Distributing
Rt. 2, Box 189D
Fayetteville, AR 72701
(Distributor for Holmes MP-83, MP-22 pistols, and
    9mm/.45 conversions of AR-15 rifle)

Demro Products
372 Progress Dr.
Manchester, CT 06040
(Manufacturer of Demro TAC-1M and XF-7 Wasp
    carbines and accessories)

Enfield America, Inc.
P.O. Box 5314
Atlanta, GA 30307
(Manufacturers of Enfield MP45 assault pistol)

Frankford Arsenal, Inc.
1047 Northeast 43rd Ct.
Fort Lauderdale, FL 33334
(Maker of custom AR-15s and 9mm conversions of
    the AR-15)

Gibbs Guns, Inc.
Rt. 2, Hwy. 411S
Greenback, TN 37742
(Distributor of Mark 45 Carbine)

Gun South
Box 6607, 7605 Eastwood Mall
Birmingham, AL 35210
(Importers of FN LAR and Egyptian AKM)

Heckler & Koch
14601 Lee Rd.
Chantilly, VA 22021
(Manufacturer of HK-91, HK-93, and HK-94)

Holloway Arms Co.
3959 W. Vickery Blvd.
Fort Worth, TX 76107
(Manufacturer of HAC-7 and HAC-7C rifles)

Holmes Firearms Co.
Rt. 6, Box 242
Fayetteville, AR 72701
(Manufacturer of MP-83, MP-22 pistols, and
    9mm/.45 conversions of the AR-15)

Interarms
10 Prince St.
Alexandria, VA 22313
(Importers of military weapons)

Intratec USA, Inc.
1190 Southwest 128th St.
Miami, FL 33186
(Manufacturers of TEC-9, TEC-9M, and TEC-9S
    assault pistols)

Iver Johnson
2202 Redmond Rd.
Jacksonville, AR 72076
(Manufacturers of M-1 Carbine chambered for .30
    Carbine, 9mm Luger, 5.7mm Johnson, and .22
    LR)

Lanchester USA
P.O. Box 47332
Dallas, TX 75247
(Importers of Sterling submachine guns and
    semiauto versions of Sterling carbine pistol)

Military Armaments Corporation
P.O. Box 1385
Stephenville, TX 76401
(Manufacturer of M10-A1 submachine gun and
    semiauto pistol)

Magnum Research, Inc.
2825 Anthony Lane So.
Minneapolis, MN 55418
(Importers of Galil rifle chambered for .223 and
    .308)

Marlin Firearms Co.
100 Kenna Dr.
North Haven, CT 06473
(Manufacturer of Model 9 Carbine chambered in
    9mm)

Michigan Quartermaster, Inc.
42317 Ann Arbor Rd.
Plymouth, MI 48170
(Distributor for Broadhead Armory's semiauto
    grease gun M3C)

MK Arms Inc.
P.O. Box 16411
Irvine, CA 92713
(Manufacturer of MK-760 submachine gun)

Odin International
818 Slaters Lane
Alexandria, VA 22314
(Importer of Valmet and CETME)

Osborne's Shooting Supplies
P.O. Box 408
Cheboygan, MI 49721
(Importer of SIG rifles)

Pacific International Merchandising Corp.
2215 J. St.
Sacramento, CA 95816
(Importer of Chinese AKS semiauto rifle)

Pars International
P.O. Box 37101
Louisville, KY 40233
(Importer of selective-fire Uzi and Mini-Uzi)

RPB
4327 A-1 S. Atlanta Rd., S.E.
Smyrna, GA 30080
(Manufacturer of M11-9mm version of MAC-11)

Sage International
1856 Star-Batt Dr.
Rochester, MI 48063
(Importer of Enfield Weapon System bullpup in
    .223)

SGW
624 Old Pacific Hwy. S.E.
Olympia, WA 98503
(Manufacturer of custom AR-15s, gun parts,
    accessories, and 9mm conversion units for the
    AR-15)

Shepherd and Turpin Distributors
P.O. Box 40
Washington, UT 84708
(Manufacturer of STEN reproduction semiauto and
    selective-fire submachine guns)

Springfield Armory
111 E. Exchange St.
Geneseo, IL 61254
(Manufacturer/distributor of M1A, M-14, M1A-A1,
    SAR 48 [FN LAR], M1 Garand, M1 "Tanker
    Garand," Beretta BM-59, BM-59 Alpine
    Trooper, and BM-59 Nigerian model; semiauto
    and selective-fire models of most weapons are
    available.)

Stoeger Industries
55 Ruta Court
S. Hackensack, NJ 07606
(Distributors of .223 MAX-1, MAX-2 Daewoo
    assault rifles)

Sturm, Ruger & Co.
Southport, CT 06490
(Manufacturers of Mini-14 and XGI rifles)

SWD, Inc.
1872 Marietta Blvd.
Atlanta, GA 30318
(Manufacturers of M-11/9mm version of MAC-11)

Universal Firearms
3740 E. 10th Ct.
Hialeah, FL 33013
(Manufacturers of semiauto M1 .30 Carbines and
    pistols)

Weaver Arms Corp.
344 North Vine St.
Escondido, CA 92026
(Manufacturer of Nighthawk 9mm Carbine)

Wilkerson Firearms
6531 Westminster Blvd.
Westminster, CA 92683
(Manufacturer of bullpup conversion kit for the
    Mini-14, M1 Carbine, and AK-47)

Wilkinson
Rt. 2, Box 2166
Parma, ID 83660
(Manufacturer of Terry and Linda 9mm Carbine
    and pistols)

Accessories and Custom Modifications

A.I.I., Inc.
Box 26483
Prescott Valley, AZ 86312
(Manufacturer of AR-15 9mm adapter kit)

Alpha Armament
218 Main St.
Milford, OH 45150
(AK-74-style muzzle brake)

ARMS
230 W. Center St.
Bridgewater, MA 02379
(Manufacturer of scope mount bracket for H&K
    rifles, magazine bolt hold-open adapter for
    H&K rifles, and NATO AR-15/M16 scope
    mount)

Armson
P.O. Box 2130
Farmington Hills, MI 48018
(Armson O.E.G. available-light dot scope)

Assault Systems
869 Horan Dr.
St. Louis, MO 63026
(Rifle cases and accessories)

Beeman Precision Arms
47 Paul Dr.
San Rafael, CA 94903
(SS-1 and SS-2 scopes and other accessories)

BMB Industries
P.O. Box 466
Cave Creek, AZ 85331
(Handguard pistol grips for AR-15, H&K firearms,
    and other firearms)

B.M.F. Activator
3705 Broadway
Houston, TX 77017
(Plastic bipod)

B-Square Company
Box 11281
Fort Worth, TX 76109
(Scope mounts for most military firearms)

Cherokee Gun Accessories
830 Woodside Rd.
Redwood City, CA 94061
(Cheekpieces for military firearms)

Choate Machine and Tool Company
Box 218
Bald Knob, AR 72010
(Manufacturer of wide range of stocks, flash
    suppressors, handguards, etc., for Mini-14,
    AR-15, Uzi, MAC-10/11, and other rifles and
    carbines)

D.C. Brennan Firearms, Inc.
P.O. Box 2732
Cincinnati, OH 45201
(Nil-flash flash suppressors for, among others, the
    AR-15, AR-18/180, and Mini-14)

Defense Moulding Enterprises, Inc.
Box 4328
Carson, CA 90745
(Plastic magazines for the AR-15, HK rifles, and
    other weapons)

Some shooters like a Thompson-style pistol grip under their weapon's handguard. Nearly identical to those of the Thompson in size and shape, but made of tough plastic that matches that used on most firearms, the BMB Industries' forward grips are available for the AR-15/M16 and H&K firearms. (Shown are the SGW 9mm Commando, top, and the HK-94, bottom.)

DTA
3333 Midway Dr., Suite 102-L
San Diego, CA 92110
(Mil/Brake muzzle compensator for H&K 91/93,
     AR-15, AR-18, and other rifles)

E & L Manufacturing
2102 W. Coolbrook
Phoenix, AZ 85023
(Rigid brass catchers for Uzi, Mini-14, AR-15,
     TEC-9, H&K rifles, H&K stock extension, and
     barrel shrouds)

Eaton Supply, Inc.
5340 East Hunter Ave.
Anaheim, CA 92807
(Manufacturer of plastic magazines for the
     AR-18/180, AR-15/M16, and HK-91)

Excalibur Enterprises
P.O. Box 266
Emmaus, PA 18049
(Night-vision equipment)

Executive Protection Products, Inc.
1834 First St., Suite E
Napa, CA 94559
(Laser sighting systems)

Fiber Pro
P.O. Box 83732
San Diego, CA 92138
(Fiberglass and composite stocks for the M14, M1A,
     Mini-14, and other rifles)

Fleming Firearms
7720 E. 126 St., N.
Collinsville, OK 74021
(Custom conversion of semiauto weapons to
     selective fire [H&K], and MP5 conversion of
     .308 H&K rifles)

Grendel, Inc.
P.O. Box 908
Rockledge, FL 32955
(Grendelite and rifle/assault pistol light mounts)

Group Industries
1127 Lavista Way
Louisville, KY 40219
(Manufacturer of .22 LR conversion kits for Uzi
     carbines)

Harris Engineering
Barlow, KY 42024
(Harris bipod)

Hydra Systems
Box 3461
Bridgeport, CT 06605
(Laser sighting systems)

JFS, Inc.
P.O. Box 12204
Salem, OR 97309
(Manufacturer of Tac-Latch III [H&K rifles], Redi-
     Tac [AR-15 sling], and Redi-Mag [AR-15])

Jonathan Arthur Ciener, Inc.
6850 Riverside Dr.
Titusville, FL 32780
(Manufacturer of Mini-14, .22 LR conversion kit,
     automatic firearms, and custom-built or
     modified AR-15s)

Laser Arms Corp.
P.O. Box 4647
Las Vegas, NV 89127
(Laser sighting systems)

Light Enterprises
P.O. Box 3811
Littleton, CO 80161
(Nightsighter night sight)

Litton
Electron Tube Div.
1215 S. 52nd St.
Tempe, AZ 85281
(Night-vision equipment)

Lone Star Ordnance
P.O. Box 29404
San Antonio, TX 78229
(Distributor of AR-15 parts and accessories)

Michaels of Oregon Company
     (Uncle Mike's)
P.O. Box 13010
Portland, OR 97213

Military Surplus Supply
5594 Airways
Memphis, TN 38116
(Camo covers for firearms)

To carry combat gear, a belt and harness with pouches, a combat vest, or some similar arrangement is needed. Lightweight commercial pouches and belts like those put out by Uncle Mike's are ideal for such use. Photo courtesy of Michaels of Oregon.

Mitchell Arms
19007 South Reyes Ave.
Compton, CA 90221
(Manufacturer of Mini-14 plastic stock)

Newman's GI Supply
RR 1, Box 782
Augusta, NJ 07822
(Combat support vests and military surplus gear)

Parallex Corporation
1285 Mark St.
Bensenville, IL 60106
(Distributor of magazines, flash suppressors, slings, cases, scope mounts, and more)

Ram-Line, Inc.
406 Violet St.
Golden, CO 80401
(Manufacturer of AR-15/Mini-14 combo mag, Mini-14 accessories, and AR-15 Laser Grip)

Sherwood International
18714 Parthenia St.
Northridge, CA 91324
(Distributor of magazines, bayonets, slings, cases, spare parts, and more)

Smith Enterprises
325 South Westwood #1
Mesa, AZ 85202
(Vortex flash suppressors for AR-15, AR-180, and other rifles)

Standard Equipment Co.
9240 N. 107th St.
Milwaukee, WI 53224
(Night-vision equipment)

Tobias Guns
Rt. 1, Box 210
Norwood Rd.
Albemarie, NC 28001
(Manufacturer of M-14, XGI, and M1A 30-round magazines)

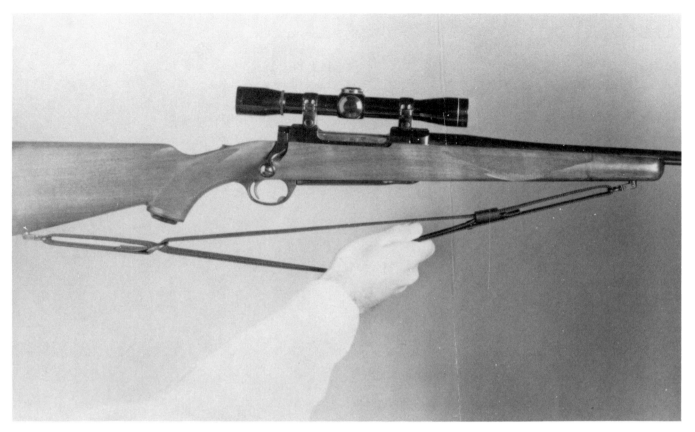

The best—and most reasonably priced—slings are those made by Uncle Mike's. Their "Quick Adjust" sling can be quickly shortened on the rifle so that it doesn't hang in the way. Photo courtesy of Michaels of Oregon.

Triple K Manufacturing Company
568 Sixth Ave.
San Diego, CA 92101
(Manufacturer of magazines for various firearms)

Westminster Arms, Ltd.
2961 Industrial Rd., Suite 531
Las Vegas, NV 89109
(Manufacturer of K-3 Bullpup stock for Mini-14,
    M1 Carbine, M-14, and others)

Williams Trigger Specialties, Inc.
RR 1, Box 26
White Heath, IL 61884
(Trigger-pull adjustments to H&K weapons and set
    trigger for H&K rifles)

Publications and Video Tapes

The following books and magazines have valuable information which will be of interest to those needing more information about small arms and weapons developments.

The American Rifleman
1600 Rhode Island Ave., NW
Washington, DC 20036
($15 per year)

AR-10er newsletter/exchange
LTC
184 Highland
Wethersfield, CT 06109

The AR-15/M16: A Practical Guide
Duncan Long
Paladin Press
P.O. Box 1307
Boulder, CO 80306

Combat Ammunition: Everything You Need to Know
Duncan Long
Paladin Press
P.O. Box 1307
Boulder, CO 80306

The Combat Shotgun and Submachine Gun
Chuck Taylor
Paladin Press
P.O. Box 1307
Boulder, CO 80306

Deadly Weapons (in VHS or Beta)
P.O. Box 375
Pinole, CA 94564

Silencers in the 1980s
J. David Truby
Paladin Press
P.O. Box 1307
Boulder, CO 80306

Small Arms of the World
Edward Clinton Ezell
Stackpole Books
P.O. Box 1831
Harrisburg, PA 17105

Soldier of Fortune magazine
P.O. Box 348
Mt. Morris, IL 61054